SPAIN

The Trials and Triumphs of a Modern European Country

MICHAEL REID

YALE UNIVERSITY PRESS
NEW HAVEN AND LONDON

For information about this and other Yale University Press publications, please contact:
U.S. Office: sales.press@yale.edu yalebooks.com
Europe Office: sales@yaleup.co.uk yalebooks.co.uk

Set in Adobe Garamond Pro by IDSUK (DataConnection) Ltd
Printed in Great Britain by TJ Books, Padstow, Cornwall

Library of Congress Control Number: 2022950313

ISBN 978-0-300-26039-7

A catalogue record for this book is available from the British Library.

10 9 8 7 6 5 4 3 2 1

For Roxani
And to the Jardines del Buen Retiro
Storm-tossed survivor and source of solace

Hombre de España: ni el pasado ha muerto, ni esta el mañana – ni el ayer-escrito. [Spaniard: neither has the past died, nor is tomorrow – nor yesterday – yet written.]

Antonio Machado, 'El Dios ibero'

I am firmly convinced that Spain is the strongest country of the world. Century after century trying to destroy herself and still no success.

Attributed to Bismarck

Nothing causes more pain to Spaniards than to see volume after volume written by foreigners about their country.

Richard Ford, *A Handbook for Travellers in Spain*

On analysing the state of dissolution that Spanish society has reached, we find some symptoms and ingredients that are not exclusive to our country but rather are general trends in European nations.

José Ortega y Gasset, *España Invertebrada*

CONTENTS

ILLUSTRATIONS AND MAPS

Plates

1. Diego Velázquez, *Las Meninas*, 1656, Madrid, Museo Nacional del Prado (P001174). © Photographic Archive Museo Nacional del Prado.
2. Voting for the constitution in 1978. Reproduced with the permission of EFE.
3. Lieutenant-Colonel Tejero on a podium after leading the takeover of Spain's parliament, 1981. Bettmann / Getty Images.
4. Supporters of Catalan independence throng Barcelona at the Diada demonstration in 2012. David Ramos / Getty Images.
5. Catalan and Spanish flags on balconies in Barcelona in 2017. Reuters / Alamy Stock Photo.
6. The Benedictine monastery of Montserrat. Joe Sohm / Visions of America / Getty Images.
7. Francisco de Goya y Lucientes, *The 3rd of May 1808 in Madrid, or 'The Executions'*, 1814, Madrid, Museo Nacional del Prado (P000749). © Photographic Archive Museo Nacional del Prado.
8. Antonio Gisbert Pérez, *Execution of Torrijos and his Companions on the Beach at Málaga*, 1888, Madrid, Museo Nacional del

Prado (P004348). © Photographic Archive Museo Nacional del Prado.

9. Manuel Azaña, 1930. Alamy Stock Photo.
10. Anarchist militia in Barcelona during the Civil War. Hulton Deutsch / Getty Images.
11. General Francisco Franco saluting nationalist troops, 1939. Keystone-France / Getty Images.
12. Exhumation of a victim of the Civil War, 2021. Carlos Gil Andreu / Getty Images.
13. Frank Gehry's Guggenheim Museum in Bilbao. VW Pics / Getty Images.
14. Empty apartments at Seseña near Madrid, 2012. Reuters / Alamy Stock Photo.
15. Feminist protesters demand the abolition of prostitution, Madrid, 2022. Europa Press News / Getty Images.
16. Pampaneira, Andalucía. Education Images / Getty Images.
17. Francisco de Goya y Lucientes, *Duel with Cudgels, or Fight to the Death with Clubs*, 1820–3, Madrid, Museo Nacional del Prado (P000758). © Photographic Archive Museo Nacional del Prado.
18. Pedro Sánchez, 2022. Europa Press News / Getty Images.
19. Alberto Núñez Feijóo, 2022. Europa Press News / Getty Images.
20. Pablo Iglesias with Ada Colau, 2019. Europa Press News / Getty Images.
21. Santiago Abascal at a Vox rally, 2022. Europa Press News / Getty Images.
22. King Felipe and Queen Letizia with their daughters, 2019. Jaime Reina / Getty Images.
23. AVE high-speed train. Jose Manuel Revuelta Luna / Alamy Stock Photo.
24. Bar terraces of Gijón, 2019. Xurxo Lobato / Getty Images.

Maps

GLOSSARY AND ABBREVIATIONS

abertzale	patriotic or nationalist in Basque
afrancesado	an admirer of France and of the Enlightenment
ANC (Assemblea Nacional Catalana)	Catalan National Assembly, a separatist social movement
AP (Alianza Popular)	Popular Alliance, conservative party formed in 1977 and merged into the PP (Partido Popular) in 1989
ayuntamiento	municipal government, town hall
BNG (Bloco Nacionalista Galego)	Galician Nationalist Bloc
cacique	political boss
cajas de ahorros	savings banks
CEDA (Confederación Española de Derechas Autónomas)	Confederación Española de Derechas Autónomas, a Catholic right-wing party in the 1930s
CIS (Centro de Investigacianes Sociológicas)	Centre for Sociological Research, the state pollster

CiU (Convergència i Unió)	Convergence and Union, a Catalan nationalist party
Ciudadanos	Citizens, a party of the centre-right which mixed liberalism with Spanish nationalism
Comunidades Autónomas	autonomous communities, or regions
concierto económico	the arrangement under which the Basque provinces and Navarre collect their own taxes
corrida	bullfight
Cortes	the Spanish parliament
crispación	tension or confrontation
CUP (Canditatura d'Unitat Popular)	Popular Unity Candidacy, a Catalan separatist party
diputación (**Catalan** *diputació*)	provincial council
EEC	European Economic Community
EH Bildu	a Basque separatist coalition that included former members and supporters of ETA
ERC (Esquerra Republicana de Catalunya)	Republican Left of Catalonia
estado autonómico	the autonomous state, the name for the quasi-federal structure of regional governments of the 1977 constitution
Estelada	the unofficial flag of the Catalan independence movement
ETA (Euskadi Ta Askatasuna)	Basque Homeland and Liberty, terrorist group formed in 1959 and dissolved in 2018
EU	European Union
exaltados	hotheads, radical liberals in the 1820s and 1830s

franquista	supporter of General Franco and his dictatorship
fueros	legal privileges
GAL (Grupos Antiterroristas de Liberación)	a police death squad active in the Basque Country between 1983 and 1987
GDP	gross domestic product
Generalitat	the regional government in Catalonia, and in Valencia
guapo	handsome
HB (Herri Batasuna)	Popular Unity, a front party for ETA
ikurriña	the red, green and white Basque flag
indignados	mainly young protesters against corruption and austerity who took to the streets in May 2011
INE (Instituto Nacional de Estadística)	National Statistics Institute
Izquierda Unida	United Left, an electoral coalition including the former Spanish Communist Party, and which itself formed a coalition with Podemos
Junts per Catalunya	Together for Catalonia, the separatist party founded by Carles Puigdemont
kale borroka	'struggle in the streets' in Basque, vandalism and intimidation practised by supporters of ETA
lehendakari	president of the Basque regional government
masia	farmhouse in Catalan
Moncloa	the complex that houses the prime-ministerial offices
Mossos d'Esquadra	the Catalan regional police force

Òmnium Cultural	Catalan separatist social movement
PNV (Partido Nacionalista Vasco)	Basque Nationalist Party
Podemos	We Can, a hard-left party founded in 2014 which later changed its name to Unidos Podemos and then Unidas Podemos ('Together we can', in the feminine)
PP (Partido Popular)	Popular Party, a mainstream right-of-centre party formed in 1989
procés	process, the name given by Catalan nationalist leaders to their drive for independence
pronunciamiento	rebellion, often bloodless, by military leaders
PSOE (Partido Socialista Operário Espanhol)	Spanish Socialist Workers' Party, referred to in the text as the Socialists
Renaixença	renaissance, a Catalan cultural movement in the nineteenth century
Senyera	the official flag of the Catalan autonomous region
sobremesa	conversation, sometimes over spirits and cigars, at the end of a meal
tertulia	a group political or literary discussion, originally in a café or nowadays on television programmes
torero	bullfighter
UCD (Unión de Centro Democrático)	Union of the Democratic Centre, electoral coalition formed by Adolfo Suárez, which governed from 1977 to 1982

ACKNOWLEDGEMENTS

I would like to thank the following who have helped me in different ways during my years of working on *Spain*: Jordi Alberich, Joaquín Almunia, José María Areilza, Tobias Buck, Tom Burns Marañon, Andrea Calvé, Carles Casajuana, William Chislett, Wolfgang Dold, Rafael Domenech, Adrián García Aranyos, Luis Garicano, Daniel Gascón, Ramón González Férriz, Victor Lapuente, Bernadino León, Sandra León, Elvira Lindo, Kiko Llaneras, Marc López, Fiona Maharg Bravo, Andreu Mas-Colell, David Matheson, Antonio Muñoz Molina, Rodrigo Orihuela, Ana Palacio, Joan María Piqué, Charles Powell, Luis Prados de la Escosura, Maite Rico, Manuel de la Rocha, Toni Roldán, Eduardo Serra, José Enrique Serrano, Pablo Simón and José Ignacio Torreblanca. None of the above are responsible in any way for the arguments of the book. Several of them would not tolerate being in the same room with others on the list. It is the writer's privilege to listen to a wide range of views. My apologies to anyone I have unintentionally omitted.

I am grateful to Sir John (J.H.) Elliott both for illuminating conversations about Spain over the past fifteen years or so and for his enthusiastic welcome for the idea of this book. It is sad that he did not live to see it in print. Many thanks to Yale's two anonymous readers of the text for their penetrating comments, and to one of them in particular for correcting mistakes of historical fact. Thanks, too, to Jordi Alberich, Daniel Gascón and Andy Reid for helpful suggestions, to Emily Upton for information about language teaching in France, to Adam Meara for the maps and to Silvie Koanda for help with the photographs.

I thank Joanna Godfrey at Yale's London office for her championing of the book and close reading of the text, as well as Katie Urquhart and the rest of the Yale team for turning it into a manufactured product. *The Economist* is accommodating of the writing of books by its staff. I am grateful to Zanny Minton-Beddoes, Robert Guest, Emma Hogan and Christopher Lockwood for enabling me to take several months away from my then day jobs to complete this book.

For many decades I have enjoyed sharing an interest in Spain with Charlie Forman, with whom I made a memorable trip to the Basque Country, Navarre and La Rioja in 1977. More recently I have also profited from sharing that interest with David Camier-Wright. As always, my chief debt is to my family. Having been sceptical about the project, my wife, Emma Raffo, whose opinion I respect above all others, thankfully became a convert, and by spotting weaknesses in the draft text helped to improve it. This book is dedicated to my daughter, Roxani Wilberg, who never misses an opportunity to come to Spain.

Madrid, June 2022

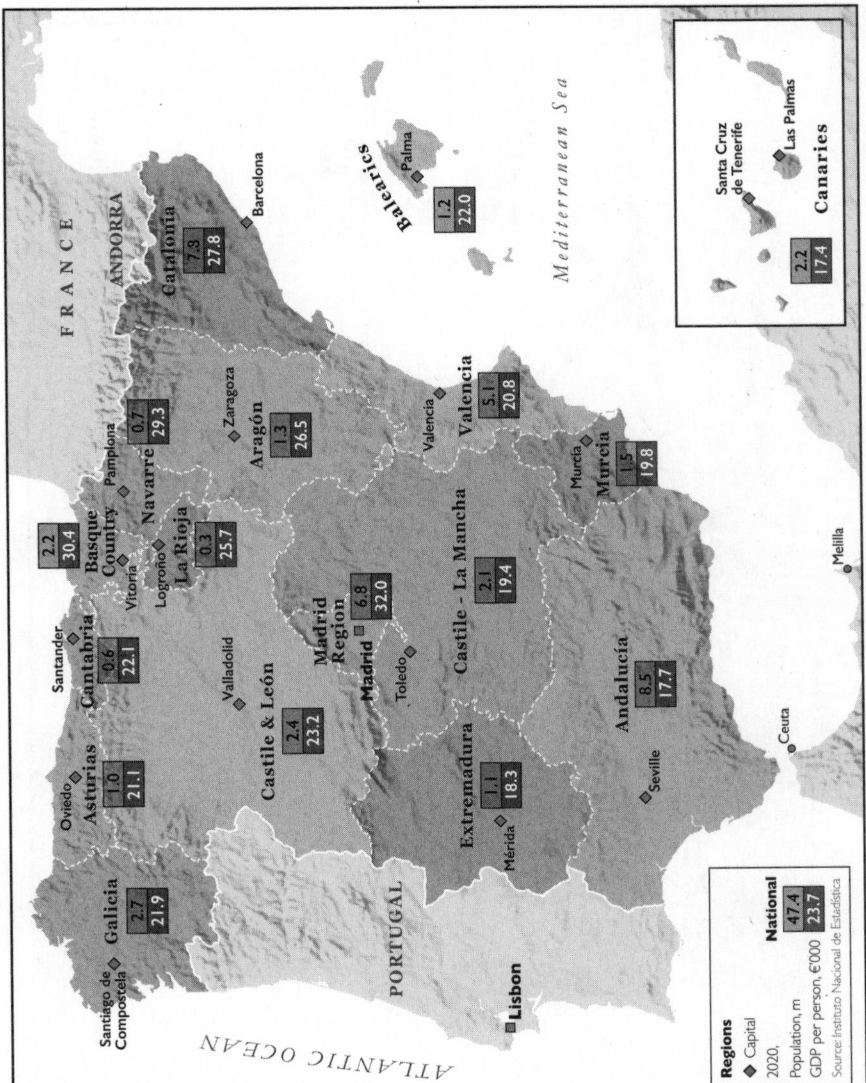

Map 1. Spain's regions.

Regions

◆ Capital

2020,
Population, m
GDP per person, €'000

Source: Instituto Nacional de Estadística

National
47.4
23.7

Canaries
2.2
17.4

Santa Cruz
de Tenerife ◆ ◆ Las Palmas

Mediterranean Sea

Balearics
1.2
22.0

Palma

Catalonia
7.9
27.8

◆ Barcelona

FRANCE

ANDORRA

Navarre
0.7
29.3

◆ Pamplona

Aragón
1.3
26.5

◆ Zaragoza

**Basque
Country**
2.2
30.4

◆ Vitoria

La Rioja
0.3
25.7

◆ Logroño

Valencia
5.1
20.8

◆ Valencia

Murcia
1.5
19.8

◆ Murcia

Cantabria
0.6
22.1

Santander ◆

Asturias
1.0
21.1

Oviedo ◆

Castile & León
2.4
23.2

◆ Valladolid

**Madrid
Region**
6.8
32.0

◆ **Madrid**

Toledo ◆

Castile La Mancha
2.1
19.4

Galicia
2.7
21.9

Santiago de
Compostela ◆

Extremadura
1.1
18.3

◆ Mérida

Andalucía
8.5
17.7

◆ Seville

◆ Melilla

◆ Ceuta

PORTUGAL

■ Lisbon

ATLANTIC OCEAN

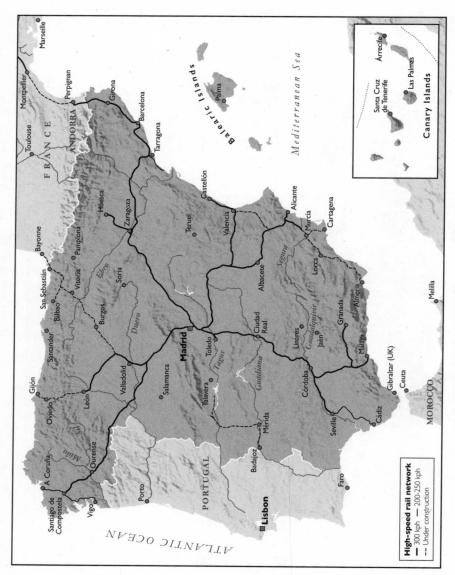

Map 2. Spain's high-speed rail network.

PROLOGUE: THE SPANISH MIRROR

At its midpoint, the extended gallery that runs much of the length of the first floor of the Prado opens onto the spacious, hexagonal Room 12. This spot is the fulcrum of Madrid's great art museum, left undisturbed even in the rehang of its collections during the pandemic. On the western side of the long gallery at that point hangs Titian's majestic equestrian portrait of Emperor Charles V at the Battle of Mühlberg. Some seventy paces away, the eastern wall of Room 12 is occupied by *Las Meninas*, Diego Velázquez's towering painting, which has come to be seen as perhaps the greatest single work in the history of European art. Ostensibly a conversation piece, a homely scene in which a sumptuously dressed princess is attended by her ladies-in-waiting, a dwarf, a dog and palace retainers, the more the viewer looks at it the more it resembles a riddle.[1]

For a start, the most prominent figure in the painting, the one who stares across at Charles V from afar, is the painter, Velázquez himself, portrayed standing before a large easel, working on a canvas that is hidden from us. But who is Velázquez looking at with his forensic gaze as he stands poised, brush in one hand and palette of reds and browns in the other? One answer is provided by a mirror on the back wall

1

which reveals the figures of the king, Philip IV, and his second queen, Mariana of Austria. It was once thought that the royal couple were merely observing the scene, that they had dropped by to greet their daughter. But the alignment of the ceiling lights shows that the reflection in the mirror is not that of the monarchs themselves but rather of the canvas that Velázquez is working on, a dual portrait of the king and queen. (Velázquez was fascinated by mirrors, and possessed no fewer than twelve.) *Las Meninas* is thus a painting about painting. It has multiple focal points. Velázquez's gaze is mimicked by that of the chamberlain, who stands in a lighted doorway beside the mirror. He is perhaps the most enigmatic figure in the painting. Is he entering or leaving the room? Things are much more complicated and uncertain than they might seem.

Velázquez worked in the final years of Spain's Golden Age, when its monarchs, although embattled, still ruled much of Europe and an empire stretching from the Andes to the Philippines. Temporarily enriched by the gold and silver of the Americas, Spain enjoyed an even greater cultural wealth, exemplified by Miguel de Cervantes and his masterpiece, *Don Quixote*; the playwrights Lope de Vega and Calderón de la Barca; Quevedo and Góngora, rival poets who detested each other; as well as Velázquez's fellow-artists, such as Zurburán, with his haunting portraits of pious monks, and Murillo, the baroque painter of the Counter-Reformation's religious ecstasy.

Yet the glitter was misleading. Contrast *Las Meninas*, painted in 1656, with the Charles V portrait, painted a little over a century earlier, and it seems clear that Velázquez, the official court painter to Philip IV, is portraying decline, albeit obliquely. He had earlier painted his king in a similar equestrian pose to Titian's image of his great-grandfather. But in his greatest work, the monarchs are off stage. They are seen through a glass, darkly. They may – or may not – be standing exactly where we, the viewers, are. So *Las Meninas* also seems to be a painting about us. No wonder it fascinated both Jorge Luis Borges, the Argentine writer of metaphysical stories and riddles, and Michel Foucault, the high priest of postmodernism.

Las Meninas plays with our sense of certainty about what we see when we look. It asks whether we only see what we want to see. And so it is with Spain. Like Velázquez's painting, the country itself has been extensively studied and dissected. Indeed, few nations in Western Europe have been the subject of such a large literature by foreign writers (especially Britons) and one that is so cliché-ridden. Spain has served as a mirror, an often distorted one, onto which observers have projected their own visions and fantasies.

Foreigners have seen, or projected, two seemingly opposed but in fact intersecting visions in the Spanish mirror. José Varela Ortega, a historian at the Complutense University in Madrid, sums these up in a 1,100-page tome published in 2019 as being 'the militant, passionate Spaniard' contrasted with 'the indolent, decadent or degenerate Spaniard'.[2] The first view is commonly known in Spain as the 'black legend', the propaganda that newly Protestant northern Europe deployed against the Spain of Charles V and his son, Philip II, who between them led the Catholic Counter-Reformation against what they saw as heresy (this battle began, in military terms, at Mühlberg in 1547, though Charles's victory there proved to be a pyrrhic one). Spain was portrayed as cruel, dark and obscurantist, under the sway of priests and the thumbscrews of the Inquisition. As in all successful propaganda, there was truth in this, but exaggeration too.

Showing prickly insecurity which may reflect the difficulty the country – indeed any country – has in coming to terms with the loss of empire, Spanish conservative thinkers have tended to present all criticism of Spain by outsiders as a product of the black legend. Far from fading, such commentary has gathered force in the past decade. A book defending Spain's colonial record against the black legend by María Elvira Roca Barea has become a surprise bestseller of over 100,000 copies since it was first published in 2016. For one of her critics Roca

Barea's argument is simply 'national-Catholic populism' ('national Catholicism' was the ideology often attributed to the dictatorship of Francisco Franco).[2] More broadly, Spaniards are often portrayed as uniquely intransigent and violent. 'If one Deadly Sin were to define the Spanish national character, it would be Pride,' claims one recent account by a British author, who goes on to forecast portentously that the country is 'destined to follow' paths involving 'bloodshed'.[3]

If the black legend was originally a response to Spanish power, a second, romantic, vision was evoked by Spain's subsequent decline. From the eighteenth century onwards, foreign observers began to view Spain as backward, a vision summed up in the sneering remark attributed to Alexandre Dumas that 'Africa begins at the Pyrenees'. For Voltaire, who unlike Dumas never visited Spain, Spaniards were an 'indolent' race. In the nineteenth century, other foreign travellers and writers began to rejoice in this supposed backwardness. They portrayed Spain as exotic as well as decadent. Their approach was 'orientalist', in Edward Said's term.[4]

Spain thus became the land of the 'Carmen' of Mérimée's novel and Bizet's opera, of lascivious women, gypsies, bandits, and song and dance. 'The only serious thing for Spaniards is pleasure, and they give themselves up to it with admirable abandon, commitment and ardour,' wrote Théophile Gautier, a visiting French writer.[5] The country's alleged lack of modernity began to be seen as a sign of the authenticity of its culture. Its popular music inspired foreign composers, such as Rimsky-Korsakov, Debussy and Ravel. The English Romantics, such as Richard Ford in his *Handbook for Travellers in Spain* of 1845, wrote of the vitality and dignity of Spaniards, a noble people who were held to be routinely betrayed by bad government and rulers (that, too, contained considerable truth). This theme was continued by two writers who indelibly fixed outsiders' view of the Spanish Civil War, Ernest Hemingway in his novel *For Whom the Bell Tolls* and George Orwell in *Homage to Catalonia*, his memoir of fighting as a volunteer militiaman against the nationalist army of General Francisco Franco.

The romantic appeal of Spain was reiterated by Franz Borkenau, an Austrian former Marxist who offered perhaps the most perceptive contemporaneous foreign account of the Civil War. He noted that almost every foreign observer, whether of the left or of the right, felt 'an almost magical attraction' to the country. He went on:

> The deep attraction of Spain consists, in my view, not so much in its [political] importance but in its national character. There life is not yet efficient; that means that it is not yet mechanised; that beauty is still more important for the Spaniard than practical use; sentiment more important than action; honour very often more important than success; love and friendship more important than one's job.[6]

One might add to this list the more basic characteristics of sun, warmth, wine and Mediterranean food – all things which for northern Europeans contributed to the sense of contrast and otherness.

The Romantics, according to Tom Burns Marañon, an Anglo-Spanish writer, 'created a series of stereotypes and those clichés now form part not just of the way others see [Spain], which matters little, but of the very mirror in which Spaniards look at themselves'.[7] Those clichés and stereotypes have surfaced in recent years, especially in foreign coverage of the Catalan conflict. And their internalisation by Spaniards has contributed to an abiding pessimism. Like Velázquez, Spaniards have for centuries had an acute sense of their country's relative decline from past greatness. Sometimes exaggerated, this declinism has coloured the country's political life. It still does.

'Travellers often become enchanted with the first country that captures their hearts and gives them licence to be free,' notes Wade Davis, a

Canadian writer and anthropologist.[8] In my case that country was Spain. I first entered it on a hot Saturday afternoon in July 1971, with two university friends. We had driven from London in a battered blue Volkswagen camper van. We crossed the border at Irún and drove into San Sebastián. I have many snapshots of memory from that and later trips. The first is of the slanting evening sun in the crowded streets of the old quarter of San Sebastián, as we walked from bar to bar, sampling squid and octopus, delicacies almost unknown in the still insular Britain of that time. In the residual heat, there was a pungent aroma of sewerage.

Spain then was a far poorer country than Britain. From Madrid, we drove south, through Toledo and then Puertollano, a stiflingly hot coal-mining town of tin-roofed shacks. After marvelling at the *mezquita*, the vast mosque in Córdoba, we stopped to buy some food at Fernán-Núñez, deep in the Andalucian countryside and surrounded by olive groves. It was a whitewashed town of dirt streets and one-storey houses with tiny windows, home to thousands of agricultural day labourers, who spent much of the year unemployed, and prematurely aged women dressed in widow's black. One was seated in her doorway pounding tomatoes for gazpacho in a stone pestle. Fernán-Núñez stuck in my mind as the poorest place I had ever seen. We drove back almost the length of Spain's Mediterranean coast, from Algeciras to Barcelona, along the N340, a slow highway. Torremolinos and Benidorm were starting to sprout forests of high rises, but much of the coast was still largely undeveloped.

Franco was still in charge, as he had been since crushing the Republic in the Civil War. The freedom I felt was purely internal, to be outside my own culture and in a different, more extrovert but still accessible one. I considered myself fortunate not to have to run the risks that Spaniards of my age did in opposing dictatorship. We were merely stopped sometimes and briefly questioned by stern civil guards in their tricorn hats, suspicious of three long-haired foreign young men. The next summer I hitch-hiked round a large segment of Spain, from Barcelona to Madrid and on to León, Asturias and Galicia. In Santiago de Compostela I fell in with a friendly group of students from the town's big university. As term was ending, one of them invited me to stay at his family home in Vigo, Spain's largest fishing port and an important industrial city. He introduced me to the art of Spanish bar-crawling on an almost non-existent budget: we would arrive in a bar just when it was serving its free *pincho* – a cup of shellfish soup here, a chunk of tortilla there, a plate of mussels somewhere else, all washed down with beakers of rough local wine costing one peseta. While I was in Vigo, in September 1972, the trade unions, which operated clandes-tinely, called a general strike. It began with a demand by workers at the big Citroën factory to limit the working week to forty-four hours, and went on to last a fortnight. I remember seeing groups of workers facing the police in otherwise deserted avenues. The national press, which operated under censorship, failed to mention what was the biggest news in Spain. The local paper had a small story about Communist agitators.

To a young and inhibited Briton, Spanish women were alluring. Arriving in a town I would join the *paseo*, the early evening stroll round and round the main square that is still a mainstay of social life in provincial Spain. Groups of young women would stare and giggle, at once flirtatious and out of bounds, with a chaperone not far away and life spent under the shadow of the priest and the confessional. In the cities I met more independent young women, who whizzed around in the sunshine on motor scooters.

Like the Romantic travellers of the nineteenth century, I was hooked. I would make three more trips to Spain in the 1970s. Even to an outsider with limited Spanish, as mine was back then, it was clear that the country was in a ferment of change. Professional people in their thirties, part of a rapidly growing middle class, would give me lifts in their cramped Fiat 500s or boxy SEAT 124s. They were keen to talk to a foreigner about their frustration at the stasis of dictatorship, and desperate to enjoy the same freedoms as their counterparts across Western Europe. They were often very kind. The only coldness I remember was on one occasion in Madrid: a young South African with whom I had shared a lift from Zaragoza took me to an uncle's flat on Calle Bravo Murillo on a stifling Saturday afternoon, as what was then a sleepy city of bureaucrats shutting down for the weekend. Perhaps understandably, the uncle, a civil servant and a *franquista*, was not overjoyed to see us, but did let us stay the night in the flat with its dark, heavy furniture. Hitch-hiking could be difficult. After waiting hours at the roadside, sometimes I gave up and took the train. The cheapest were called 'Rápido' or 'Exprés'. They stopped at almost every station and took many hours to get anywhere. With few motorways and no high-speed trains, Spain seemed like a much bigger country than it feels now.

In 1972 Franco was almost a mummy. On his summer holiday in Galicia, the newspapers dutifully published photos of the elderly dictator fishing, his face hidden by dark glasses. In November 1975 he died, in his bed. At last, a transition to democracy began. On regular visits to Spain over the next three decades I saw a country swiftly transforming. It became an outwardly prosperous European nation, 'normal' at last. Political scientists stopped lamenting Spanish 'exceptionalism', the notion that 'Spain is different' in the words of an official tourist slogan dreamed up under Manuel Fraga, Franco's information minister in the 1960s (a job title that revealed the nature of the regime).

In 2008, just as a property bubble was bursting amid the financial crisis that shook the United States and Europe, I reported and wrote a 14-page Special Report on Spain for *The Economist*. I found a country on the verge of a deep slump about which it was mostly in denial. There were clear signs of the clash that would come in Catalonia. I titled the report 'The party's over'. It touched a nerve in Spain. That edition of *The Economist* sold more than 20,000 extra copies on

Spanish newsstands. In May 2016 I moved to Madrid, and have lived there since.

Today Spain is a country where, superficially at least, progress has largely halted. The past dozen years have been hard ones, starting with the bursting of a property bubble and an economic slump between 2008 and 2012. Although a vigorous recovery followed, at times what Spaniards call *convivencia* (getting along together) has been strained. What seemed to be a robust democracy has suffered multiple jolts. Many of its institutions, from the monarchy to the courts and the political parties, have been called into question. The biggest shock came in Catalonia, where nationalism turned to separatism. In the autumn of 2017 Catalonia's devolved government, in the hands of separatists, organised an unconstitutional referendum and a unilateral declaration of independence. In response the Spanish state placed a dozen separatist leaders on trial and jailed them in a move that seemed incomprehensible to many outsiders. And then came the Covid-19 pandemic, which hit Spain and its economy harder than many of its neighbours and exposed failures of governance, as it did everywhere.

The Catalan events, in particular, prompted a revival of stereotypes, especially among commentators in Britain and the United States. In many portrayals, including their own, Catalan leaders were seen as representing an oppressed nation. Since Orwell, Catalonia has occupied a particular place in the romantic imagination. And many outsiders are all too ready to detect Franco's ghost at work in contemporary Spain. They and some Spaniards argue that the country is paying the price for what is held to have been 'a pact of forgetting' during the transition to democracy. 'The ghost of Franco still haunts Catalonia', opined *Foreign Policy* magazine in October 2017. 'Ghosts of Civil War haunt Spain in its Catalonia madness', echoed *The Times* in February 2019.

In the aftermath of the Catalan autumn of 2017 Antonio Caño, then the editor of *El País*, the country's leading newspaper, complained to me: 'There is always some *inglés* who tells us that Spain is different. Spain is not different.' In important ways, that is true. This book will argue that the country is not falling prey to atavistic authoritarianism and that the ills of Spain over the past, turbulent decade are not principally due to any original sin surrounding the birth of its democracy. They are in many ways those of other democracies around the world in the 2010s, in Europe, the United States and Latin America: hubris, austerity, populism, polarisation, poor leadership and the struggle to adapt to a rapidly changing world of globalisation and technological change.

Partly in response to austerity but also to political strains, Spain has suffered three successive versions of populism: two are new parties, Podemos on the hard left and Vox on the radical right, and the third is Catalan separatism (although it carries other meanings too). In many respects, the drive for Catalan independence can be bracketed with Brexit and Matteo Salvini's Liga in Italy as among the most powerful populist-nationalist revolutionary movements in Western Europe. But the Catalan clash can also be seen as just the latest iteration of Spain's centuries-old, and still unresolved, battle to reconcile its regional diversity with national unity.

The issues revealed by Spain's recent travails are thus not just profound but they are also of wider significance. What is a nation, and does it automatically require its own state? Should nations or regions in twenty-first-century European democracies have the right to self-determination? Can referendums ever resolve divisive questions? Spain exemplifies other contemporary issues too. How can and should countries deal with a traumatic and divisive past? Is 'historical memory' a democratic duty or a partisan political project? Why does Spain have such persistently high unemployment, and how can it overcome the legacy of two deep slumps? Does rapid social change necessarily prompt a conservative backlash? How can democratic politicians work together to provide coherent and reformist government in a fragmented and polarised political system? And can parliamentary monarchies survive misconduct by monarchs? The remainder of this book will address these questions. In doing so it will sometimes look back, especially in chapters 3, 4 and 5. History doesn't determine – but it does influence – how people think about the present. The book will also at times look sideways, to assess how Spain is similar to other Western European democracies and in what ways history, geography, customs and ideas have made it different.

That these questions have arisen with such force is all the more poignant because in the quarter-century or so after 1975 Spain had been such a success story. Despite everything, it remains so in many ways, as this book will also endeavour to show. In 2017 I went back to Fernán-Núñez. The houses were of two or three storeys, with some blocks of flats. The streets were lined with cars. There was a certain bustle about the place. The shops included a Chinese supermarket. Señora Juana, a 78-year-old who was sitting outside her home in the autumn sunshine, said that much had changed. 'More people have land, and many have studied,' she said. Some commute to Córdoba, 30 kilometres away but now quickly reachable by the motorway that has replaced the old road. She has three children. The eldest, a daughter, studied tourism and works in Mallorca, the second is a local policeman and the youngest works as a plasterer. There are few better places in which to live than Spain. Yet if the country cannot find a path of political renewal, the permanence of its achievements will be in doubt.

CHAPTER 1

THE UNRAVELLING

In the summer of 2008 Sir John (J.H.) Elliott, a British historian who was one of the foremost authorities on Spain's imperial apogee in the sixteenth and seventeenth centuries, presented a sharp-eyed paper at Menéndez Pelayo University in Santander in which he forecast that 'the period between 1975 and 2000 may come to be seen in retrospect as a [second] golden age of Spanish history'. He went on to say that the years since 2000 'have seen the falling of shadows over what for a quarter of a century had seemed an increasingly sunny landscape'. The shadows he mentioned included polarisation, the re-emergence of dogmatism and 'narrow-minded nationalism and localism'. To them would soon be added economic slump.

Ten years later, when Spain's political world marked the fortieth anniversary of the constitution and the transition to democracy after Franco, those shadows had all but obscured the sun. Since 2008 Spain has been buffeted by setbacks and changes that have unfolded with dizzying speed, leaving almost no institution untouched. The anniversary celebrations, which included a special session of parliament in December 2018, were thus bittersweet, imbued in some quarters with wistful nostalgia. At the turn of the millennium Spain's swift move from Franco's long dictatorship to parliamentary democracy, with little violence and through negotiated agreements, was still widely hailed as exemplary. Now, a significant minority of political opinion in Spain, both on the left and on the right, rejects the constitutional settlement, though for different reasons. Writing on the anniversary in *El País*, the newspaper of the left-of-centre political establishment, Felipe González, the Socialist prime minister from 1982 to 1996 and the country's elder statesman, urged politicians to recover the spirit of dialogue and understanding that had marked the process known in Spain simply as the 'transition'. 'Let's not open new trenches after we filled in those that caused so much suffering,' he urged.[1]

Spain's post-1975 transition broke almost two centuries of relative decline, political instability and episodes of fratricidal conflict, punctuated by periods of reform and revival. Between 1812 and 1975 Spain saw six different constitutions, seven successful military *pronunciamientos* (bloodless coups), four royal abdications, two dictatorships and four civil wars. The last and worst of these – known to the world simply as *the* Spanish Civil War – was the conflict of 1936–39, triggered when Francisco Franco and several fellow generals staged an initially unsuccessful military coup against a centre-left Popular Front government representing an unstable parliamentary republic, and Hitler, Mussolini and Stalin all intervened.

As Western Europe enjoyed peaceful, prosperous democracy in the decades after the Second World War, while Spain suffered Franco's iron rule, outside observers worried about the country's seeming backward exceptionalism. So did many Spaniards. Two powerful ideas guided the transition, both widely shared across much of the political spectrum. The first was that it was imperative to avoid any repeat of the Civil War of 1936–39 which cost some 300,000 to 350,000 lives (out of a population of around 25 million) in addition to a further 20,000 or so executed in the repression that followed the conflict.[2] The second imperative was that Spain should become a normal Western European country. The transition was the result of pacts between modernising moderates in the Franco regime, who knew that social peace and integration into Europe required democracy, and an opposition rendered pragmatic by decades of exile, prison or clandestinity.

The process was pushed along from above by King Juan Carlos, whom Franco had designated as his successor as head of state, and, from mid-1976, by the new monarch's chosen prime minister, Adolfo Suárez, a previously obscure *franquista* functionary of shrewd political instincts.[3] Pressure for freedom came from below, too, in the form of strikes and protests. Once Franco was dead, many prohibitions quietly fell away before they were formally lifted, like flakes of dead, clotted skin from a scab. Travelling in Spain in those years I found a self-confident sense among many younger people that they would create their own freedoms.

There was resistance, too. Suárez faced down pressure from the army when he legalised the Communist Party, long the main internal opposition to Franco, ahead of a general election in June 1977 – the first democratic election since 1936. Ahead of the vote I spent a week in the Basque Country. I attended a big Socialist rally in a cavernous sports hall in Bilbao in which González, a lawyer from Seville who was the party's young and attractive leader, stressed that 'socialism is freedom' against a backdrop of the party's new social-democratic symbol, a hand clutching a red rose. More atmospheric was a meeting with local Socialist candidates in a tightly packed fishermen's hall on the coast of Vizcaya. After decades in the shadows, left-wing politics had emerged into the open, in all its sectarian effervescence. In the rusting industrial suburbs of Bilbao along the banks of the River Nervión, at rallies of Euzkadiko Ezkerra, activists waved the *ikurriña*, the red, green and white Basque flag, only legalised months before. The party represented a minority within ETA, the Basque terrorist organisation, which embraced the new democracy. The majority current in ETA senselessly continued to bomb, murder and kidnap for decades, a source of tragedy and tension.

Suárez's newly formed Union of the Democratic Centre (UCD) won a majority in the 1977 election, with the Socialists coming a strong second. To general surprise Alianza Popular (AP), the conservative party formed by Manuel Fraga and other former Franco ministers, fared poorly. Events then moved rapidly: in two intense and heady years dictatorship was dismantled. The new Congress was tasked with drawing up a democratic constitution. The work was done by a committee of seven, on which the Communists, the AP and the Catalan nationalists, as well as the two biggest parties, were all represented. All but one of Spain's previous constitutions had been dictated by the winning side in internal conflicts and rejected by the losers and were thus rendered ephemeral. This time the constitutionalists were determined to reach broad and durable agreements. Beyond its assertion of civil and political freedoms and socio-economic rights within a market economy, the new charter involved two historic compromises. The left accepted a parliamentary monarchy instead of the republic it had fought to defend in the Civil War, whereas the right accepted devolution in place of Franco's unitary, centralised regime.

This second compromise was expressed in Article 2 of the constitution which affirmed the 'indissoluble unity of the Spanish nation' while going on to 'recognise and guarantee the right to autonomy of the nationalities and regions that comprise it'. This awkward formulation was an attempt to satisfy the claim of Basques, Catalans and Gallegos to be 'nations' without alienating conservatives. On paper there were two other, clearer approaches that might have been adopted. One was federalism, favoured by both Socialists and Communists and the most logical solution to the Spanish conundrum of reconciling diversity and unity. But a chaotic and short-lived federal republic in 1873 had given the term an enduringly bad name, especially on the right (see chapter 4). The other approach would have been to grant home rule solely to

Catalonia, the Basque Country and Galicia, giving due recognition to their sense of difference, of being cultural nations and not just Spanish regions.

But the political leaders were not wholly in control of events during the transition, and there was a widespread sense among Spaniards that democracy should involve the devolution of power. Even before the constitution was drawn up, Suárez had agreed to the provisional restoration of home rule in Catalonia, through an accord with Josep Tarradellas, the president of the Catalan government-in-exile. In October 1977 Tarradellas made a triumphal return to Barcelona after thirty-eight years in France. When he proclaimed to the welcoming crowd 'Ja sóc aquí' ('Now I am here') it was far more than a statement of the obvious. A preliminary agreement for Basque home rule followed. Tarradellas recognised the unity of Spain and accepted the right to autonomy (home rule) of other Spanish regions. In December 1977, amid a generalisation of regional sentiment, demonstrations for autonomy in Andalucía mobilised up to 1.5 million people. Other places, such as the Canary Islands, which had never before seen nationalist political movements, made similar demands.

Even as the constitutional committee of the Cortes (parliament) was deliberating, Suárez's government decreed 'pre-autonomous' entities in a dozen regions. That was ill-advised: it pre-judged the constitutional debate and made restricting autonomy to the historic three unviable.[4] In the end the constitution's Title VIII on the Territorial Organisation of the State was muddled and contradictory. It guaranteed 'the right to autonomy' of 'nationalities and regions' in that awkward fudge, but without defining or naming them. It attempted to establish two different classes of territorial unit: those whose autonomy derived from a statute approved by referendum (Article 151) and those where the Cortes approved autonomy (Article 144). The former were supposed to enjoy more powers, more quickly. In the end that distinction was abandoned. In a solution known as *café para todos* (coffee for all) Spain was divided into seventeen 'autonomous communities', plus the enclave cities of Ceuta and Melilla on the Moroccan coast. Each was to have its own elected parliament and government.

The *estado autonómico* (autonomous state), as it was called, was in some ways a deft compromise, a kind of federalism that dare not speak its name. It worked well at first, and in many ways it has changed Spain for the good. The regions run education, health and social services, and much cultural policy and economic regulation. Catalonia and the Basque Country have their own police forces and run their prisons. By 2017 the regions were responsible for 38% of total public spending (and local governments a further 15%).[5] Yet Title VIII stored up problems which have exploded in the past decade. Decentralisation was open-ended. It was asymmetric, but in the course of time it would prove to be not sufficiently so to satisfy Catalan and Basque nationalists who wanted more than just administrative decentralisation.

The framers of the constitution tried hard to avoid the flaws that had contributed to the demise of the 1931 Republic and the lurch to Civil War. They wanted to create strong, stable governments. The electoral system is based on proportional representation but, by awarding a minimum of three seats to each of the fifty provinces, it gave a bonus to the majority party as well as over-representing rural areas. Governments can only be overthrown by censure if their opponents secure a majority for an alternative candidate for prime minister. And the constitution is hard to reform: to change its core provisions requires approval by a three-fifths majority in both chambers of parliament, then an election, then reiterated approval by three-fifths in the new parliament and finally a referendum. This rigidity, too, would over time create new problems.

In December 1978 the constitution was approved in a referendum. It was the third national vote in two years, but 67% of the electorate turned out of whom 87% voted Yes. That figure was higher in Catalonia; only in the Basque Country did the new charter receive the support of less than a majority of the electorate (only 45% turned out there, of whom 69% voted in favour). The Basque Nationalist Party had objected that the constitution talked of 'updating' their region's *fueros* (legal privileges), which they saw as primordial rights.

The transition had two further pillars. While the constitutional deliberations were under way, a parallel negotiation quickly produced a socio-economic agreement, called the 'Moncloa pacts' (after the prime-ministerial offices). In return for the recognition of trade union rights and a commitment to expand social spending, the left agreed to a mixed economy and wage restraint (Spain, which imports nearly all its oil, had been badly hit by the steep rise in oil price in 1973). The other pillar was a sweeping amnesty law, approved in October 1977. This covered 'all acts of a political purpose, whatever their outcomes may have been' committed up to the election of June that year. It thus included ETA prisoners who had been convicted of murder, who were released. It also guaranteed that those who worked for the Franco regime would not be investigated or prosecuted for the 'crimes and misdemeanours that may have been committed by state authorities against the rights of others'. This prevented any purge of the armed forces, the police or the judiciary.

Over time the amnesty would become the single most controversial feature of the transition. It would be dubbed 'the Pact of Forgetting'. That is a misnomer: Spanish society has remembered the Civil War and *franquista* repression copiously in the years since, with an outpouring of books, films and commemorations (see chapter 5). What the amnesty did was to prevent the application of 'transitional justice' and the punishment of *franquista* officials. But amnesty had been a demand of the Communist Party and the left since 1956, and nobody in Spain, or indeed the world, was talking about transitional justice in 1977. That there was no purge also reflected the balance of forces in the late 1970s.

Under the aegis of the constitution and the transition settlement, Spain seemed to have slain its historical demons and assuaged chronic sources of unrest. Late but massive urbanisation from 1950 onwards took the sting out of agrarian conflicts. The economy had begun decades of rapid growth in the late 1950s, when Franco junked the autarky of the Falange, Spain's version of Mussolini's Fascist Party, and handed economic management to Catholic technocrats from Opus Dei. The Socialists led by González won a landslide victory in 1982 and governed for the next fourteen years. They updated the economy, shutting down antiquated state-run smokestack industries. They strengthened Franco's rudimentary welfare state, providing free health care and education for all, and reducing poverty. The Catholic Church, overmighty for centuries, faded as younger generations stayed away from mass. After a failed coup attempt in 1981, fronted by a preposterous lieutenant-colonel of the Civil Guard, the army came to terms with democracy. Spain's entry into the North Atlantic Treaty Organisation (NATO) in 1981, endorsed by a subsequent referendum organised by González, was an important step in the process by which the armed forces came to accept that their role is to protect against external rather than internal threats.[6] Spain's entry to the European Economic Community (EEC) in 1986 (along with Portugal) set the seal on its convergence with democratic Western Europe. 'Europe' quickly became a pillar of the new Spain's identity.

The country had also swiftly moved from Franco's gerontocracy to a young leadership: when Franco died, King Juan Carlos was 37, Suárez 43 and González just 33. The country swiftly shook off the dead hand of *franquista* press censorship as well as the hypocritical, patriarchal moralism of the Church. Democracy ushered in a creative cultural frenzy, in which Spaniards embraced sexual openness, drugs and unbridled individual freedoms. Though Barcelona had long been Spain's cultural vanguard, in the 1980s Madrid's *la movida*, portrayed in the early films of Pedro Almodóvar, led the new counter-culture.

By 1996, after four terms in office, the Socialists were politically tired, their record marred by reported episodes of corruption and abuses in the long struggle against ETA terrorism. The conservative opposition had regrouped as the Popular Party (PP), which brought together AP and many from the defunct UCD. It had a new young leader, José María Aznar, a former tax inspector who had briefly been the regional president of Castile and León. He had narrowly escaped an ETA assassination attempt in 1995. He moved the PP away from its *franquista* origins towards something more akin to Christian Democracy, a move rewarded with electoral victory in 1996.

Peaceful alternation in office is the hallmark of a consolidated democracy, and so the transition was complete. In his two terms, Aznar concentrated on economic reforms, including privatisations. He was determined that Spain should qualify to join the eurozone, as it did. While González had been an important player in Europe, Aznar was an Atlanticist who thought the way to expand Spain's international influence was to seek closer ties with the United States. Whether or not he was right, he failed to persuade Spaniards of that. Spain joined the US-led coalition in the invasion of Iraq in 2003, although it did not deploy combat troops. Polls showed that 90% of respondents opposed the invasion. His personal unpopularity may have prompted Aznar to say he would not seek a third term (a meritorious decision in a country where leaders tend to cling on indefinitely). Even so, Aznar's chosen successor as leader of the PP, Mariano Rajoy, seemed poised to win the election in 2004. But on the morning of 11 March, three days before the vote, ten bombs exploded simultaneously on several Madrid commuter trains, killing 191 people and injuring more than 2,000 in the country's worst-ever terrorist attack. Aznar tried to pin the blame on ETA; officials pressed the media to do so too. When it quickly became clear that the perpetrators were Islamist extremists, many Spaniards were outraged at this deceit – and confirmed in their view that the Iraq venture had made the country vulnerable. A huge turn-out of voters gave the Socialists, under a new and inexperienced leader José Luis Rodríguez Zapatero, a narrow and wholly unexpected victory.[7] This episode injected lasting poison into the political system, with both the main parties accusing the other of playing dirty.

Zapatero (when their first, patronymic surname is a common one, such as Rodríguez, Spaniards tend to be known by their second, maternal one) represented a new generation whose political lives had not been shaped by dictatorship. Although he had studied law, his only profession was politics; he had entered parliament aged 26 and unexpectedly won the Socialist leadership in a primary by campaigning against the party's old guard. With striking green eyes and a tactile manner, he was certainly a political animal. He was dismissed by some as a lightweight. Because of that, and his physical appearance, he was cruelly dubbed 'Bambi' by Alfonso Guerra, González's deputy.[8] Zapatero was more cunning and ruthless than that description allowed. But he would prove to be a disappointment. In hindsight, he seemed in many ways as if he wanted to be the first prime minister from Podemos, a hard-left party which did not exist until 2014, rather than a moderate social democrat in the mould of González. His decision to withdraw the 1,300 Spanish peacekeeping troops that Aznar had sent to Iraq after the US invasion was popular at home and honoured a campaign commitment. But the manner in which he carried it out – abruptly and with no consultation – soured Spain's relationship with Washington for years to come.[9] It also suggested a deep-streak of anti-Americanism in Zapatero that would become more pronounced after he left office.

In Aznar's second term, when the PP had an absolute majority in Congress, and then under Zapatero, the consensual approach that underlay the transition began to break down (it had already weakened in González's last term). It was replaced by what Spaniards call *crispación*, meaning tension. To some extent this was simply politics as usual, and a sign of the growing self-confidence of Spanish democracy. But it had a destructive side. Commentators began to compare the national political debate to a painting by Goya in the Prado in which two men face off against each other, swinging heavy clubs even as both sink into a quicksand (see plate 17). Zapatero began a 'culture war', seeking wedge issues with which to provoke the PP. Some of his reforms represented welcome modernisation of social norms. They included same-sex marriage, a law against domestic violence and the promise of public money for the care of elderly or disabled people. These measures 'strengthen the idea of citizenship' and made for a 'more creative, more tolerant society', Zapatero told me when I sat down with him for an hour at the Moncloa palace, the prime-ministerial offices, in September 2008. Most Spaniards agreed with him. But the measures provoked the conservative bishops who headed the Catholic Church into organising protests against the government. Rajoy, smarting from his election defeats, was happy to support them. Zapatero thus manoeuvred the PP into portraying itself as more reactionary than the average Spaniard – and perhaps more than it really was.

Two other initiatives were even more controversial. One was a new Catalan statute of autonomy (see chapter 3). The other was a Law of Historical Memory. This offered government money and help for the relatives of victims of the Franco regime, often dumped in unmarked graves, to find and rebury their dead. That righted a clear wrong. The law also called for all plaques on public buildings or street names commemorating the old regime to be removed. More generally, the law left many, and not just on the right, queasy, in that the government appeared to be upholding a particular view of the Civil War rather than leaving the matter to Spanish society. The opposition also attacked Zapatero for holding talks with ETA (which were inconclusive), though both Aznar and González had done the same.

Spain's economy had continued to grow strongly, unemployment had fallen steadily and living standards had converged towards the European average. This was the culmination of an extraordinarily successful four decades, from 1960 to 2000, in which Spain became one of only a dozen countries in the world to make the leap from middle-income to high-income (developed) status. Joining the EEC helped but the cornerstones for growth had been laid during the later period of Franco's rule in which policymaking became technocratic, the economy became increasingly open and market-oriented, and private investment boomed.[10] In 1986 Spain's income per person was only 68% of the EEC average; by 2007 that figure had risen to 90% of the average of the European Union's (EU's) then fifteen members. Spanish business became increasingly self-confident and global. By 2008 the list of the world's 500 biggest firms by market value compiled by the *Financial Times* included fourteen from Spain, up from eight in 2000.

Entry into the euro in 1999 meant that Spain suddenly enjoyed Germany's low interest rates – but without German competitiveness. Cheap money fuelled a housing boom. On the outskirts of every Spanish city and town, and even some villages, arose neat rows of houses or blocks of flats. When the first signs of the credit crunch hit the American and European economies in 2007, Spain was building 700,000 new housing units a year – more than France, Germany and Italy combined. Only a small proportion of those homes were required to meet the increased demand generated by a wave of immigration that saw Spain's population jump from 40 million to 45 million between 2000 and 2008. Many of the new arrivals found jobs on building sites. The government subsidised home ownership. As Spaniards got richer, they poured their savings into housing. Jesús Encinar, an entrepreneur who founded idealista.com, an online estate agency, told me in 2008 that Spain had about 50% more homes than households. Many middle-class families acquired second homes near the beach, or in their grandparents' village, or as an investment. There was no tax on empty property.

There was another factor driving the housing boom: the powerful, and allegedly sometimes corrupt, nexus between local politicians, property developers and the *cajas de ahorros* (savings banks) that in 2008 accounted for half of the country's financial system.[11] Spanish towns are typically quite dense, ending abruptly in open countryside. Building on vacant land required the *ayuntamiento* (the municipal government) to extend the town limits by re-zoning rural land for development. The *ayuntamiento* was entitled to 10% of the development land. Selling this 10% back to the developer became a main source of revenue for many municipalities. Sometimes councillors took bribes to approve new developments.[12] The third side of this triangle was the *cajas*. Their original remit was to act as non-profit savings and loans outfits and devote the proceeds to local good causes. But deregulation allowed them to operate beyond their home patch, and they were colonised by local politicians.

The *cajas*, too, stumped up much of the money for the herd of white elephants that trampled Spain's landscape and finances during the last years of the economic boom, the product of the puffed-up ambitions of regional and municipal politicians and the voracity of construction bosses. There were airports with no flights, as at Ciudad Real and Castellón. There were toll motorways with few cars, as around Madrid at a cost of billions to the taxpayer, or more modestly a €120 million tramway in Jaén that has never operated. There were cultural centres with little culture, such as a museum of Iberian culture in Jaén (again), which remained almost empty a decade after it opened, or the City of Culture in Santiago de Compostela, an assemblage on a hillside overlooking the town which resembles a ski-jump designed by a drunk. And then there were the hundreds of thousands of flats with no inhabitants, many on the wrong side of motorways from the beach.

The construction sector came to account for 12% of Spain's GDP (gross domestic product), when in any other developed country 5% is normal. Regulators failed to step in. It appeared that mid-level officials at the Bank of Spain, the central bank, charged with monitoring the financial system were too close to the banks; the Bank had warned that house prices were overvalued back in 2003, but that prompted an outcry and it became more timid. It had also insisted on counter-cyclical provisioning by the banks, but only to a modest extent. To a degree, the whole country was complicit in the bubble. 'It was a national mistake,' said Pablo Hernández de Cos, the governor of the Bank of Spain since 2018. 'What we didn't know was that the bursting of the property bubble would coincide with an international financial crisis.'[13]

The party came to a sudden halt in 2007 when the European Central Bank raised its interest rate. The economy sank into recession, and credit flows dried up. Spain was caught naked: a current account deficit of 10% of GDP could no longer be financed, and Spanish banks found no takers in financial markets for their bundles of mortgage loans. In September 2008, when I interviewed scores of Spanish politicians, officials and business leaders for an *Economist* Special Report, I found a few (including Pedro Solbes, the long-serving finance minister) who were aware of the gravity of the situation. Plenty of others, starting with Zapatero, were in denial. We spoke days after Lehman Brothers, an American investment bank, had gone out of business, triggering financial market chaos. 'Once calm returns to the international system, we will return to growth without the Spanish economy having suffered structural damage,' Zapatero told me. He mistook what was a structural problem for a cyclical one, and tried to fight the slump with demand-priming measures, such as a pension increase and a short-lived grant of €2,500 for the parents of newborn babies. A decade later, in a world of low interest rates, greater tolerance for fiscal deficits and greater aversion to austerity, he might have got away with it. But those were not the conditions in the eurozone during the great financial crisis. Zapatero's Spain was in part a victim of the European authorities' zeal to defend their still fledgling currency with austerity. Spain entered recession in a strong fiscal position, with a surplus in 2007 and a public debt at a low 36% of GDP (compared with Italy's 44% in that year or 44% in the United Kingdom). But as the recession undermined tax revenues, the deficit soared (it peaked at 11% of GDP in 2009). The European Commission and Angela Merkel, the German chancellor, pressed Zapatero into a humiliating retreat. With the support of the PP, in 2011 the Cortes approved an amendment to the constitution mandating budget balance over the medium term and giving legal priority to debt payments over other public spending commitments. Zapatero's government also pushed through modest reforms of the labour market and pensions.

A few months later Rajoy and the PP won an absolute majority in a general election. Having begun his career as a property registrar in Pontevedra in Galicia, Rajoy had steadily worked his way up the PP hierarchy. His flaws were obvious: in public he seemed a plodding and cautious bureaucrat. Nobody could accuse him of having anything as daring as a vision. He had the caginess of a typical *Gallego* (Galician), of whom it is jokingly said that if you meet them on the stairs you never know if they are going up or going down (rather like the chamberlain in *Las Meninas*). His qualities, and he had them, were less evident. In private he could be affable, witty and razor-sharp. He was quietly ruthless, clinging on to his job as leader of the PP despite two election defeats, and seeing off an attempt by Aznar to unseat him at a party conference in 2008. He was dogged and determined, not easily thrown off course. If Aznar had displayed touches of both libertarianism and Thatcherism, Rajoy was a genuine conservative in the mould of Edmund Burke, a moderate rather than an ideologue who thought change a regrettable inevitability, to be managed as best one could.

Rajoy took office in the depth of slump. The continuing problems of Spanish banks weighed upon the country's sovereign credit rating. Spain was widely expected to be forced to seek a full-scale bail-out from the European Commission (and with it the policing of the 'men in black', as international financial officials came to be dubbed). Unemployment peaked at 27% in 2013 when 6.3 million Spaniards were out of work. Then a robust recovery began (see chapter 7). This was partly due to favourable circumstance, such as the fall in international interest rates; the determination of Mario Draghi, the president of the European Central Bank, to do 'whatever it takes' to save the euro; and generally low oil prices. But the revival also owed much to Rajoy's reforms. Three measures were particularly important.

First, the government at last cleaned up the financial system. Helped by the promise of a €100 billion loan from the EU, of which only €40 billion was used, it merged or shut down scores of the broken *cajas*. It nationalised four insolvent banks, including Bankia, a big one. Bankia was the result of a forced merger in 2010; its main constituents were Caja Madrid and Bancaja of Valencia. In 2011 it listed its shares on the Madrid stock exchange. Its managers punted the shares to its customers as a safe investment. Within months, Bankia had to be nationalised again. Its shares were worthless, wiping out the savings of tens of thousands of people. Bankia's chairman, Rodrigo Rato, Aznar's finance minister who then went on to head the International Monetary Fund (IMF), was eventually convicted, along with many other senior managers, for embezzlement for having issued themselves with undeclared credit cards which they used for private purchases they never repaid.[14] Again, the Bank of Spain had failed in what was its main function after the creation of the euro: to ensure the stability of the financial system. 'One of my main missions', admitted Hernández de Cos, 'is to restore the reputation of the bank.' He was more outspoken than his predecessors in warning of risks facing the economy.

Second, after a slow start Rajoy began to get the public finances under control. Rejecting calls to accept a Greek-style general bail-out of the economy, he was vindicated when this proved unnecessary. He thus was able to cut the deficit gradually, keeping political control over the process (he had irritated European Commission officials when he unilaterally but realistically raised Spain's deficit target for 2012 from 4% of GDP to 5.8%). The government paid off the arrears that regional administrations had run up with their suppliers, which added up to 5% of GDP. That saved many small businesses, according to a minister. Rajoy also held the nominal value of pensions steady (since Spain saw several years of price falls, that meant they increased slightly in real terms) and extended the period for which unemployment benefit was paid.

Third, the government pushed through changes to the rigid labour laws. After years in which Spanish labour costs had risen faster than the European average, the reform allowed for the devolution of wage-bargaining to firm level. Although rarely invoked, this forced restraint on the unions. For fair dismissals, redundancy pay was cut from forty-five days per year worked to a still generous thirty-three days, making lay-offs more bearable for companies. The unions hated the reform. But it meant that when the economy started growing again, jobs were created much more swiftly than in the past.

'Spain has passed from being a country on the brink of bankruptcy to a model of recovery that provides an example to . . . the European Union,' Rajoy proclaimed in 2015.[15] He was right, but many Spaniards, still suffering the effects of the slump, did not see it that way. As well as the notorious case of Bankia, the crash exposed other examples of malfeasance.[16] Unlike Italy, Spain is not systemically corrupt. But an unfortunate by-product of regional autonomy was to create one-party fiefs, in which politicians came to enjoy a sense of impunity and entitlement, and in some places corruption flourished at a local level (see chapter 9).

In November 2012, in the depth of the recession, I made a reporting trip to Barcelona and Madrid. The Spanish capital, in particular, seemed depressed, with many empty shops and boarded-up businesses. Spaniards were in a furious mood. A one-day general strike saw many health service workers of the Madrid regional government, who faced cuts, and swindled savers parade down the Paseo de la Castellana on a cold and gloomy day. Groups broke away to demonstrate outside banks. Evictions of mortgagees who couldn't keep up with their payments were met with other protests. In a particular injustice, under Spanish law those who handed back the keys of their property were still liable for the balance of the mortgage debt.

The combination of recession, austerity and corruption is politically toxic in any democracy. In Spain it spawned the *indignados*, the crowds of mainly young people who occupied city squares across the country in protests that began on 15 May 2011 and lasted for weeks. Organised through social media, it was a new kind of protest movement, one that would be swiftly copied elsewhere, notably by Occupy Wall Street later that year. The movement died away, but it presaged a far-reaching shift in public opinion, fuelling two new parties. On the left Podemos (We Can) mixed Peronist populism with Leninism. It was scornful of the quality of Spanish democracy. It claimed that the transition was a capitulation to *franquismo*, which it saw as continuing to have a hold over Spain's 'deep state'. On the centre-right Ciudadanos (Citizens), a small party formed by a group in Barcelona disillusioned with what they saw as the Catalan Socialists' temporising with nationalism, blossomed into a national party. Mixing liberalism (in the British sense) with an increasingly vocal Spanish nationalism, for a time it claimed inspiration from France's Emmanuel Macron. It was the beneficiary of the anger of many former PP voters at corruption.

It was noteworthy that public anger did not prompt either violence or social tension but rather found its outlet in these institutionalised channels. But there was a cost. The political system fragmented. Since 2015, Spain has suffered weak minority governments, when it has been able to form them at all. The Catalan nationalists had morphed into separatists and were no longer so readily available for the horse-trading in which they had propped up past governments in return for the concession of further powers. An election in November 2015 saw the PP lose sixty-four seats in the Congress of Deputies, though it still beat the Socialists, who lost twenty seats. Podemos, with sixty-five seats, and Ciudadanos, with forty, both entered the Congress for the first time. Months of paralysis ensued. Pedro Sánchez, the new Socialist leader, reached an agreement with Ciudadanos on a programme of economic and political reforms. Between them the two parties had 130 of the 350 seats in the Congress of Deputies. They failed to get the approval of the PP or Podemos to form a government. As Felipe

González noted: 'we've moved to an Italian-style parliament, but without Italians to manage it'.[17]

A repeat election followed in June 2016. Opinion polls suggested that Podemos would overhaul the Socialists, just as in Greece Syriza, an initially far-left party, had replaced PASOK, the traditional social-democratic party. At an ebullient Podemos rally in Seville a week before the election, Iñigo Errejón, its deputy leader, exclaimed: 'We are rubbing up against it with our fingertips. Our moment is now.' It didn't happen. Although Podemos forged a coalition with Izquierda Unida (United Left), the former Communist Party, the two forces combined won a million fewer votes than they had secured separately in November and they failed to gain additional seats. The opinion polls in this period tended to underestimate the support of the traditional parties. And the surprise result of the Brexit referendum, held three days before the election, may have discouraged some voters from pursuing political experiments.

In the event, Rajoy gained fourteen seats and won the support of Ciudadanos to govern. But he was still ten seats short of a majority. Sánchez came under great pressure to agree that the Socialists would abstain in the investiture vote to provide the country with a government. He repeatedly refused, saying 'No is No' (a phrase that seemed to sum up the political climate of negativity and that would come back to haunt him). That prompted the Socialists' powerful regional leaders to band together and oust their general secretary at a tumultuous meeting of the party's executive. Rajoy got his government as sixty-eight of the eighty-three Socialist deputies abstained.

With the economy on the mend, Rajoy's minority administration had to face another big challenge – that to the constitution and the unity of Spain posed by Catalan separatism, culminating in the unconstitutional referendum on independence organised on 1 October 2017 by Carles Puigdemont, the president of the Generalitat, as the Catalan regional government is known. In response to his unilateral declaration of independence later that month, the government temporarily imposed direct rule from Madrid in Catalonia. Two conceptions of democracy were in conflict. Puigdemont's was plebiscitarian, majoritarian (although he didn't have one) and populist in that it was based on popular mobilisation and the invocation of 'the people' against an imagined enemy. Spain's constitutionalist politicians – the Socialists as well as the PP – defended a representative democracy anchored by the rule of law and respect for minority rights. At issue, too, was whether nationhood should be an overriding identity and value in twenty-first-century Europe, justifying any means to a national end (see chapters 2 and 3).

After his ousting from the Socialist party leadership, Sánchez resigned his seat. His career seemed to be over almost before it had begun. But his uncompromising stance was popular among the party rank and file. Against all forecasts, and against the party establishment, he got his old job back, storming to victory in a primary in May 2017 against Susana Díaz, the Socialist regional president of Andalucía, one of the party's few remaining leaders of working-class origin but an old-fashioned tub-thumping machine politician. Sánchez was a smooth, middle-class economist from Madrid, who had worked as a staffer for Carlos Westendorp, a Spanish diplomat, when the latter was United Nations (UN) representative in Kosovo. Tall and handsome, Sánchez was said to be sensitive about being dubbed *el guapo*, his looks counting for more than his intellectual calibre. He was the first Spanish prime minister in the modern period to speak fluent English, and was at ease among European leaders. He was bold as well as resilient. His moment came in May 2018. Rajoy was celebrating having at last won approval for his minority government's budget. The next day came a bombshell: the High Court convicted twenty-nine former PP officials in a long-running case in which Rajoy himself had given evidence as a witness. The court found that they had set up a 'system of institutionalised corruption' involving kickbacks on public contracts. It sentenced Luis Bárcenas, the party's former treasurer, to thirty-three years in prison for his role in the scheme.[18] The court also cast doubt on the credibility of the prime minister's evidence.[19] Sánchez pounced, filing a censure motion, while Albert Rivera, the young leader of Ciudadanos, demanded an immediate general election.

Rajoy's position was untenable. For years he had argued, in the context of the separatist demand for an independence referendum in Catalonia, that the rule of law was the foundation of democracy and that court decisions must be upheld. For the first time in Spain's restored democracy, a censure motion against the prime minister triumphed. After Rajoy had spoken against the motion the previous day, he retired with a group of close allies to the private room of a nearby restaurant where they spent the next eight hours, much of that time in a titanic *sobremesa* of whisky and cigars. He emerged, the worse for wear, into the flashes of the press pack.[20] His critics saw that as contempt for parliament. But it showed the common humanity of a leader who had remained a modest, ordinary man. There was something very Spanish about that last lunch – food, drink and conversation as the unchanging priorities of life. Rajoy resigned his seat and returned to his job of decades before, as a property registrar in a seaside town near Alicante, before arranging his transfer to Madrid. He was the ultimate civil servant. His party's brushes with corruption were his downfall (there was no serious evidence or finding that he was personally corrupt) but in any event he had seemed weary, worn down by the Catalan clash and out of touch with many Spaniards' post-crisis concerns over inequality.[21]

Sánchez refused to call an election, a decision that won him the lasting personal animosity of Rivera, whose party was briefly ahead in the opinion polls. With just eighty-three seats in the Congress, Sánchez embarked on a government of symbols and gestures. He appointed a cabinet with a majority of women. The government ordered the disinterment of Franco's remains from the Valley of the Fallen, the dictator's grandiose memorial to his victory in the Civil War (though legal obstacles meant this would not be carried out until October 2019). It decreed a big increase in the minimum wage. And it held preliminary, and inconsequential, talks with the Catalan regional government. With no prospect of approving a budget, Sánchez called an election for April 2019. The Socialists did well, winning 123 seats, but not quite as well as they had hoped, perhaps because Sánchez was lacklustre in back-to-back TV debates. The PP under Pablo Casado, its new leader, had veered right, facing the threat of Vox, a new party of the hard right. Hurt by its association with corruption the PP suffered its worst-ever result in a national election, losing more than half it seats. Former PP voters turned to both Vox and Ciudadanos.

Spain (and Portugal) had hitherto stood out in Europe for the absence of a populist-nationalist party, though in some respects the Catalan separatists qualified in their part of the country. Political analysts argued that Franco had inoculated Spaniards against far-right nationalism. Time and circumstances weakened that immunity. A splinter from the PP, Vox was above all a reaction to the threat of Catalan secession and what its leaders saw as Rajoy's pusillanimous handling of this. It burst on to the political scene in a regional election in Andalucía in late 2018, taking 11% of the vote. It denounced illegal immigration, and upheld conservative family values and what it saw as traditional Spanish culture, such as bullfighting. It was anti-feminist and represented the Spanish male id. It jumbled together a Catholic conservative nationalism similar to that of Poland's ruling Law and Justice party and Trumpian anti-globalist populism. In its programme, it called for an abolition of regional autonomy and a return to a centralised state. In that sense it represented a repudiation of the constitution. Vox did less well in the general election than some polls had predicted, but still won 10% of the vote and twenty-four seats. For the first time since the 1970s, the far right was represented in the Spanish parliament.

There was one clear route to forming a strong reformist government that might have been able to tackle slowing economic growth, the dysfunctional labour market and the Catalan conflict: a centre-left coalition between the Socialists and Ciudadanos (which held 180 seats between them). Unforgivably, Rivera had repeatedly vetoed this option during the campaign, preferring to try to overhaul the PP as the dominant party on the right, a mission in which he failed. This stance prompted several prominent figures in Ciudadanos to leave the party. Sánchez might have done more to try to persuade Rivera, but he seemed reluctant to leave space to his party's left by moving to the centre. Instead, the Socialists engaged in hasty and amateurish negotiations with Podemos. These failed. Set on the risky course of subjecting jaded voters to yet another election, Sánchez explained that he 'wouldn't be able to sleep at night' had he agreed to a coalition with Podemos. 'There can't be two governments in one,' he said.

His gambit backfired. In the repeat vote in November 2019 the main winner was Vox, which, with fifty-two seats, became the third-biggest force in the Congress. The Socialists lost three seats and Podemos seven. The electorate put most of the blame for the impasse on Rivera: Ciudadanos suffered a crushing rejection, hanging on to only ten of its fifty-seven seats. Rivera swiftly resigned and left politics. Swallowing his earlier words, Sánchez soon announced that he had reached an agreement for a coalition government with Pablo Iglesias, Podemos's leader. Their combined forces were twenty-one seats short of a majority. The government was invested in the parliament with 167 votes to 165 and 18 abstentions. It gained the support of the Basque nationalists and four small regional outfits, and the abstention of Esquerra (one of the Catalan separatist parties) and EH Bildu, the successor party to ETA. Alfredo Pérez Rubalcaba, Sánchez's predecessor as Socialist leader, had earlier rejected this alliance with separatists as a 'Frankenstein government'. Sánchez promised a 'progressive' coalition: at Podemos's insistence its joint programme included repeal of Rajoy's labour reform as well as steep rises in taxes. At least Sánchez had tried to answer González's point about Italian politicians: for the first time in the modern democratic period, Spain had a coalition government (it had been one of only two countries in the EU, in company with Cyprus, not to have had one previously).

Within two months this fledgling administration was faced with the Covid-19 pandemic. On 14 March 2020 it imposed a state of emergency, centralising control over health care and policing, and a national lockdown which would last until 20 June. Even so, Spain was one of the European countries worst hit by the first wave of the virus. Thousands of elderly people suffered harrowing deaths alone in care homes which lacked medical staff. Shortcomings in the previously prized health system were exposed: with its functions having been decentralised, the health ministry was a shell of aged bureaucrats awaiting retirement. It struggled to organise the procurement of vital medical equipment, leaving this largely in the hands of the regions.

The economic impact of the pandemic was disproportionately severe in Spain. GDP contracted by 10.8% in 2020, the worst performance in Europe, and recovered less than half of the lost output in 2021. There were two reasons for this. One was that tourism (13.5% of GDP) and other face-to-face services made up such a large slice of the economy. The second was that the failure of both Rajoy and Sánchez to cut the deficit more aggressively meant that Spain had less fiscal space than other European countries to take compensatory measures. Even so, thanks to unlimited support from the European Central Bank, it was able to do much more than in the 2008–13 slump: up to 4 million workers, at the peak, were furloughed and received government payments. The government guaranteed emergency credits worth €140 billion to businesses. It also introduced a permanent and genuinely progressive measure: a targeted minimum income guarantee, aimed at reducing Spain's scandalously high child poverty rates and plugging a hole in the welfare state. As Russia's invasion of Ukraine and rising inflation brought further difficulties, forecasters eventually reckoned that the economy would not surpass its pre-pandemic size until 2024.

Like many other governments, Sánchez's team made mistakes in handling the pandemic. In particular, they were a few days too slow in imposing the lockdown. But the conservative opposition at first made more errors: Casado veered erratically between offering critical support at a time of national crisis to making life as difficult as possible for the government at the cost of the national interest. He refused to support a continuation of the state of emergency, the only legal instrument the government had for a national response to the pandemic. Sánchez's response was to shrug, and hand responsibility for the design of restrictions on movement and gatherings to the regions. When a second wave hit in the autumn of 2020, the government secured parliamentary approval for a second, six-month state of emergency. But Sánchez left it to regional governments to implement controls as they saw fit as further waves of the virus hit. The country had discovered that it had decentralised health care without arranging for effective means of crisis co-ordination between centre and regions. The National Statistics Institute (Instituto Nacional de Estadística – INE) reported that there were 75,000 more deaths in 2020 than in 2019 – one of the highest mortality rates in Europe in relation to population.

In the short term, the government emerged strengthened from the ordeal. But that effect quickly wore off. Having offered weekly television broadcasts during the first wave, the prime minister all but disappeared. Rather than lead the fight against the pandemic, he preferred to take credit for vaccinations (organised by the EU) and to talk of the European recovery funds (of which €140 billion in grants and loans were assigned to Spain). Sánchez did manage gradually to implement a social-democratic programme, with further big rises in the minimum wage, increased paternity leave and the legalisation of euthanasia. His government partially repealed Rajoy's labour and pension reforms, and took steps to cool the Catalan conflict (see chapter 9). He could claim to have brought a precarious stability to Spain. But his and the country's future seemed to hang mainly on the strength of economic recovery, and there the signals were mixed (see chapter 7).

In 2012, when Spaniards were suffering the depth of the slump and mass unemployment, they were surprised by the news that King Juan Carlos had fallen and broken his hip while elephant-hunting in Botswana in the company of Corinna Larsen, a Danish woman who, at the time, went by her ex-husband's aristocratic surname of Zu Wittgenstein. Many were angered. The Spanish Bourbons had a chequered history, having been ousted three times between 1808 and 1930. Juan Carlos owed his job to Franco's Law of Succession. He had made up for this lack of legitimacy of origin by his actions in the transition, especially his intervention to halt the 1981 coup attempt. His clubbable, down-to-earth manner won him many friends. He was an active ambassador for Spain and Spanish business abroad. Spaniards didn't all turn into monarchists, but a large majority became 'juancarlistas'.

Yet Juan Carlos evolved into a Shakespearian figure. 'Instead of maintaining the prudence that had guided him when he felt weak, he lowered his guard, thinking himself strong, and made mistake after mistake,' according to José Álvarez Junco, a historian.[22] The king's outward bonhomie hid deep insecurities. Born in Rome, at the age of 10 he was taken from his Swiss boarding school to be educated in Spain, and to become a bargaining chip between his father, Don Juan, and Franco. His elevation as the dictator's successor prompted a breach with his father. He later told a friend: 'Since I was small I always heard talk at home of economic problems. For us, money was a matter of constant problems.'[23] Historically, the Bourbons had been notorious womanisers. Juan Carlos appeared to 'collect lovers as if they were state gifts', as Lucía Méndez, the political commentator of *El Mundo* newspaper put it.[24] Queen Sofia, his long-suffering and widely respected wife, was rarely seen with him in public.

Juan Carlos appeared a victim not just of his own weaknesses but of changing circumstances and standards. A legacy of the transition and its uncertainties was that the media covered him with a protective cloak of secrecy – until the Botswana episode blew that away. At the start of his reign he had shrewd mentors who guided him through the transition. Thereafter, there was nobody there to place limits on his behaviour. The royal household is small and staffed by cautious civil servants and former diplomats. He appeared to believe that he was immune from scrutiny. He never grasped that his role required his behaviour to be exemplary and deprived him of the right to a private life.

His reputation never recovered from the elephant hunt. According to the Centre for Sociological Research (CIS), the state pollster, trust in the monarchy fell from a high of 75% in 1995 to a low of 37% in 2013. The monarchy's standing was hurt, too, by the conviction of Iñaki Urdangarin, a former Olympic handball player who married the Infanta (princess) Cristina, the younger of Juan Carlos's daughters. Despite having a well-paid role in a private company, Urdangarin set up a consultancy that extracted contracts from regional governments for non-existent work. For that he was sentenced to six years and three months in jail in 2017.[25]

Juan Carlos abdicated the throne in 2014 in favour of his son, Felipe, taking the title of 'emeritus king'. Felipe is a much more modern figure: educated partly in the United States, he married a commoner, Letizia Ortiz, a former television journalist. He comes over as level-headed and intelligent, if slightly dull. Reigning as Felipe VI he restored some of the monarchy's shine. He cut ties with his sister, Cristina, and her husband.

But then controversy involving Juan Carlos erupted again. A Swiss prosecutor opened an investigation into a $100 million gift to Juan Carlos from the Saudi king in 2008, paid into one of two offshore foundations linked to the former monarch. The foundation transferred €65 million to Corinna Larsen in 2012.[26] The Swiss investigation was wound up in 2021 with the prosecutor saying he had been unable to prove any link between the gift and the award, three years later, of a €6.7 billion contract to a Spanish consortium for a high-speed rail line between Mecca and Medina.[27] In March 2022, the Spanish national prosecutor's office also dropped its investigation after failing to find sufficient evidence of criminal activity. It said that the events under investigation had either lapsed under the statute of limitations or had occurred when Juan Carlos enjoyed immunity as the reigning monarch. His lawyers insisted that the former king had not done anything wrong.[28] In the meantime, Juan Carlos had announced his withdrawal from public life in 2019. Larsen's lawyers claimed that King Felipe was a beneficiary of the two offshore foundations. In a televised statement in March 2020 Felipe announced that he was renouncing his inheritance and cancelling his father's annual salary of €194,232.[29] In 2020 and 2021 Juan Carlos's lawyers made payments totalling €5.1 million to the tax authority in respect of donations their client had received.[30]

Podemos and the Catalan separatists tried to use the royal scandals to force the cause of a republic on to the political agenda. The issue was a difficult one for Sánchez. Part of the Socialist base is sympathetic to republicanism, but the party is loyal to the constitution and thus the monarchy. The government pressed Felipe to evict Juan Carlos from the Zarzuela palace, where he had lived for fifty-eight years. In August 2020 that happened. Juan Carlos promptly flew on a private jet to Abu Dhabi and was still living there two years later. According to someone who visited him there, he was miserable and pining for home. Remarkably, seven successive generations of the Spanish Bourbons experienced exile, self-imposed or not, or banishment.[31] Felipe soldiered on. But polls showed that the monarchy had lost appeal among the young, those on the left and in Catalonia and the Basque Country. Its main strength is inertia.

The slump of 2008–13 and its aftermath placed severe strains on Spanish society. Many younger Spaniards had to delay their plans for a career, a house of their own and children. The hubris of the boom turned to depression and a sense of fragility. Seemingly solid institutions had fallen into disrepute, from the banks to the courts. Political polarisation and fragmentation replaced consensus and stability: a two-party system splintered into five, not counting peripheral nationalist and regionalist groups. In all, sixteen separate political organisations were represented in the parliament, up from ten in 2004. No government has had a majority since 2015; in his first two years in office, Sánchez failed to gain approval for a budget, operating on Rajoy's 2016 accounts. In the process the transition – the founding pact of Spanish democracy, with the monarchy at its centre – has come into question.

Many of Spain's problems – greater inequality, high public debt, unsustainable pensions and political fragmentation, for example – were those of other European democracies. What was unique to it was what Spaniards called the 'territorial problem', its peripheral nationalisms. For much of the democratic period the most acute tensions were in the Basque Country. But ETA's terrorism discredited its cause, and full independence has never commanded much public support there. It is Catalonia that is Spain's most persistent headache.

CHAPTER 2

A CATALAN AUTUMN

On Friday 27 October 2017 a revolution failed in Barcelona. That afternoon, at the urging of Carles Puigdemont, the president of Catalonia's devolved government, the region's parliament approved a resolution 'constituting the Catalan republic as an independent and sovereign state'. On the grand marble staircase of the parliament building several hundred mayors from towns and villages across Catalonia, banging their staves of office, mobbed Puigdemont. That evening a euphoric crowd of several thousand chanted 'Freedom!' and caroused in front of the Palace of the Generalitat, the part-medieval seat of the Catalan government in the Plaça Sant Jaume in the heart of Barcelona's Gothic Quarter. 'It's a dream, it's marvellous,' David Regalos, an estate agent, told me as I threaded my way with difficulty through the packed crowd. 'It may hurt the business I work in,' he admitted, 'but I'm thinking of my children's future.' He had brought his teenage daughter to witness what he thought was history in the making.

But as dusk fell with an autumnal chill, the dream was revealed to be delirium. A stuttering counter-revolution was already under way. Even as the crowd celebrated, in Madrid the Senate approved, for the first time, the activation of Article 155 of Spain's 1978 constitution in order to suspend Catalonia's regional autonomy and impose direct rule by the national government. In this, Mariano Rajoy, Spain's conservative prime minister, had the support of Pedro Sánchez and the Socialist opposition. Puigdemont and his councillors were nowhere to be seen. They hadn't even lowered the Spanish flag that fluttered above the entrance to the palace alongside the scarlet and gold bars of the *Senyera*, the official Catalan standard.

The declaration-of-independence-that-wasn't marked the climax of a campaign to break away from Spain launched by Catalonia's nationalist leaders in 2012. In pursuing that campaign Puigdemont, who had become president of the regional government in 2016, was less cautious than his predecessors. An affable former journalist with a Beatle haircut, Puigdemont had previously served as mayor of the historic town of Girona, part of the nationalist heartland in the Catalan interior. He pledged himself to hold a referendum, asserting a 'right to decide' on independence. That was in contravention of Article 2 of the constitution and its proclamation of 'the indissoluble unity of the Spanish nation'. The constitution upheld the right to regional self-government but not to secession. When I sat down with him in his office in the Generalitat on a dank winter's day in December 2016 he was insistent that blocking the referendum would be 'bad news for democracy'. He was prepared to negotiate the timing, but not the principle. 'We won't easily renounce it. I think we've earned the right to be heard.' It sounded reasonable enough. In fact, it was an existential challenge to Spanish democracy.

With 7.5 million people and accounting for around 19% of Spain's economy, many Catalans have long felt their territory to be a country apart, with its own language, history and culture. But since its emergence in the nineteenth century, the mainstream of Catalan nationalism had always sought *autonomía* (home rule) within Spain. Granted in full by the constitution, that has come to mean that the Generalitat runs not just schools and health care, but its own police force and prisons and a host of other services besides those. It even set up a dozen 'embassies' abroad. Only a small minority of Catalans ever yearned for independence.

Then suddenly 'minority became multitude', as Enric Ucelay-Da Cal, a historian of Catalonia, put it.[1] That multitude first appeared on 11 September 2012 for the Diada – Catalonia's national day, which marks the fall of Barcelona to the new Bourbon king of Spain in 1714, at the end of the War of the Spanish Succession. The organisers claimed 1.5 million people took part; others, more realistically, put the figure at a still huge 600,000. Emboldened by the vast crowd, Artur Mas, Puigdemont's predecessor, called a regional election two years early to seek a mandate to turn Catalonia into 'a state within Europe' and for 'the right to decide' on its status. Many balconies in Barcelona, by tradition a socialist and anarchist city, began to be draped not just with the *Senyera* but increasingly with the *Estelada*, which adds a blue triangle with a white star and is the banner of the independence movement. Mas, a rather grey and cautious economist, began to strike public poses as Moses, arms outstretched, leading his people to the promised land.

Three things explained the swing in nationalist opinion towards independence. The first was a bungled attempt to write a new autonomy statute which engendered resentment towards Madrid (see next chapter). Second, the turn to separatism by the nationalist leadership coincided with Spain's economic slump and years of austerity. Mas, whose Convergència i Unió (CiU) party was broadly conservative and Christian Democratic in inspiration, had been cutting public spending. In June 2011, as part of the anti-austerity movement of the *indignados*, demonstrators surrounded the Catalan parliament as it was set to debate the regional budget. A humiliated Mas and his councillors arrived by helicopter to avoid the angry crowd. Third, some members of the CiU, which had been in power in the Generalitat from 1982 to 2002, were being investigated for financial irregularities.[2] For its critics, the launching of the *procés*, as the nationalists called their drive for independence, was a smokescreen to obscure these economic and political problems. For some of the nationalist leaders it was merely a tactic, aimed at extracting more money and powers from the national government. But Rajoy, trying to stave off national bankruptcy, was in no mood to entertain the Generalitat's demands.

At the regional election in 2012 CiU lost votes and seats, though mostly to Esquerra Republicana de Catalunya (ERC), a previously small left-wing nationalist party which in 1989 adopted the cause of independence but had joined the Catalan Socialists in the regional government from 2003 to 2010. Mas had failed to win his mandate for a state. But Rajoy's government in Madrid seemed to underestimate the extent to which the independence movement had acquired momentum. Towns in the Catalan interior began holding their own unofficial referendums. These culminated in a regionwide vote in November 2014, called by Mas but organised at arm's length from his administration by separatist social movements. This was ignored by Rajoy. Next Mas called another snap election, claiming it would have the character of a plebiscite on independence. CiU and ERC ran on a joint slate, but again the nationalist camp fell short of a majority of the popular vote. Its junior member, a far-left organisation called the Popular Unity Candidacy (CUP), demanded Mas's head as its price for supporting a new government, leading to Puigdemont's anointment.

Puigdemont promised to press ahead with the independence *procés*. Officials in Madrid were confident that he would back down. They trusted in a backchannel to Oriol Junqueras, the slippery leader of Esquerra who was Puigdemont's vice-president. But in September 2017 Puigdemont and Junqueras used their narrow majority of seats in the Catalan parliament to ram through laws calling a 'binding' referendum on independence on 1 October and 'disconnecting' the region from Spain. The referendum law stated that the ballot was to be followed by an automatic declaration of independence if a majority voted Yes, whatever the turn-out. The second law gave Puigdemont the power to organise a new republican state and to appoint its judges. These laws violated not just the constitution but also Catalonia's autonomy statute (any change to this required a two-thirds majority in the parliament) and their approval forty-eight hours after their introduction contravened the Catalan parliament's rules, prompting the opposition to walk out before the vote. 'In one day, they are trying to liquidate the Constitution and national sovereignty,' said Rajoy. 'Nobody will liquidate Spanish democracy.' The most eloquent speech in the Catalan parliament that day was by Joan Coscubiela, a former Communist and trade union leader who represented the Catalan affiliate of Podemos. 'I don't want my son to live in a country where the majority can block off the rights of those who don't think as they do,' he declared.

The Constitutional Tribunal immediately struck the laws down, but Puigdemont went ahead with the referendum regardless. At a press conference with foreign journalists in mid-September he hid any nervousness behind cocky defiance. He insisted that, whatever the turn-out, the vote would be binding: 'this time it's organised by the institutions, not civil society'. Rajoy trusted in the courts and police to prevent the ballot. One of his officials said of Puigdemont, quoting a song by Sting: 'every step you take, I'll be watching you'. But Puigdemont was a step ahead: over the weekend of 1 October, activists occupied schools for use as polling stations. Undetected by the security services, the independence movement had procured 10,000 plastic ballot boxes in China. They were imported through Marseilles and stored on the French side of the border before being distributed under the nose of the police.

Not for the first time, on the morning of 1 October 2017 I woke up in the wrong place. I had travelled to Barcelona ahead of the referendum weekend. But I assumed that the panoply of measures taken by the Spanish government would ensure that there was no voting. 'The referendum won't happen,' Rajoy had categorically declared in August. So on the afternoon of Saturday 30 September I took a train to Vic, halfway between the Pyrenees and the French border. The journey of 70 kilometres took about eighty minutes. The poor state of their suburban trains is a matter of justified grievance for Catalans. A prosperous town of 45,000 people, with the remains of a Roman temple, an ancient cathedral and a thriving meat-processing industry, Vic is sometimes called 'the capital of Catalan Catalonia', the separatist heartland. Every building on the medieval town square was adorned with flags, banners or posters in favour of the referendum. A gigantic banner saying simply 'Yes' was strung across the centre of the square. It was hard to find a sign in shop windows or on the street that was not solely in Catalan, although the law states that Castilian Spanish is also an official language in Catalonia. The young waitress in the restaurant where I had dinner had difficulty translating some words on the menu from Catalan to Spanish.

I woke up the following morning to find, not far from my hotel, a couple of hundred people quietly queueing up to vote at a polling station housed in a school. Two Mossos officers (police from the Generalitat's own force) were looking on impassively. The polling station was staffed by a mixture of citizens picked by lot, as in a normal election, and volunteers. There were voting slips on tables next to the plastic ballot boxes stamped with the logo of the Generalitat. 'Catalonia is already different. It's a new European state,' enthused Dolors Solà, a representative of Puigdemont's Junts per Catalunya (Together for Catalonia) party. At another polling station across town, where several hundred were waiting to vote, I tracked down Ana Erra, the mayoress of Vic, a teacher and long-standing supporter of independence. Voting was slow because of IT problems, she said, but she expected 90% to vote. 'This is a city with a great sense of history. We've maintained our traditions and desire to be what we are. After six years asking for talks [the referendum] is the only thing we have left.'

While the morning was proceeding quietly in Vic, in Barcelona the riot police were trying to evict activists from schools to prevent voting. I rushed back to the Catalan capital in a taxi, but by the time I got there at lunchtime the police had withdrawn and people were peacefully queueing to vote. Rajoy had failed to stop the referendum happening. The scenes of police wielding truncheons against defenceless resisters were a propaganda disaster for Spanish democracy. In fact, many of the news pictures that day were fake, some of them distributed by Russian servers.[3] Only a handful of people were injured by the police, not hundreds as the Catalan government claimed. A much-reproduced picture of a grey-haired woman with a bleeding skull turned out to be from a previous occasion and involved the Mossos. According to the unverifiable count of the Catalan authorities, 43% of the electorate voted, 92% of them (or 2 million people) in favour of independence.

But, although they seemed to be the winners of the day, Puigdemont and his supporters had touched a void. They had nowhere further to go. Their strategy had been to force a confrontation. This was explicitly stated in a document called Enfocats that the police found at the home of Josep Maria Jové, one of Junqueras's aides. The plan was 'to generate a democratic conflict with broad citizen support, aimed at creating political and economic instability, that forces the State to agree to negotiate separation . . . or a forced referendum.' A unilateral declaration of independence 'will generate a conflict that, well managed, can take us to our own state'.[4] This document said much about the nature of the separatist project: it was driven from the top by the authorities of the Generalitat, who had no sense of constitutional loyalty although they were legally the local representatives of the Spanish government.

They were convinced that 'Europe' would force Rajoy into that negotiation. They expressed certainty that 'Europe' would welcome an independent Catalonia because they were pro-European and because it would be a net contributor to the budget, as if that was all those in Brussels were worried about. In that, their intelligence was as faulty as Rajoy's. Angela Merkel, among many others, had no time for them. 'The principle of territorial integrity shouldn't be touched,' she said in the presence of Rajoy at a European summit in Malta in March 2017. 'We should say loud and clear that nationalisms and separatisms that seek to weaken the EU are contrary to modern patriotism.'[5] That seemed to be a reference to 'constitutional patriotism', the concept championed by Jurgen Habermas, a German social-democratic philosopher. He meant that the norms and values of liberal democracy are a healthier basis for political attachments than nationalism.

The most they got from 'Europe' were cautious statements shortly after 1 October from Jean-Claude Juncker, the president of the European Commission, and Donald Tusk, his counterpart at the European Council, condemning violence and calling generically for dialogue. At the European Council meeting later that month the leaders lined up behind Rajoy.[6] No outsiders recognised the 'right to self-determination' of less than half of Catalonia. It soon became clear that the whole thrust of the *procés* had been to get to the referendum and the declaration of independence, with no thought or plans as to what would come next.

Puigdemont came under heavy pressure to pull back from declaring independence. He was in close contact with Iñigo Urkullu, the nationalist president of the Basque regional government, who had been trying to mediate between Puigdemont and Rajoy since July. In the early hours of 26 October Puigdemont decided to call yet another regional election. That would have stalled both the declaration of independence and the approval of Article 155. According to Lola García, the political editor of *La Vanguardia*, Barcelona's main newspaper, Puigdemont told a lengthy meeting of his parliamentary group: 'I don't want to be the president of a virtual country. . . . I refuse to go around the world handing out business cards of a non-existent republic.'[7]

That would indeed be his fate. His words were greeted by cries of 'traitor' from some in the meeting. Those cries were echoed on social media and by students demonstrating in the Plaça Sant Jaume the following morning. Puigdemont backed down. He texted Urkullu to tell him of 'difficulties in sticking to the decision'.[8] He would later claim that he had desisted from the election because Rajoy had failed to offer guarantees that Article 155 would not be implemented. But at no point in his communications with Urkullu had he raised this issue. Having called into being a mass movement for independence, the separatist leaders had become its prisoners. Their own division, into three rival parties and two social movements (one was called the Catalan National Assembly, or ANC, and the other Òmnium Cultural), created a logic of competitive radicalisation that had driven the *procés* forward since 2011. Esquerra and Junqueras sometimes presented themselves as a moderating force. But on 26 October it was Esquerra that threatened to accuse Puigdemont of betrayal, apparently calculating that this would benefit it if there was a regional election. It was one of many recent examples in Catalan and Spanish politics of tactical considerations trumping longer-term strategy.

In that frenzied autumn of 2017 in which the world's media descended on Barcelona, the counter-revolution quickly gathered force. In a short televised message on 3 October, King Felipe had stressed that it was 'the responsibility of the legitimate powers of state to assure constitutional order and the normal functioning of institutions'. His intervention was criticised by some for lacking a paragraph in Catalan empathising with the frustrations of the nationalist half of Catalonia. But it was widely seen as rallying a demoralised government and reassuring the non-nationalist half that, as he said, 'they are not alone, nor will they be: that they have the full support and solidarity of the rest of Spaniards and the absolute guarantee of our rule of law in the defence of their freedom and their rights'.[9]

The independence drive, and the king's encouragement, roused the previously passive half of Catalonia that wants to stay in Spain. They took to the streets in demonstrations almost as big as the separatist ones. More than 4,000 businesses moved their domicile out of Catalonia in search of legal certainty. Across Spain the national flag suddenly appeared on balconies. That was new: since Franco's death Spaniards had been circumspect about public displays of nationalism, a creed discredited by its abuse by the dictator. The generation that made the democratic transition (who are now mostly in their 70s and 80s) put far more stress on achieving a democratic state than on the Spanish nation. Their children lost that inhibition.

Humiliated on 1 October, the Spanish state hit back, in the form of prosecutors and courts. Puigdemont and twenty-four other separatist leaders were charged with crimes ranging from rebellion to misuse of public funds, potentially attracting prison sentences of up to twenty-five years. But Puigdemont had quietly vanished the day after his unilateral declaration of independence, turning up in Belgium. Five other separatist leaders fled variously to Belgium, Scotland and Switzerland.

The nationalists threatened to respond to direct rule from Madrid with mass civil disobedience. In the event, this didn't amount to much beyond a one-day strike which was not backed by the main union confederations. To reduce tensions, Rajoy had used his powers under Article 155 to call a fresh regional election in Catalonia for December. This changed little: Puigdemont's coalition again fell just short of a majority of the popular vote while winning a majority of seats (Catalonia's electoral law grants a disproportionate number of seats to the interior at the expense of Barcelona). One novelty was that Ciudadanos was the single most-voted party (with 25%). Its leader, Inés Arrimadas, a young Catalan-speaking migrant from Andalucía, rallied the anti-independence electorate. 'Their illusion is to stop being Spaniards. Ours is to cut hospital waiting lists,' she told a few hundred people who had turned out on a cold December evening, days before the vote, for a rally next to the Espanyol football stadium in Cornellà de Llobregat, a Barcelona suburb.

A dozen of Puigdemont's former colleagues, including Junqueras, went on trial in February 2019 before seven justices in the plenary hall of Spain's Supreme Court in Madrid. Decked out with black marble, its *belle époque* décor is oppressive rather than exuberant. Most of the defendants had been in jail since November 2017. Puigdemont himself had been arrested when travelling through Germany in 2018 only for the High Court of Schleswig-Holstein to refuse to extradite him for rebellion on the grounds that the evidence would not have warranted the charge there. He was safe in Belgium, which has a long and dishonourable record of refusing to comply with European extradition warrants against Spaniards, including ETA terrorists.

In fifty-two sessions, stretching into June, 422 witnesses gave evidence, as the country relived the events of the Catalan autumn of 2017. Many lawyers were sceptical that the prosecution could prove rebellion, a charge designed to deal with military coups and which implies the use of large-scale violence. In fact, the *procés* had been remarkably peaceful. More appropriate, and less inflammatory, would have been the lesser charge of disobedience, which lawyers for most of the defendants admitted in their closing speeches, and which would have involved merely disqualification from office and a fine, rather than jail. One line pursued by the defence was that the declaration of independence had never happened, since it was not published in the official bulletins of either the Generalitat or the Catalan parliament. Clara Ponsatí, Puigdemont's education councillor who, to avoid arrest, fled to Scotland where she held a university post, claimed that the whole thing had been a 'bluff' which had got out of hand.

In the event, the court dismissed the charge of rebellion but found nine of the leaders guilty of sedition (and four of misuse of public funds). In a unanimous verdict it stated that they had 'led the citizenry in a public and tumultuous rising' which prevented the application of law and decisions of the courts. Junqueras got thirteen years in prison and six other former officials terms of ten to twelve years. Jordi Sánchez and Jordi Cuixart, the leaders of ANC and Òmnium respectively, each got nine years. They were accused chiefly of organising a large demonstration for many hours outside one of the Generalitat's offices to intimidate a team of prosecutors who were searching it. Since neither of the two Jordis (as they became known) held public office, their sentences seemed especially disproportionate. But the court took the view that the social movements had operated in close concert with the Generalitat, which indeed seemed to be the case.

The sentences prompted a week of rioting in Barcelona, with nightly fires and barricades, which to some on both sides of the political divide conjured up the *rosa de foc* (rose of fire), the name given to a wave of church burnings by anarchists in the Catalan capital in 1909.[10] The jailed leaders were not political prisoners, as the separatists claimed. As the prosecutors repeated, they were tried and sentenced for their unconstitutional and illegal actions, not their ideas. But they were politician prisoners, sentenced to long prison terms for political acts, and that was highly unusual in a European democracy.

For many outsiders Spain's failure to allow a referendum and its persecution of the Catalan leaders were incomprehensible, undemocratic and repressive. That view was, of course, promoted by the Generalitat, which devoted effort, staff and public money to propaganda abroad. It was much better at it than the plodding Spanish government. 'It's possible that we are losing the propaganda war,' Alfonso Dastis, the foreign minister, conceded in a briefing for foreign journalists in September 2017. 'We don't want to do propaganda. We want to tell the truth. It's difficult to counteract such nonsense.'

The harshness of the state's reaction was provoked by the enormity of the actions of Puigdemont and Junqueras. The achievement of constitutional democracy had cost Spaniards decades of suffering.

Despite the long-standing unhappinesses of some Catalans and Basques, Spain has been a nation with more or less the same borders since the sixteenth century. Were Catalonia to vote for independence, the Basques would almost certainly follow (and the Balearics might well seek to join Catalonia). For many Spaniards the break-up of their country, and the departure of some of its richer regions, is unthinkable. They complained of the naivety of David Cameron, the British prime minister, who trusted that he would win the Brexit referendum of 2016 but who ended up allowing the narrowest of ephemeral majorities in a binary vote on a complex issue to wreak irrevocable change (and many would say damage) to his country's economic condition and place in the world.

Some Spaniards saw the Catalan parliament's laws of 6 and 7 September as amounting to a 'postmodern coup', in the title of a book by Daniel Gascón.[11] Officials in Madrid insisted that no other Western European democracy would have acted differently if faced with such a challenge. Far from being unique, Spain's constitutional protection of the nation's territorial unity is the norm in continental Europe, as the Supreme Court noted. 'No European constitution exists that recognises "the right to decide",' it stated. Indeed, constitutional tribunals in Germany and Italy had recently barred referendums on separation, in Bavaria and Alto Adige. Nor does the United States allow secession. Czechoslovakia, with its 'velvet divorce' of 1993, and Canada and Britain, where national governments have allowed independence referendums (but may be less willing to do so in the future) are exceptions. As for Article 155, it is a close copy of Article 37 of Germany's Basic Law, its constitution.

But many in Spain also blamed Rajoy for the lack of a more imaginative political response to the separatists and for allowing events to get so far. When Artur Mas allowed the unofficial referendum of 2014, 'I would have warned of Article 155 while offering talks,' Felipe González told me. Rajoy's approach was simply to apply the law. Polls consistently showed that a majority of Catalans wanted a referendum on their region's status, agreed by the national government. They also showed that a majority in Spain believed Rajoy should negotiate, and that his intransigence was helping the separatist cause. The opposition complained of the outsourcing of politics to judges and prosecutors.

Officials disagreed. Given the binary nature of the demand for a referendum, negotiation was hard. 'We are convinced that time will deflate this issue,' a senior official handling the Catalan conflict said in March 2017, seven months before the referendum. 'Junqueras wants to be [regional] president. We are convinced he won't go to the end. We think they will call a referendum, the Constitutional Tribunal will annul it and they will call an election.' That showed how much the government misread its adversaries. Conservative commentators repeatedly compared the *procés* to a *soufflé* that would soon subside. It didn't. 'The soufflé is of granite,' Joan B. Culla, a Catalan historian, remarked to me in Barcelona ahead of the referendum. He was right. The jailing of their leaders was felt in separatist Catalonia to be a humiliation.

Because of this sense of humiliation, the separatist defeat of 2017 did not immediately translate into a change in the balance of power in Catalonia. The separatist parties again won a majority of seats in a regional election in February 2021. For the first time they also won a majority of votes (51%, divided among four parties) but the import of this was blunted by a record low turn-out of under 54%, compared with 79% in 2017. The pandemic was partly to blame for that, but so was a generalised feeling of political disillusionment. Ciudadanos suffered a similarly crushing defeat as it had nationally in 2019. The Catalan affiliate of Sánchez's Socialists, led by Salvador Illa who had switched shortly before from being the health minister in the national government, became the largest single party (with 23% of the vote). The election saw a change within the nationalist camp: Esquerra, with 21% of the vote and thirty-three parliamentary seats edged ahead of

Junts, Puigdemont's party. Pere Aragonès, Junqueras's deputy, became the first Esquerra president of the Generalitat since the 1930s.

Four months after the election Sánchez decreed pardons for the nine prisoners, freeing them from jail. That was a bold move: the conservative opposition accused him of betraying the rule of law, and of rewarding Esquerra for propping up the government in votes in the Spanish parliament. Many of the prisoners showed no remorse. Only Junqueras admitted that the referendum was not seen as 'fully legitimate' by part of Catalan society and that a unilateral road to independence was 'neither viable nor desirable'. The pardons stopped short of the full amnesty demanded by the Generalitat; they were conditional on not breaking the law again and did not revoke a ban on holding public office that ran for the same period as the original jail sentences. Puigdemont, who had been elected to the European Parliament, remained in legal limbo, along with Ponsatí and two of the other fugitives. After the refusal of courts in Germany and Italy to extradite them, the instructing magistrate of Spain's Supreme Court sought a ruling from the European Court of Justice as to the validity of the European arrest warrants against them. Whichever way it rules, Puigdemont was likely to remain an irritant for the Spanish government.

While the pardons divided Spaniards as a whole they were widely welcomed in Catalonia. Sánchez was soon vindicated. The pardons swiftly ceased to be a national issue and they drained much of the emotional poison from the conflict. In July 2021 I returned to Barcelona for my first visit since the start of the pandemic and found the atmosphere more relaxed than at any time since the independence *procés* began. There were far fewer *Esteladas* on balconies. While not renouncing the goal of an agreed referendum Aragonès and Esquerra agreed to open talks with the national government. These began with bread-and-butter issues such as infrastructure. Nobody expected them to be quick or easy. But they offered a way back to a degree of political normality. By mid-2022 the Generalitat's official pollster found that support for an independent Catalan state had fallen to 41%, the lowest level since the start of the *procés*, while 52% were against. Given other options, such as the possibility of a state within a federal country, only 34% favoured independence.[12] 'Since 2017 Catalonia has been digesting a political failure,' Illa told me. 'The problem now is to find ways of living together again, both among Catalans and between Catalans and other Spaniards.'

In 2018, eight months after the referendum, I returned to Vic. Now almost every building on the town square had a banner calling for the release of the separatist prisoners and for 'democracy'. I went to see the mayor at the town hall, a small palace of honeyed stone dating from the fourteenth century on a corner of the square. Alongside the *Senyera* and the stars of the EU, a Spanish flag fluttered from a pole on the roof. An apologetic banner almost covered it, explaining that the presence of the offending flag was by judicial order. Erra was both defiant and rueful. 'They think that with prison and repression they will make us disappear. With this they make the breach bigger,' she said. Independence will take longer than people thought, she admitted, it wasn't simply a matter of declaring it, as people had hoped. 'The unilateral route will be very difficult, it hasn't worked as we thought.' But, she added: 'I think eventually we will get at least a referendum. We are a people who have a language, a history, a culture.'

At the other end of the railway line, the trains from Puigcerdà and Vic terminate at L'Hospitalet de Llobregat. Wedged between Barcelona and its airport, with 260,000 people L'Hospitalet is the second most populous municipality in Catalonia. It was long a dormitory for factory workers who had migrated from elsewhere in Spain, its treeless streets among the densest in Europe, intersected by a tangle of railway lines. Around a quarter of its present residents were born outside the EU, many in Latin America. L'Hospitalet boasts a twenty-first-century district of gleaming offices and hotels and Barcelona's new trade fair, host to the Mobile World Congress. In the municipal library and cultural centre, housed in a former textile factory, there was an exhibition of Andalucian *mantillas* when I visited. After Barça, the football team with the largest fan base in L'Hospitalet is Real Betis, the pride of Seville. This is the Catalonia that looks to the rest of Spain, the world and the future. Its children are taught in Catalan at school, but here they speak Spanish in the playground and at home. Although some balconies in L'Hospitalet were draped with the *Estelada*, its dominant political traditions are those of socialism and anarchism. 'We won't forget the contempt that was shown' by the separatists for those who disagree with them, L'Hospitalet's Socialist mayor, Núria Marín, told me. Her father was Basque, her mother from Navarre. 'The problem isn't just between Catalonia and Spain, but within Catalonia. There can't be winners and losers here.'

CHAPTER 3

THE INVENTION OF CATALONIA

For the outsider, that Catalonia should be the site of a bitter political conflict might seem surprising. Few corners of the globe feel
more privileged. Wedged between the Pyrenees, the Mediterranean
and the rivers Ebro and Noguera, Catalonia has it all in terms of physical beauty and cultural creativity: the rugged coast of the Costa Brava,
the wooded hills and fertile plains and valleys of the interior, a remarkable architectural history from medieval to modernist, a strong business tradition, a great European city in Barcelona, a generally prosperous
standard of living, exquisite wines from Priorat, Montsant and
Ampurdan, and a rich and innovative gastronomy manifested in two
restaurants (El Bulli and Cellar de Can Roca) that have topped the
world rankings. Its people like to pride themselves on their *seny*, a
Catalan word meaning their wisdom or common sense. Yet when it
comes to politics, as Jaume Vicens Vives, a distinguished historian and
Catalan nationalist of the mid-twentieth century noted, they have
more often acted with its opposite: *rauxa* or emotional impulsiveness.
And time and again Catalans have been internally divided at crucial
moments. These are not manifestations of a presumed essential national
character – they are simply a historical pattern. They sometimes give

rise to an uncanny sense of *déjà vu* when studying the history of Catalonia. But there are other patterns, too. While conflict, violence and mistrust have formed one strand in the relationship between Catalonia and the rest of Spain, the two are bound together by many other threads. Different in some ways, Catalans are far more like other Spaniards than they are like anyone else. Despite everything, opinion polls in 2020 showed that around two-thirds of respondents in Catalonia feel Spanish to a greater or lesser degree and only a quarter purely Catalan.[1] If there was evidence that the settled view of the overwhelming majority of Catalans was to break away, it would be hard to deny the case for a referendum. But that has never been the case.

The fears that some Catalans expressed to me in 2017 – that their land was moving towards a sectarian conflict in the manner of Northern Ireland – have fortunately ebbed. But there are still two Catalonias, often within the same town or city, that don't talk or listen to each other much. Puigdemont's claim to represent *un sol poble* (a single people) is false.[2] It is a basic reason why the independence drive has failed, so far. But that is not how the separatist movement sees it. The referendum, Puigdemont stated when he called it, was the 'exercise of the legitimate right to self-determination that a millenarian nation like Catalonia enjoys'.[3] That claim to nation-statehood is based on history, language and culture, as Vic's mayor Ana Erra said.

Some supporters of independence try to distance themselves from nationalism, because of its right-wing and racist connotations. They claim to stand for an open-minded internationalism and argued that the drive for independence was all about participatory democracy. This position is expressed by Francesc-Marc Álvaro, a Catalan journalist sympathetic to independence, in a recent, well-informed book:

Academics and students of national questions know that Catalan nationalism is a nationalism of a civic kind, not ethnic or essentialist.

... The civic character of Catalanism passed automatically to separatism and that has underlined the framework of the demand for
independence, which is 'more democracy' not 'more identity' nor a
supposedly pure identity.[4]

This assertion goes hand in hand with the argument that opponents of
Catalan independence were guilty of Spanish nationalism, which is
held to be inherently nasty. The implication was that Francoism hadn't
really died and that Catalonia had been uniquely its victim, and
continued to be so. Puigdemont, in an op-ed in November 2017,
claimed that what was at stake was 'democracy itself'.[5] These claims
provided a 'progressive', left-wing veneer to what was at bottom a
right-wing movement. Independence is not, on the whole, the cause of
the working class in Catalonia: polls show that its support is greater
among the better-off. Symptomatically, almost half of Franco's designated mayors at the end of the dictatorship became candidates for
CiU, the main nationalist party, in the first democratic elections (most
of the rest stood as independents).[6] Nevertheless, the nationalists'
contentions were lapped up with little questioning in much foreign
commentary.

In fact, Catalan nationalism and separatism are very much about
identity. Álvaro acknowledges this, contradicting his own argument,
when he writes later about the demand for recognition of 'identity,
sense of belonging and collective memory'.[7] Talking to those who
attended separatist rallies, what came over was a generalised sense of
victimhood which jumbled together history, practical matters of money
and infrastructure and identitarian questions. 'The way they are trying
to hang on to Catalonia is like they did with the colonies,' Sergi Cercos,
a manager from Vilafranca del Penedès, a town in *cava* country west of
Barcelona, told me during the Diada demonstration of 2017. Many
younger supporters of independence felt an emotional disconnection
with the rest of Spain. 'We don't feel Spanish,' Cercos's friend, Sergi

Rubió, said. 'They don't like us at all,' Joana Reñe, a young nurse, said as she stood in the crowd outside the Catalan parliament as it was poised to declare independence. 'They say Catalan is a dialect and that Catalans are tight-fisted.' Ana Erra echoed this: 'at bottom they don't like us,' she told me in 2018.

So is there a solid basis to Catalonia's claims to nationhood and statehood? 'The right to decide' is a simple and seductive slogan. But international law recognises a right to self-determination only in cases of colonisation, invasion or gross denial of human rights. None of those things applied in Catalonia, much though the separatists tried to claim otherwise. One of the more bizarre things about covering the Catalan events was to be in the prosperous, sophisticated surroundings of Barcelona and to hear officials from the Generalitat solemnly compare Catalonia with war-ravaged Kosovo or Lithuania as it emerged from Soviet totalitarianism. It was hard to keep a straight face.

Nevertheless, since the Generalitat gained control over education many Catalans have been taught to believe not just that Catalonia is an ancient nation – and by implication, a former sovereign state – but also that governments in Madrid have repeatedly oppressed it, treating it as a colony, and that Spain has been ruled in the exclusive interests of Castile. The historical record is more blurred. Certainly, in the past four centuries governments have sometimes acted in heavy-handed and oppressive ways that were contemptuous of Catalonia. (Many on the right in the rest of Spain see Catalonia as chronically disloyal, materialistic and selfish.) But the nationalist claims are at most half-true. The Catalan nation, as conceived by the separatists, is a prime example of what Eric Hobsbawm, a British historian, called 'the invention of tradition'. This practice involves 'the use of ancient materials to construct invented traditions of a novel type for quite novel purposes' and often involves 'semi-fiction' or even forgery.[8] This applied widely in Europe during the second half of the nineteenth century under the inspiration of the Romantic movement and the emergence of nationalism in the aftermath of the French Revolution. Spanish nationalism is not free of such invention: for example, histories written in the nineteenth century ascribed the start of the 'reconquest' of Muslim Spain by Christian rulers to the Battle of Covadonga in Asturias in the early eighth century. Modern historians doubt that it took place. And the 'reconquest' was in fact a conquest since there was no meaningful continuity between those Christian rulers from the far north and the Visigothic kingdom in Spain of the fifth to seventh centuries whose capital was in Toledo. In the case of Catalonia, the official nationalist narrative has a particularly flimsy relationship to historical fact.

The origins of Catalonia lie in the County of Barcelona, a lordship in the Hispanic march, a buffer established by the Franks to protect the Carolingian empire against the Arabs and Berbers who had invaded Iberia in the eighth century. The counts of Barcelona eventually freed themselves from obeisance to the kings of France, and by the mid-twelfth century had established dominion over the other lordships in the territory that is today Catalonia. But medieval Catalonia was a dynastic, patrimonial entity; unlike say Scotland, it was never clearly an independent nation, recognised as such by others, and less still a state. Through dynastic marriages the counts of Barcelona came to possess, temporarily, a large chunk of southern France. To their west emerged the Kingdom of Aragon, based on Christian lordships in the valleys of the central section of the Pyrenees, which grew in importance with its capture of Zaragoza from the Arabs. In 1137 the County of Barcelona merged, by marriage, with its neighbour. The king-counts of Aragon would come to rule over a remarkable Mediterranean empire including Valencia, the Balearic Islands, southern Italy and trading posts as far afield as Greece. Certainly, Catalonia was the most dynamic part of the kingdom until around 1350 when Valencia overtook it. But the king-counts were normally crowned in Zaragoza, not Barcelona.[9]

The raw material of (re)invented Catalan tradition lies in this period, in the Middle Ages. The Arab invasion drove many Christian peasants to the refuge of the tight Pyrenean valleys. There they built Romanesque churches decorated with frescoes of simple, powerful beauty, many of which have been transferred to the splendid National Museum of Catalan Art in Barcelona. The Frankish nobility established a more developed feudal system there than elsewhere in Spain, where the 'reconquest' of Muslim territory took several centuries. The Catalan countryside became home to fiercely independent yeoman farmers; their solid farmhouses, the *masias*, were the basis of a conservative, Catholic, patriarchal society. Barcelona developed a powerful merchant class. The city's magnificent Barrí Gòtic, with one of the most extensive collections of medieval public and religious buildings in Europe, is testament, in stone and in the soaring, slender arches of churches such as Santa María del Mar, to their wealth. At this juncture, Madrid was no more than a fortified former Arab-Berber village lost in the Castilian *meseta*.

The Kingdom of Aragon was marked by a greater respect for local laws and by less centralised rule than Castile. Feudal institutions of government and social contract developed in Catalonia, as they did in Aragon proper and Valencia. The Useages of Barcelona, a document drawn up in 1068, expressed the legal foundations of the Catalan feudal order. The *corts*, an assembly representing the nobles, high clergy and the more prosperous merchants, met every three years, to approve the king's requests for taxes and laws. In Catalonia, the *corts* had a permanent standing committee of twelve members, known as the *diputació del general* or Generalitat, a name that would be revived in the twentieth century. Barcelona was run by the *Consell de Cent* (council of a hundred), which mainly represented the big merchants. In the nationalist narrative, these institutions were proto-democratic. Thus, to buttress his claim to lead a millenarian nation, Puigdemont styles himself the 130th president of the Generalitat, claiming continuity with this medieval institution, although there is no similarity beyond the name between it and the contemporary regional government. The reality is displayed in large paintings of the Valencian *corts*, which still hang in the stone-floored hall where they used to meet in the fifteenth-century Palace of the Generalitat in Valencia. They depict the bishops, the military nobility and the merchants of the towns. Missing are the peasant masses and the urban artisans. Today, textbooks in Catalonia refer to the 'medieval Catalan state' or 'the Catalan empire', while nationalist historians talk of the 'Catalan-Aragonese Federation'. These terms were not employed at the time to designate a political entity that contemporaries knew as the Kingdom of Aragon. Indeed, it was only around the time of the union with Aragon that the terms 'Catalan' and 'Catalonia' were first recorded, according to Jordi Canal, a Catalan historian who teaches at the School of Advanced Studies in Social Sciences in Paris.[10] In *El Cantar de Mio Cid*, an epic poem first published around 1200, the Catalans were still referred to as 'Franks'.

After 1300 Catalonia fell into decline. When the king-count of Aragon died without an heir in 1410, three representatives from each part of the mainland kingdom chose as his successor Fernando de Antequera, of the Castilian royal house of Trastamara. This would give rise, in 1479, to the union of the crowns of Castile and Aragon in the persons of Isabella and Ferdinand, the Catholic monarchs. They ruled a 'composite monarchy', not a unified nation state, as some conservative Spanish historians argue.[11] The two territories remained separate entities. Aragon retained its own system of government.

Catalonia was subjected to centralising demands from the Habsburg monarchy in the seventeenth century, when the Count Duke of Olivares, Philip IV's chief minister, attempted to extract money and men for campaigning in the Thirty Years' War. As part of that conflict, France declared war on Spain in 1635, invading Catalonia. The army of Philip IV expelled the invaders but was then faced by an uprising against the billeting of troops and other exactions. Several hundred *segadors* (reapers) rioted in Barcelona; Pau Claris, the canon of Urgell and president of the *Diputació*, declared a republic, which lasted a week, and invited France to protect it, proclaiming Louis XIII as Count of Barcelona. The French stayed for twelve years, during which part of the Catalan nobility fled to Castile. Under the Treaty of the Pyrenees of 1659 France kept the counties of Cerdanya and Roussillon, the part of the original Hispanic march to the north of the Pyrenees. According to J.H. Elliott, 'the revolt of 1640 left a permanent legacy of bitter memories in the Court [in Madrid], just as it did in Catalonia itself – a legacy that would have a lasting influence on the Crown's policies towards the Catalans.'[12]

Conflict returned when Charles II, the last Spanish Habsburg, died childless in 1700, triggering the War of the Spanish Succession. His will named Philip, the Duke of Anjou and grandson of Louis XIV, as his heir. Fearful of the expansion of French Bourbon power, a coalition of England, Austria, Holland and later Portugal backed the rival claim of Archduke Charles of Austria. After his proclamation Philip V visited Barcelona where he was well received and swore to respect traditional privileges. But anti-French feeling in Catalonia was strong, especially in the interior, following past invasions, and the Church, too, sided with the Austrian camp. The Vigatans, the gentry of Vic and surrounding areas, rebelled against Philip and signed a pact with England. After military defeat in La Mancha, the Austrian and English forces withdrew, recognising Philip. Barcelona (but not the rest of Catalonia) fought on to the bitter end against a monarch who never forgave it for having switched sides. Some 40,000 Spanish and French troops besieged the city, defended by around 5,000, mainly militias, under Rafael Casanova, the head of the *Consell de Cent*. Part of the Catalan nobility and bourgeoisie deserted to Philip's forces. After fourteen months of siege, and with some 7,000 dead, on 11 September 1714 the city surrendered.

It was a crushing defeat that became a powerful national myth which still resonates. It is commemorated at the El Born Centre of Culture and

Memory in the barrio of La Ribera in the heart of old Barcelona. This occupies a former fruit and vegetable market, a splendour of wrought iron and glass. Beneath what was the market floor, archaeologists recently exposed half a dozen cobbled streets and the foundations of the houses that lined them, demolished by the conquering Bourbon army in order to build the fortress that would dominate rebellious Barcelona for almost two centuries, and whose remnant now houses the Catalan parliament. Defeat marked 'the true end of the Catalan nation', a didactic panel in the museum explains. 'The freedom of Catalonia and its rights and constitutions would soon be entirely eliminated.' Again, this is to impose modern democratic language on a very different historical reality.

Catalonia's national day is celebrated on 11 September. The tercentenary of the defeat provided an emotional spur to the independence *procés*: Artur Mas talked of winning at the ballot box in 2014 what was lost in 1714. In historical fact, the war was both international and intra-hispanic, in which most of the crown of Aragon fought most of Castile. But large minorities in both backed the other side. Catalan supporters of Philip, who held several towns in the interior, were known at the time as *botiflers*, a word that is now used as an insult by separatists to designate Catalans who disagree with them.

The defeat of 1714 brought medieval Catalonia to a belated end, and ushered in what would become its modern replacement. In victory, Philip imposed an absolute, centralised monarchy in the mould of his grandfather, Louis XIV. In Catalonia this took the form of the *Nueva Planta* (new plan) of 1716, which abolished the *corts* (which had only met twice since 1640), the *Consell de Cent*, the charters of privileges and the University of Barcelona, and made Castilian Spanish the language of public administration and the law courts. The new plan preserved Catalan civil law and granted an amnesty. But Philip stationed an occupying army in Catalonia and turned Barcelona into a garrison city with the building of the fortress of the Citadel, as the museum of the Born so poignantly reveals.

Nevertheless, Bourbon rule would give greater impetus to an incipient revival of Catalonia after centuries of decline, as it became an integral part of a united Spain. Catalans were granted equal access to trade and administrative posts in Spanish America. The Catalan industries of wine, brandy and textiles profited from access to the Spanish and American markets. By the end of the eighteenth century the Catalan cotton textile industry had become the biggest outside Lancashire, the 'first true industrial complex in modern Spain'.[13] It depended on protectionism: under pressure from Catalonia, the Spanish government imposed a tariff on cotton goods.

Industrialisation brought far-reaching social and political changes. It increased the gulf between rural Catalonia and Barcelona, and brought new class conflicts in the city. Above all, it gave birth to a national consciousness in Catalonia that had not existed in the Middle Ages or in 1714. This began in the 1830s with a cultural movement, known as the *Renaixença* (Renaissance), which promoted the Catalan language and 'national' history and traditions. Catalan had remained the spoken vernacular. It now underwent a literary revival, featuring poetry competitions (known as 'floral games'), publishing and, in 1879, the first daily paper in Catalan. Pompeu Fabra, an engineer and amateur linguist, published the first Catalan dictionary and grammar, always choosing the vocabulary and usage that was most distant from Castilian Spanish. The Diada began to be celebrated by the end of the nineteenth century. The *Renaixença* involved, too, the recovery, or invention, of traditional folklore, such as the *sardana* dance (akin to a more somnolent version of Scottish country dancing) or the extraordinary human towers known as *castells*. 'Els Segadors', a song about the rebellious reapers of 1640, was adopted as the Catalan national anthem. Urban professionals spent their weekends in organised exploration of the Romanesque villages of the Pyrenean valleys looking for the essence of Catalonia. To twenty-first-century eyes, much of it looks very twee, but not so different from the practices of the English and Scottish Romantics.

Catalanism, as this cultural movement became known, was closely linked to Catholicism, and priests were among its prime movers. But it was also heavily influenced by Romanticism, especially in its German and British variants. The Scottish romances of Sir Walter Scott were an inspiration; so was Wagner, the subject of a craze in Barcelona's opera house, the Liceu, in the 1880s and 1890s.[14] (In Madrid Verdi was always more popular.) The Catalanists also imbibed the ideas of Johann Gottfried Herder, a German philosopher who believed that a nation was an organic essence defined by language, rather than a cultural and political construction as theorists think today. Artur Mas once described Catalans as 'more German and less Roman' than other Spaniards, despite their land's abundance of Roman ruins.[15] It was certainly true, in architectural terms, that in Catalonia the Gothic was more prominent than the Baroque. Even Catalan *modernisme* – the artistic and architectural movement with which Anton Gaudí, Barcelona's greatest architect, was associated – was partly backward-looking.

Much of the peasantry felt its way of life threatened by capitalism and embraced Carlism, a traditionalist and above all anti-liberal Catholic movement (see chapter 4). Rural Catalonia saw heavy fighting in the first (1833–40), second (1846–49) and especially third (1872–76) Carlist wars. In Barcelona and other towns, the mass of the population had other concerns: the growing working class suffered harsh labour conditions in the new factories and worse housing conditions than Dickensian London. The Catalan capital's population density in the mid-nineteenth century was twice that of Paris, according to a study by Ildefons Cerdà, the forward-looking civil engineer and utopian socialist who planned Barcelona's Eixample (Expansion), its new city.[16] Desperate, many of the workers turned to insurrection and anarchism. Barcelona became the most insurrectionary city in Europe: strikes, barricades and bombs, along with police torture and military repression, became a way of life. An often violent struggle between anarchist and Catholic trade unions and their respective gangster gunmen peaked between 1917 and 1923.

In this context, Catalanism evolved from a purely cultural movement into a political one: Catalan nationalism. This was a project of the expanding bourgeoisie and professional middle classes, who felt their interests threatened both by anarchism and by the relative weakness of the Spanish state in distant Madrid. That weakness was highlighted by what became known as the 'disaster' of 1898, when Spain suffered a crushing defeat at the hands of the rising United States in the Spanish-American War, losing its remaining American and Asian colonies – Cuba, Puerto Rico and the Philippines (see chapter 4).

Catalan nationalism had several currents. One, which briefly became dominant in the 1930s and again in the 1960s and 1970s, is republican, socialist and federalist; there are echoes of this today in some leaders of Esquerra and in the Catalanism of the regional affiliate of the Socialist party. Another, conservative, current draws on the Carlist inheritance of traditionalism and localism. Carlism was a profoundly reactionary movement in the purest sense of the word. It was not coincidental that the areas of Carlist influence in the nineteenth century – the Pyrenees, the central plain of Catalonia and the Ebro valley among them – are the areas of greatest separatist strength today. Berga, a town not far from Vic that was Carlism's headquarters in its third war, has a mayor from the CUP. In the Second Carlist War the headquarters of Carlism's commander, General Ramón Cabrera, was at Amer, Puigdemont's birthplace near Girona.

The dominant current in Catalan nationalism from the 1880s until 1930, and again in the 1980s and 1990s, was conservative and Catholic but pro-business and more modern. This was the stance of the first nationalist party, the Lliga de Catalunya, whose founders included Enric Prat de la Riba, a lawyer and writer, and Francesc Cambó, a businessman, politician and patron of the arts. It represented the industrialists, bankers and professional classes. It approved a programme, drawn up by Prat, of home rule for Catalonia as an autonomous region within Spain, with Catalan as its official language. All public jobs were to be reserved for Catalans, either by birth or naturalisation – a sign of the insecurities engendered by the arrival of immigrants from elsewhere in Spain to work in the factories. The Lliga was pledged to economic protectionism. Its cause was strengthened by the 'disaster' of 1898; Cuba had been a big export market for Catalonia and had a significant Catalan expatriate community. The Catalan bourgeoisie had backed Spain's unyielding military repression of Cuban rebellions; it then blamed the Spanish government for its failure. The events of 1898 'turned Catalanism from a minority creed into the vehicle for a generalised protest', as Raymond Carr put it.[17] By 1914 the Lliga had achieved a limited degree of home rule; Prat de la Riba became the president of a Mancomunitat, or Commonwealth, which amalgamated the powers and authorities of the four Catalan provinces. Prat was not a separatist; he believed a federal Spain was the most Catalonia could aspire to. 'Age-old living together has created bonds with the larger unit of Spain which could not be broken,' he wrote.[18] But in a tension that became familiar more recently, he wanted to use the Mancomunitat to build a nation. His plans were cut short by his early death. Cambó, a minister in several national governments, would attempt to deploy Catalan nationalism as a force to reform Spain. He failed.

The Catalan bourgeoisie were in despair at continuing anarchist agitation. They applauded when, in 1923, General Miguel Primo de Rivera, the captain general of Barcelona, staged a *pronunciamiento* which replaced parliamentary government with dictatorship. Some 4,000 well-dressed Catalans went to the station to see Primo off on his journey to Madrid. They would be disappointed. In a milder foretaste of the Franco regime, Primo shut down the Mancomunitat and banned the use of Catalan in schools. That doomed the Lliga's brand of moderation.

When the failure of Primo's dictatorship brought down the monarchy, it was Francesc Macià, an elderly former army colonel and farmer who had broken with the Lliga, who proclaimed a Catalan state within what he hoped would be an Iberian federal republic from the balcony of the Barcelona town hall in the Plaça Sant Jaume on 14 April 1931. Together with Llúis Companys and others he had founded ERC weeks before. They swept to victory in Catalonia in the municipal elections that had taken place on 12 April, in which Companys was elected as mayor of Barcelona. The provisional government of the newly proclaimed Spanish Republic swiftly offered a statute of home rule. The Cortes approved this the following year; it made both Catalan and Spanish official languages in Catalonia and brought the Generalitat back into being for the first time since 1714. 'I was a separatist from the Spanish monarchical state,' Macià said. 'We don't want the Statute in order to distance ourselves from the other peoples of Spain.'[19]

Less than four years later Companys, a labour lawyer and journalist who had become president of the Generalitat on Macià's death, appeared on its balcony to proclaim a 'Catalan state within the Spanish federal republic'. This coincided with an armed rising in Asturias against an elected right-wing government in Madrid. The 'Catalan state' lasted ten hours before Companys and its other leaders were arrested. 'Even if we lose, Catalonia will win because we need martyrs who will tomorrow assure definitive victory,' Companys said.[20] Puigdemont might have said the same.

Companys represented the federalist republican wing of Esquerra, but he felt pressure to prove his nationalist credentials. The party also contained an ultra-nationalist wing, led by Josep Dencàs and Miquel Badia, who had founded a youth movement and a militia, clad in olive-green uniforms. Companys had made Dencàs, a doctor from Vic, his councillor for the interior and Badia the chief of police. They prosecuted a murderous feud with the anarchists. Dencàs's movement 'represented Catalan nationalism in its most intransigent form: in fact, it was Catalan fascism', according to Gerald Brenan in *The Spanish Labyrinth*, his classic account of the background to the Spanish Civil War, published in 1943.[21] Dencàs told the Italian consul that he was 'militarising' Catalan youth and that his militia were 'action squads of pure fascist essence'.[22] He had promised armed support for Companys's proclamation. In the event he fled, to Mussolini's Italy. Later historians have qualified Brenan's statement. In the judgement of Ucelay-Da Cal, there was not an organised Catalan fascism, but there were plenty of Catalan fascists.[23]

Companys was sentenced to thirty years in prison but was quickly pardoned when the left-wing Popular Front won the election of 1936. His triumphant return was watched by Manuel Chaves Nogales, an outstanding Spanish journalist of the 1930s, whose reports from Barcelona in March 1936 have an uncannily contemporary ring to them. He wrote: 'One million people in the streets. Not a single policeman. The spectacle is beautiful.' The same could be said of the Diada demonstrations. Chaves saw Catalan nationalism as a sentimental movement: 'Let us recognise that Catalonia has this incalculable value: that of turning its revolutionaries into pure symbols, since it can't make them perfect statesmen.' Like others, he reckoned that the most capable Catalans went into business and that the region had poor political leaders: 'Perhaps someone [in Catalonia] should trouble themselves to fill their time with a task that is perhaps not completely superfluous: to govern, to administer, to do something for the people, something more than offering them the occasion and pretext for these dazzling spectacles.' That could have been written of Catalonia any time in the past decade or so. Chaves concluded that: 'separatism is a rare substance that is used in the political laboratories of Madrid as a reagent of patriotism, and in those of Catalonia as glue for the conservative classes.'[24]

The illusions of Catalan nationalism would be brutally shattered by the attempted coup of 18 July 1936 against the Republic led by Franco and other generals which triggered the Spanish Civil War. As with so many previous events, the Civil War exposed divisions in Catalonia.

Barcelona saw a proletarian revolution led by the anarchists and other left-wing groups, so vividly described by Orwell. The Generalitat of Companys was largely a bystander, tolerated by a Central Committee of Anti-Fascist Militias, which held the real power until this was prised from it, the following year, by the Comintern and the Republican government in Madrid, in the interest of prosecuting the war against Franco. Some 400 members of the Lliga were among the 6,000 people murdered by the anti-fascist militias in Catalonia between July and December 1936. Carlists, Catalan members of the Spanish Falange (the fascist party) and monarchists either crossed to Franco's side or went into exile, in fear for their lives.[25] Cambó fled to Mussolini's Italy. The Popular Front government in Madrid had little time for Catalan nationalism. 'I am not making war on Franco to allow a stupid and provincial separatism to sprout in Barcelona,' declared Juan Negrín, the Republic's prime minister. 'There is only one nation: Spain!'

When Franco's forces invaded Catalonia at the end of the war in January 1939, some 400,000 refugees, gaunt, hungry and cold, crossed the French border into exile. Others cheered the victorious army on the streets of Barcelona. Many hoped that Franco would liquidate the left but recognise in Catalan nationalism a conservative ally. Instead, Franco's victory closed, for decades, a circle that had begun with the *Renaixença*. Joan Estelrich, a writer close to Cambó, confided to his diary: 'a year ago, liberation day, all of Catalonia was unanimously for Franco and the Movement; it was the moment to undertake a policy of moral conciliation, of Spanish integration. Then have come the disappointments; all of Catalonia feels, rightly or wrongly, harassed.'[26] There was doubtless exaggeration in this, but it explodes the myth that Catalonia and Catalan nationalism was uniformly anti-Franco and anti-fascist. Far from it.

In the event, Franco and his Spanish nationalist generals would prove to have a particular animus against Catalan nationalism, which they saw as traitorously divisive. Companys, captured by the Gestapo in German-occupied France, was returned to Spain and summarily executed by firing squad in the grounds of the fortress of Montjuic overlooking Barcelona. To the repression that Franco's dictatorship imposed across Spain (see chapter 5), in Catalonia it added the dismantling of the cultural machinery of Catalanism. It was 1714 all over again, only more so. The use of the Catalan language in all public contexts was banned. Even Christian names were Castilianised: Jorge for Jordi, Dolores for Dolors and so on.

Rebuilding Catalan nationalism took decades and, as in the nineteenth century, began with culture before moving on to politics. In 1962, a Catalan publishing house, Edicions 62, opened in Barcelona; a Catalan-language bookshop followed and in the coming years Catalan began to be taught (as if it were a foreign language) at the University of Barcelona and then in secondary schools. The Catholic Church, and in particular the Benedictine monastery of Montserrat and its abbot, Aureli Maria Escarré, played an important role in an incipient civic revival of Catalanism. Escarré sheltered and promoted an organisation of Catholic Catalanists.[27] One of its members was Jordi Pujol, who would be the central figure in Catalonia in the last quarter of the twentieth century. The son of a businessman who made money partly by evading exchange controls, Pujol studied medicine and worked as a salesman for a pharmaceutical firm in which his father owned shares. That job meant he made many journeys by car around Catalonia, which gave him detailed knowledge of the region and a network of contacts. Pujol, a man as big in ambition as he was short in physical stature, first achieved prominence thanks in part to Franco's police. In 1960, at a concert in the Palau de la Música in Barcelona – a temple of the *Renaixença* associated with the revival of popular song – attended by several of Franco's ministers, a group of activists began to sing 'El Cant de la Senyera', a banned Catalan anthem. The police beat them up, confiscating pamphlets written by Pujol. Alerted, he opted not to flee. After being arrested, tortured and tried, he served two years of an eight-year prison sentence.

Free again, with other nationalists he bought a small bank, moving it to Barcelona and renaming it Banca Catalana. He used the bank's patronage to try to gain hegemony over cultural activities.[28]

As many of Franco's prohibitions fell away in the 1960s, Pujol's Catholic conservative nationalism was seemingly sidelined by other political currents. A Communist-led front became the main anti-franquista organisation in Catalonia. Barcelona became the cultural capital of Spain, the centre of publishing (in Spanish), art and dissent, a development which owed little to Catalanism. In the 1977 general election the Socialists won in Catalonia. It was Josep Tarradellas, a Republican and former member of Companys's administration, who extracted the restoration of the Generalitat from Adolfo Suárez. But Pujol moved astutely, negotiating with the government on the new statute of autonomy, approved in 1979. Compared to the 1931 version, this granted wider powers to the Generalitat over education, culture, language policy and health, but less on public order and justice. It established Catalan and Spanish as joint official languages and followed the constitution in defining Catalonia as a 'nationality', rather than a nation.

Pujol had founded a party, the Democratic Convergence of Catalonia (CDC), in 1974 which soon entered a coalition with Unió, a Christian Democratic party. CiU, as the coalition was known, won a surprise victory in the first regional election in 1980. Pujol became president of the Generalitat, a job he would keep for the next twenty-three years. His political project was *fer país*: to make a country. He had absorbed two lessons from the past. The first was a horror of political adventurism. He was resolutely pragmatic. Rather than rock the boat, he would seek advantage in Madrid where he could. This approach became known as *peix al cove* (netting the fish, or a bird in the hand). When first Felipe González and then José María Aznar needed the CiU's parliamentary votes in Madrid, Pujol was happy to provide them. His price was additional powers for the Generalitat. In a deal negotiated between Mariano Rajoy and Pujol and known as the Pact of the Majestic, after the Barcelona hotel where it was sealed, in 1996 Aznar agreed to transfer policing power to the Generalitat. That led to the formation of the Mossos. Pujol turned down requests to provide ministers in Spanish governments. Rather than Cambó's efforts to reform Spain, Pujol's model was that of Prat de la Riba. For similar reasons, Pujol was palpably unenthusiastic about the Barcelona Olympic Games of 1992, which were widely seen as a transformative success for the city and for Spain.

The second lesson Pujol had absorbed concerned the importance of trying to win over the working class, and especially its large immigrant segment, to Catalan nationalism. He saw this not just in terms of social policy, but also in terms of identity. In the 1960s Catalonia saw a fresh wave of rapid industrial growth. Franco's regime chose to site a big SEAT car factory at Martorell, in the Llobregat valley. Immigrants flocked in, from Andalucía, Murcia, Extremadura and Galicia. Pujol had written in 1968 that they were 'men who come from lands that are nationally and socially dislocated. . . . These immigrants need, and also have the right to enjoy, a national community. And in Catalonia that national community is Catalan.' The task was, he went on, 'the defence, strengthening and perfection of Catalonia's national personality'.[29]

The Catalan language is at the heart of the nationalist project. Linguists tell us that language has two basic functions: as a means of communication and as a tool to forge a common identity. Pujol was well aware of that. 'A people is a fact of mentality, of language, of feelings,' he wrote. 'It is a historic fact, and it is a fact of spiritual ethnicity. Finally it is a fact of will. In our case, however, it is in an important sense an achievement of language.'[30] Catalan is not a dialect, as Franco's officials claimed. Like Castilian, it descends from Latin, but independently so, and from a later and more demotic version than the more formal, upper-class language which, with Arabic accretions, would eventually emerge as Spanish.[31] Catalan has a literature, although this was meagre until the nineteenth-century *Renaixença*. Before then its outstanding figure was Ramon Llull (1235–1316), a remarkable monk and philosopher from Mallorca, who wrote an encyclopaedia and novels in Catalan and engaged in a scholarly dialogue with Islamic thinkers.

The cornerstone of Pujol's language policy was total immersion in Catalan, which is the sole language of teaching in all public schools in Catalonia under a regional law of 'linguistic normalisation' of 1983, which was also supported by the Catalan Socialists. In a mirror image of Franco's policy, it is Castilian Spanish that is now taught as a foreign language. Initially, this approach commanded a broad consensus, since it was seen as repairing the linguistic damage inflicted by Franco and aimed at achieving a bilingual society. In its own terms, the law has worked: the Generalitat reported in 2019 that 81.2% of residents can speak Catalan and 65.3% can write it (up from 31.5% in 1981). That is despite a wave of immigration between 2003 and 2008, which means that more than a third of the population was born outside Catalonia. According to the Generalitat, Catalan is the mother tongue of 31.5% while Spanish is for 52.7% (down from 55.1% in 2013). Reflecting the education policy, Catalan is the 'language of identification' of 36.3% while Spanish is for 46.6%.[32] So while Catalan is in no danger, the continued prevalence of Spanish means that for Catalan nationalists the language policy is a non-negotiable totem, despite the controversy it now attracts.

A small minority of parents publicly chafe against not being able to educate their children in Spanish. Article 3 of the constitution says that Castilian is the official language of state: 'all Spaniards have a duty to know it and the right to use it' while 'other Spanish languages will also be official in the respective autonomous communities in accordance with their statutes'. The Constitutional Tribunal has ruled that 'nothing permits that Castilian not be a language of teaching'.[33] The Supreme Court and the High Court of Catalonia have interpreted this, somewhat arbitrarily, to mean that at least 25% of all teaching, including at least one other subject in the curriculum, should be in Castilian

Spanish. This has not been applied in practice, according to the Asamblea por una Escuela Bilingüe, a pressure group. It analysed the language practices of 2,500 schools in Catalonia and found that there was no teaching in Spanish in preschool, an average of two hours a week in primary schools and three in secondary.[34] Over the past ten years or so around eighty parents have won court orders requiring their children to be taught at least 25% in Spanish. In some cases they have suffered ostracism and abuse; in others, schools have quietly implemented the rulings. In November 2021 the Supreme Court said that the 25% quota should be applied in all schools in Catalonia, a ruling that the Generalitat initially said it would ignore. Yet it turns out that it is the courts, rather than the Generalitat, that are in line with the preferences of most voters. A research project that interviewed 1,500 Catalans in October 2021 found that on average they wanted around half of teaching time to be in Catalan, a quarter in Spanish and a fifth in English. Even those who voted for pro-independence parties wanted a fifth of teaching to be in Spanish.[35]

The Generalitat subsidises publishing in Catalan. But more books in Spanish than in Catalan are sold in Catalonia: only 26% of sales in 2017 were in Catalan, though that figure rises to 48% if school textbooks are included.[36] Many of the best-known Catalan writers, such as Eduardo Mendoza and Juan Marsé, have chosen to write in Castilian. The Generalitat, in turn, complains that Spanish democracy continues to belittle Catalan. Speeches in the lower house of parliament (though not in the Senate) have to be in Spanish, and not in Catalan, Euskara (Basque) or Galego (Galician). Few other Spaniards learn Catalan. Until recently, the Cervantes Institute, Spain's equivalent of the British Council, ignored writers in the language. The PP has challenged Catalonia's language policy in the courts. The conservative opposition was outraged when, in 2020, Sánchez's coalition government removed from a new education law any reference to the teaching of Spanish in regions with a second official language. It was done at the insistence of

Esquerra, whose votes in parliament Sánchez sought and gained to approve his budget. The Catalan Socialists are in favour of implementing the court rulings.

Catalan nationalists are surely right when they point to their language as a source of cultural wealth for Spain. On the other hand, the policy of favouring Catalan has been taken to rigid and intolerant extremes. Businesses have been persecuted for signs in Spanish. Some Catalan officials childishly refuse to answer journalists' questions posed in Spanish. Catalonia risks turning its back on the opportunities offered by Spanish, which is spoken as a native language by 489 million people around the world and by 585 million in all, according to the Cervantes Institute.[37] 'If Barcelona wants to continue to be the capital of publishing in Spanish, it has to do something,' said Ricardo Cayuela, the director of Penguin Random House in Mexico, in 2018. Cayuela, who happens to be a great-grandson of Companys, added: 'It's cultural suicide not to feel Borges, Vallejo or Neruda as your own just because of an artificial conflict with Madrid.'[38]

What makes the language issue so political is that both sides in Catalonia are aware that support for independence is higher among those with Catalan-speaking parents. The promotion, or imposition, of the language is linked to a cultural policy aimed at building the Catalan nation. School history classes, to the critics, are exercises in indoctrination. The Madrid government has never proved that, but in practice the national school inspection system doesn't operate in Catalonia. The public media in Catalonia – a television channel (TV3) and a radio station – broadcast purely in Catalan and promote the nationalist worldview. For many people in rural Catalonia, these media provide the only news they get (apart from the similarly confirmatory biases of social media). On TV3 'you can't talk in Castilian unless you're Lionel Messi,' Francisco Moreno, a publisher in Barcelona, complained to me.[39] When it was founded in the early 1980s TV3 aspired to be a quality public service broadcaster. But it was quickly captured for the nationalist cause. Its annual budget from the taxpayer is €245 million and it has more than 2,100 staff. But the radicalisation of its coverage during the *procés* led it lose audience share, to 14% in 2021 compared with 20%–30% in the past. Even the Audiovisual Council of Catalonia, a regulatory body set up by the Generalitat, has criticised its lack of impartiality. The council found that between March and August 2020 TV3 interviewed seventy-seven politicians who favoured independence and only twenty-five who were against. It similarly conducted 130 interviews with members of the Generalitat and only four with representatives of the Spanish government.[40]

For nationalists, the ultimate goal is to create a new nation state that encompasses the *països catalans* – the places where the Catalan language still survives to a lesser or greater extent. They include Roussillon and Cerdanya across the border in France, as well as the Balearic Islands and Valencia (although they have their own versions of Catalan). The weather map on TV3 is of the *països catalans*. The forecast informs viewers whether it will rain or shine in Perpignan but is silent about the weather in Madrid or Zaragoza.[41]

Spaniards would be wise to look at Quebec, where the measures taken over the past half century to safeguard the place of the French language, in the province and in Canada, have played an important role in defusing Quebecois separatism. Recognising Catalan as the dominant language of education is a small price to pay for keeping Catalonia in Spain. In turn, the Generalitat could be more flexible in allowing teaching and the public use of Castilian without compromising the principle of immersion. Protecting a language and a cultural heritage doesn't have to be a weapon of identity politics – unless, of course, that is the aim.

What turned 'minority into multitude', autonomism to separatism, was partly the success of Pujol's nation-building efforts and the advent of new generations that had no adult memory of the dictatorship and the transition. It was partly, too, the general distemper generated by austerity. But it was also a chapter of political accidents, and of insensitive fumblings by governments in both Barcelona and Madrid. One of the first of these stemmed from the rivalry between Pujol and Pasqual Maragall, the successful Socialist mayor of Barcelona between 1982 and 1997 who had organised the Olympic Games. Catalonia had settled into a pattern where the Socialists were the largest party in national elections but Pujol's CiU dominated regional ones. In the regional election of 2003 at which Pujol stepped down Maragall was determined to unseat the CiU from the Palau de la Generalitat. To do so he attempted to compete on the terrain of Catalan nationalism, promising a new, enhanced statute of autonomy. There was little public demand in Catalonia for this. It was something that Pujol, ever averse to adventurism, had resisted. 'It would open a process of uncertain consequences,' he said in 1996.[42] How right he turned out to be.

The Socialists duly beat Artur Mas and the CiU by just 7,000 votes (or 0.3% of the total). To gain a majority, Maragall formed a coalition with Esquerra (and a small left-wing group). It was the first time that an openly separatist party had entered government in Catalonia. By making a new statute the priority Maragall missed a historic opportunity to offer a coherent rival project to Pujol's for Catalonia. Instead, he embarked on what Jordi Amat, a Catalan writer, has called 'a conspiracy of the irresponsibles'.[43] The draft new statute was drawn up by a team headed by Carles Viver Pi-Sunyer, a former justice of the Constitutional Tribunal who, in 2017, would write the notorious law of 'disconnection'. It was a voluminous document, with 223 articles where 57 had sufficed in the 1979 statute.[44] It sought to achieve by the back door a constitutional reform that would establish in Spain something close to a confederation (an association of sovereign states). It asserted the notion that Catalonia had historic rights that legitimised an increase in its sovereignty and powers and a bilateral relationship with the Spanish state.

At Maragall's final campaign rally in 2003 Zapatero, the Socialist leader, had promised to support a new statute approved by the Catalan parliament. Nobody expected him to win the next national election; as with David Cameron and the Brexit referendum, it was a promise made primarily for internal political purposes and not one intended to be kept. Yet, thanks to the Madrid bombings, the Socialists won the 2004 general election (see chapter 1) and, like Cameron, Zapatero was required to keep his word. The PP organised a public campaign against the new statute. In response Catalan nationalists organised a demonstration in which, for the first time, they embraced the idea of a sovereign 'right to decide'. Under pressure, Zapatero negotiated amendments with Artur Mas to the text of the statute, which merely served to alienate Esquerra. Following approval in the Spanish parliament, the statute was submitted to a referendum in Catalonia in a climate of public indifference. The turn-out was 48%, of whom 74% voted Yes. Shortly afterwards Maragall retired from politics, suffering from early-onset Alzheimer's disease.

What turned the saga of the statute into a turbocharger of growing separatist sentiment was a flaw in the constitution: the Constitutional Tribunal was not required to rule on the constitutionality of the document before it was put to the voters. Instead, it ruled four years later. The tribunal declared fourteen articles unconstitutional, mainly those that proposed to create an autonomous judiciary in Catalonia. It modified other clauses. In an article that declared Catalan 'the normal and preferred language' it deleted 'preferred'. It upheld the preamble which declared Catalonia to be a nation; but it said that this was a historical and cultural term which lacked legal value.[45] The separatists claimed that the tribunal had rendered itself illegitimate and used its ruling as justification for independence. When the Baltic states won their independence in the early 1990s Pujol had observed that 'Catalonia is like Lithuania but Spain is not like the Soviet Union.' But now he threw in the autonomist towel. Nationalism had had arguments to reject independence, he wrote. 'Now it doesn't.'[46]

In 2007 the Platform for the Right to Decide, a sovereigntist organisation set up during the row over the statute, organised a large demonstration in protest at the problems of Barcelona's suburban train service. It was a characteristic of the *procés* that existential issues were jumbled up with the humdrum. The financial crisis of 2008 turned fiscal issues into a matter of much grievance in Catalonia, at least after Artur Mas had switched from champion of austerity to Moses leading his people to the promised land. Under Spain's quasi-federal financing system Catalonia transferred more revenue to the rest of the country than it got back. That was because the system embodied the principle of solidarity, of transfers from richer regions to poorer ones. But many Catalans saw the transfers as disproportionate. The Generalitat also argued that Catalonia got less than its fair share of public investment.

Andreu Mas-Colell, one of Spain's most brilliant economists who was Mas's economic councillor, wanted Rajoy to agree to change the rules governing regional financing. He proposed that Catalonia should have a similar fiscal deal to the Basque Country and Navarre, which collect their own taxes and hand over an agreed amount to Madrid, keeping the rest. Since they are among the richest regions in Spain this arrangement goes against the principle of solidarity. But it has existed since the 1830s and no democratic government dare overturn it. 'For us, the essential thing was the capacity to levy our own taxes and to have decision-making powers over all resources spent in Catalonia,' Mas-Colell told me. But Rajoy, immersed in avoiding a fiscal bail-out from the EU, rejected this out of hand. The problem for Spain was that Catalonia's economy is far bigger than those of the Basque Country and Navarre.

Behind these demands was a nagging anguish that Catalonia was no longer ahead of the Spanish pack. Under the aegis of the constitution of 1978 and the *estado autonómico*, the rest of the country had started to catch up. Maragall had lamented that Catalonia was 'losing its specific weight in Spain and very probably also in the world'.[47] A few months before the Constitutional Tribunal's verdict on the new statute all of the region's main newspapers had published a joint editorial entitled 'The dignity of Catalonia' in which they complained of a new centralism afoot in Spain, led by the PP. Many moderate Catalanists expressed the view that the initial impetus for decentralisation set by the transition had been lost, and that Spain was increasingly being organised for the benefit of Madrid.

The backbone of Catalonia's economy is manufacturing and medium-sized family businesses. Spain's entry to the EU opened new export markets. But only a few of these firms have grown to be multinationals. Barcelona has an important research base. But globalisation has tended to favour Madrid, with its air bridge to the Americas. Spanish multinationals, some of them privatised such as Telefónica, tended to cluster in the capital. While Barcelona is hemmed in between mountains and sea, Madrid has plenty of space to expand, sprawling out across the Castilian *meseta*. Since Aznar, Spanish governments have favoured Madrid, at least as seen from Barcelona. The AVE high-speed train lines were a particular bugbear: they form a hub and spoke network, linking much of Spain to Madrid. Seen from the capital, this is about integrating a large country. Seen from Catalonia it is discriminatory at best, and at worst a conspiracy to downgrade Barcelona, which only gained a high-speed line to the French border in 2013. Barcelona and Valencia, Spain's second and third cities, still lack a high-speed link, though it is now under construction. Barcelona had good claims to be treated as Spain's co-capital. 'I want [it] to be Munich, not Marseilles or Lyon,' a politically influential businessman in the city told me. Yet government agencies were nearly all placed in Madrid, with the exception of the judicial academy (the government also sited a supercomputer in Barcelona). Zapatero moved the telecoms regulator to the Catalan capital but its presence was short-lived; Rajoy merged it into a broader regulatory agency based in Madrid.

When Franco died in 1975 Catalonia's economy was 25% bigger than that of the Madrid region. By 2018 the GDP of Madrid, with 6.6 million people, had overtaken that of Catalonia, which has 7.6 million. The PP, which has governed the Madrid region since 1995, attributes this economic growth to its business-friendly policies, which include cuts in regional taxes totalling €53 billion since 2004. 'We think there is a direct correlation between the lowering of the tax burden and economic growth,' Javier Fernández-Lasquetty, Madrid's economic councillor told me. Certainly, Catalonia in part had itself to blame for its relative decline. The prolonged uncertainty generated by the independence process, and the possibility that Catalonia would find itself out of the EU, dampened business confidence. But Catalans were not alone in reckoning that Madrid extracted undue benefit from the presence of central government agencies and national institutions, and that its tax cuts constituted unfair fiscal 'dumping' as Ximo Puig, the Socialist president of Valencia put it.

In 2014 Pujol dropped a bombshell: the patriarch of modern Catalonia admitted that his family had bank accounts in Andorra from which they had regularly drawn undeclared income. His statement was a response to a police investigation of the Pujol family finances, going back decades. A judge of the National Court in Madrid would eventually charge Pujol, his wife and their seven children with racketeering, money laundering and tax evasion.[48] He stated that they had abused their privileged political position to accumulate a fortune, which the police financial crimes unit estimated at €290 million. Pujol claimed that the money in Andorra was a bequest from his father (even if that was the case, he should still have declared it for tax purposes). At least part of the funds, the judge concluded, came from illegal commissions paid by firms in return for help in obtaining public contracts, land re-zoning and other favours from the Generalitat.[49] One of the sons, Oriol Pujol, who had entered politics and became the general secretary of Convergència, was convicted in 2019 of influence trafficking, taking bribes and forging documents in a case involving the award of concessions to run official vehicle testing centres in Catalonia.[50] In a parallel case, Fèlix Millet, who for thirty years had run the Palau de la Música in Barcelona, confessed to acting as another channel for the charging of commissions on the Generalitat's public contracts. At his trial in 2017 he admitted that the standard commission was 4%, that he pocketed 1.5% and the rest (totalling €6.6 million on the ones involved in the case) went to finance Convergència.[51] That doomed politically both Artur Mas and Convergència, although it changed its name to the Democratic and Europeanist Party of Catalonia (PdeCat). Puigdemont had no time for it, setting up his own political vehicle, Junts per Catalunya. So much for the notion that Catalonia could morally 'regenerate' Spain.

Far from provoking self-criticism, these revelations coincided with an increasingly populist turn in Catalan nationalism as it evolved into separatism. Populism, properly described, involves a political method that centres on the definition of a people, a leader and an enemy. In the separatist narrative, Catalans were defined as *un sol poble*, as we have seen; those who disagreed with independence were 'bad Catalans' or *botiflers*, their views to be ignored. Quim Torra, a publisher and former insurance manager who was Puigdemont's nominee as his successor as president of the Generalitat, once wrote that: 'It's not natural to speak Spanish in Catalonia. And when someone decides not to speak Catalan they are turning their back on Catalonia.' In other words, only part of the population of Catalonia constituted the Catalan people, and only that part counted. After the referendum, banners appeared saying *el poble mana, el govern obeeix* ('the people command, the [Catalan] government obeys'). As for the leader, there was Artur Mas transformed into Moses; or Carles Puigdemont who successfully turned himself into the personification of resistance. There was always a strong cult of the leader in Catalan nationalism, from Macià to Puigdemont. Pujol may have founded a party, but he was never a party man. The enemy, of course, was Madrid or Castile, just as it was 'Brussels' for the Brexiteers or 'the swamp' or the 'globalists' for the supporters of Donald Trump.[52] 'Spain robs us' became a popular slogan. In 2013 a historical institute attached to the Generalitat organised a symposium entitled 'Spain against Catalonia'.

The referendum, a device often favoured by populists, became a solipsistic obsession for an independence movement that seemed to lack a handbrake. Both Mas and Puigdemont had presented Rajoy with lists including many other demands, mainly concerning money and infrastructure. The government offered to negotiate on these. But there was only one demand that mattered, and that was for the vote. It was pursued without regard for the lack of sufficient popular support, and without serious assessment of the political constraints in Madrid or the priorities in Brussels or Berlin, or the likely reaction in all those places to unconstitutional action. As Álvaro points out, this reflected a lack of experience and knowledge of Madrid politics among the new generation of nationalist leaders which was fully reciprocated in the Spanish capital's ignorance of the changed political realities of Catalonia.[53] It seemed symbolic that on Rajoy's fleeting visits to Barcelona, he tended to stage events at a hotel in the port area as if, like Francisco Pizarro during the conquest of Peru, he needed to be near his escape ships. 'The problem is that in Catalonia they [i.e. the Generalitat] want to do politics without governing and in Madrid they want to govern without doing politics,' noted Joaquim Gay de Montellà, the head of the main Catalan business association.[54] The PP reckoned that a hard line against separatism gained it votes in the rest of Spain.

This populist tendency in the independence movement shaded into a racist suprematism in the disdain of some separatists for Spain and other Spaniards. Unlike Basque nationalism, its Catalan equivalent was not ethnically based. Nevertheless, among some there was a subliminal narrative of racism, that Catalans were Europeans, the 'south of the north', while Spaniards were, it was insinuated, Africans or *gitanos* (Roma). Mas's comment about Catalans being 'more German and less Roman' was typical. Prat de la Riba had written that 'the Catalan race' was 'European' while Spaniards were 'African' or 'Berber'.[55] Junqueras once tried to claim, misquoting a study by the University of Rotterdam, that Catalans were genetically different from other Spaniards, more similar to the French.[56] Andalucians, one heard often in Catalonia, were lazy scroungers. 'They've spent so much money on Andalucía and it hasn't reduced unemployment,' an official of the Generalitat complained to me. 'Here we work to get ahead, in other parts they take benefits and don't work,' Jaume, the retired owner of a family machinery business, told me as he queued to vote in the referendum in Vic. Racism was explicit in writing by Torra, who had been the director of the Born Cultural Centre and was an enthusiast for Dencàs, the quasi-fascist separatist of the 1930s. In a series of xenophobic articles, he described Spaniards as 'carrion-eaters, snakes, hyenas' and 'wild beasts in human form'.[57] On being sworn in as president he apologised for these articles, though without suggesting he had changed his views. Josep Sort, a candidate for Junts in the February 2021 Catalan election, tweeted of Ada Colau, the Podemos mayor of Barcelona since 2015, that 'She is no more than a hysterical Spanish whore: we will cleanse [Catalonia of] Spaniards, I promise it.' He was forced to resign.[58]

It would be unfair to infer that the sentiments expressed in these comments were shared by the majority of the 2 million or so who favoured independence. They always stressed their anti-racism. Like the rest of Spain, in the twenty-first century Catalonia had absorbed large numbers of immigrants from outside the EU with little friction. And other Spaniards were often guilty of anti-Catalan stereotyping. The underlying point is that while some of those 2 million may have thought the conflict was about democracy, as did Brexiteers, the identitarian character of Catalan nationalism is impossible to deny. And since Catalonia is not, and has never been, a colony, its nationalism commands no automatic moral superiority over the Spanish variety.

Amartya Sen has pointed out that as human beings we all have multiple identities (related to our gender, work, hobbies, preferences and so on). 'The imposition of an allegedly unique identity is often a crucial component of the "martial art" of fomenting sectarian confrontation,' he went on.[59] This is the basis of what is now called identity politics. It is this divisive highlighting of a one-dimensional Catalan identity based on language that is at the heart of the drive for independence. Torra was open about this: 'Catalanism has to base itself on a fierce defence of our identity and culture, our pride in being Catalans.'

If Catalonia is indeed a nation, it is a cultural one, and not 'millenarian'. In other words, the Catalan nation was invented in the nineteenth century through the *Renaixença* and the Catalanist cultural movement. That effort was successful because it had plausible raw materials on which to draw, above all in the Catalan language. But more than many nations it is a plural one. In places like Vic, the Spanish state is barely present, limited to a small office of the national police that issues passports and the social security office that pays pensions. But that gave the separatist movement a false sense that independence would be swift and painless. Prat de la Riba's comment about the ties that bind from 'age-old living together' with the rest of Spain remains true. When Catalan officials insisted to me, as they often did, that it was 'too late' for a reformist solution to the conflict they were placing populist sentiment above political rationality.

There is no inherent reason that a cultural nation requires a state. The world has only around 200 nation states but some 6,000 languages. Almost all nation states, except those that have practised ethnic cleansing, include cultural minorities. As José Álvarez Junco, a Spanish historian of nationalism, has written:

The big question . . . is why from the existence of some differentiated cultural characteristics we should deduce that the human group that bears those characteristics should command the governance of the territory which it inhabits. It would seem that from an approach based on the defence of ethnic or cultural peculiarities only a conclusion of a cultural kind should be deduced: the demand that the fundamental expressions of that culture should be respected, or promoted or subsidised.

Once political control of the territory is achieved by the nationalist group that insists on its cultural specificity 'it will tend to eliminate the cultural heterogeneity it finds in the area it controls', Álvarez Junco goes on.[60]

On the other hand, in rejecting the notion that Catalonia is a cultural nation with its own specificities, Spanish nationalists are refusing to acknowledge the everyday reality lived, like it or not, by several million people in Catalonia. The rest of Spain needs to accept that Catalanism is a valid sentiment, and not inherently subversive. Much the same goes, on a smaller scale, for Basques. And if it is to retain democratic legitimacy in the long term, the existing nation state of Spain has to work better for all its citizens, including those millions of Catalans and Basques. That, in turn, means accepting that Spain lacks the cultural and political uniformity of, say, France, which has long been a desired, but frustratingly unattainable, model for some Spanish political elites. This Spanish diversity is a result of history and geography.

CHAPTER 4

WHY SPAIN IS NOT FRANCE

The small town of Frómista, lost in the monotonous tawny plain of northern Castile, owes its clutch of ancient churches to its position on the medieval pilgrimage route to Santiago de Compostela. But it also bestrides another communications artery. Just outside the town is an impressive run of locks on the canal of Castile, a grandiose project conceived in the mid-eighteenth century. Its aim was to connect the wheat lands of Castile with the port of Santander. Building began in 1753, but was often interrupted by lack of funds. In 1831 a cash-strapped monarchy privatised the project. By the 1850s scores of barges plied along its roughly 200 kilometres, split between three branches. But it never reached Santander, which required boring tunnels through the Cantabrian mountains. The opening of a railway line running parallel to its main branch through Frómista killed the economic viability of the canal before it was finished.

During Spain's Golden Age wheat and sheep assured Castile's economic – and demographic – predominance within the Iberian Peninsula. From the eighteenth century onwards it lost ground economically to Catalonia, the Basque Country and the coastal regions generally. Catalan textiles and Basque iron were the pioneers of Spain's industrial revolution. Valencian oranges and the wines of Jerez flour-ished as export industries. All benefited from easy access to ports and maritime transport. Castile faced geographical obstacles, of distance and of the mountain chains which stand between it and the sea in all directions. After Switzerland, Spain is the most mountainous country in Western Europe as well as being large in area by European standards. All this delayed the emergence of a national market. The canal was a quixotic attempt to overcome those obstacles and achieve more geographically balanced economic growth. This continuing imbalance would have a fundamental impact on Spain's development, as this chapter on the relationship between state, people and territory during the crucial formative period of the modern Spanish nation from 1808 to 1936 will explain.

In addition to its transport difficulties, Castile's cereal farming was inefficient, its land unproductive, its villages depopulating. Antonio Machado, the great Spanish poet of the early twentieth century, memo-rably captured a melancholy decline that had begun two centuries earlier:

> Castilla miserable, ayer dominadora,
> envuelta en sus andrajos desprecia cuanto ignora.
> ¿Espera, duerme o sueña?
> . . . sobre sus campos aun el fantasma yerra
> de un pueblo que ponía a Dios sobre la guerra

> [Poverty-stricken Castile, yesterday dominating,
> Wrapped in its rags scorns that of which it is ignorant.
> Is it waiting, sleeping or dreaming?
> . . . over its fields lies the ghost
> of a people that set God to wage war][1]

Castile retained political power. While other urban centres began to grow, Madrid remained the capital of a multinational empire. *Solo*

Madrid es corte ('only Madrid is the court') went the phrase, after a failed attempt by the Duke of Lerma, a corrupt seventeenth-century courtier, to move the capital to his home town of Valladolid. But there was a corollary: Madrid was only the court, and little more. Its population in 1750 was around 140,000, compared with some 600,000 in both London and Paris. As Richard Ford, an English travel writer, put it a century later 'the capital has a hold on the ambition rather than on the affections of the nation at large'.[2] Under Felipe V (1700–46), and especially Fernando VI (1746–59) and his half-brother Carlos III (1759–88), the Bourbons made a determined effort to modernise Spain, to arrest its slide into penury and to turn it into a centralised absolute monarchy. Free of the dynastic commitments of the Habsburgs, they fought fewer expensive foreign wars. They reorganised the administration of their American colonies, clawing back more revenue from local elites. To run Spain and its empire they turned to career bureaucrats, many of whom were inspired by the ideas of the French Enlightenment. These civil servants promoted industry, setting up royal factories (such as for porcelain, glass and cloth), mostly around Madrid. Francesco Sabatini, Carlos III's favourite architect, left his mark on the capital, creating a new Royal Palace, elegant boulevards adorned with classical sculptures, a Botanical Garden, ornamental gateways such as the Puerta de Alcalá and a large hospital that is today the Reina Sofía art museum. José Moñino, who was the chief minister from 1777 to 1792 and was ennobled as the Count of Floridablanca, planned a network of roads radiating from Madrid, of which 1,100 kilometres and 322 bridges were built by 1788. The sunny official mood of these years is rendered in Francisco de Goya's tapestry designs of aristocratic life and his portraits of the court and of officials and thinkers, several of whom he counted as friends and patrons.[3]

Had this state-building and reform continued uninterrupted for another two or three generations, Spain might well have become a very different country. But it didn't. First the quality of government declined under Charles IV (1788–1808). And then Spain was dragged into war again. Manuel Godoy, a young guards officer and royal favourite, had replaced Floridablanca. He allied with the Directory governing post-revolutionary France and declared war on Britain, leading to the loss of the Spanish fleet – the guardian of its trade with its American colonies – at the Battle of Trafalgar. In 1807 Napoleon Bonaparte dispatched a French army through Spain to attack Portugal, a British ally; he soon mounted a full-scale invasion of Spain itself. He locked up Charles IV (who had abdicated) and his son Fernando VII in Bayonne and installed his own brother, Joseph, as king of Spain. That triggered a popular rebellion and seven years of war in which Spanish, British and Portuguese forces fought the French empire. Known to Britons as the Peninsular War, Spaniards call it the War of Independence. For Napoleon, it was his 'Spanish ulcer'; its bleeding of his armies, with some 200,000 dead, contributed greatly to his eventual defeat.

For Spain, the war and its ramifications constituted a disaster unmitigated by eventual victory. There are no precise estimates of casualties but more than 300,000 Spaniards were killed. The slaughter, cruelty, rape, destruction and misery were all reported by Goya, in a series of harrowing etchings called *Fatales consequencias de la sangrienta guerra en España con Buonaparte* – 'Fatal consequences of the bloody war in Spain against Bonaparte' – or simply 'The Disasters of War'.[4]

In the power vacuum the war entailed, mainland Spanish America, smarting under the Bourbon reforms, broke away, though it would take years of fighting for its constituent parts to obtain independence. But in Spain itself the war quickly came to be seen as marking the birth of the modern nation, expressed in the very term 'war of independence', which was coined in the 1820s. Spain is an old country: the Catholic monarchs in the early sixteenth century ruled a territory with almost exactly the same borders as the present-day ones, a rare case of geographical continuity in Europe. But in those days 'España' was identified primarily with the monarchy, though the term also harked back to Roman Hispania and the Visigothic kingdom which preceded the Arab-Berber invasions. It gradually acquired political, linguistic and cultural connotations in the subsequent centuries. The Bourbons founded the Spanish Royal Academy (of the Spanish language) in 1714, the Royal Academy of History in 1738 and another of fine art. 'From long before 1808 a Spanish identity had been being formed, the embryo of that nation which was going to take flight from then on,' as José Álvarez Junco has explained.[5]

Spanish national identity and nationalism are thus not inventions of Franco. They go back about as far as their French equivalents, for example. If modern nationalism dates from the Battle of Valmy of 1792, when a French citizen army fought for the then-revolutionary idea of popular sovereignty rather than a monarch, the Spanish experience of the war against Napoleon bore some similarities. Antonio de Capmany, a Catalan economic historian who died in 1813, described it as a cause of a new kind: 'it's a home-made war, it's a war of the nation . . . more than of soldiers'.[6] Some of the most stubborn resistance to Napoleon came in Catalonia, which played a full part in this national cause. This national epic and its high human price were fixed in the imagination of later generations of Spaniards by Goya in a pair of paintings in the Prado. *The Second of May 1808* portrays the rising of the Madrid populace against Napoleon's troops. Cuirassiers and Mamluk mercenaries in the emperor's service hack at the crowd who through sheer weight of numbers are unhorsing them. The terrible reprisal comes in *The Third of May*, otherwise known as *Los Fusilamientos* ('The Executions'). It shows prisoners lined up in the dark of the small hours against a cemetery wall as a French firing squad does its brutal work. Several have already fallen in a bloody mess. The focus is a man in a white shirt, kneeling, with terrified eyes and arms spread wide in vulnerability and defiance. Ordinary people have become the protagonists of Spanish history.

Spain's experience of the war gave the world two new words. One was 'guerrilla', to describe the irregular bands that took on the French. The insurgent warrior had entered Spanish political life, where they would stay. But the other was 'liberal'. The war and its dislocations and ruptures unleashed a long and tangled struggle over the political definition of the country's newly reinforced national identity, in difficult circumstances. The 'fatal consequences' of which Goya spoke were indeed severe. The war and the loss of much of its empire knocked Spain back by decades. In 1829 its foreign trade was still only a third of its volume of 1785.[7] Spanish America had provided a third of public revenues in the eighteenth century. Most of that had gone. What remained was a financially weak state ill-equipped for nation-building – far less so than the state bequeathed to France by Napoleon. It would be rebuilt, but that initial weakness would have far-reaching consequences.

Much writing about Spain tends to assume that its post-1815 history was darkly 'exceptional' in Western Europe, that Spain was indeed different. This, of course, begs the question as to what countries were 'normal'. Yes, Spain lagged behind Britain in economic growth and the achievement of democratic stability. But look beyond the surface turmoil of government instability, and it is striking in other respects how closely developments in Spain paralleled those of its neighbours. Many of the themes of Spanish history in this period are common to Western Europe: they include the contest between absolutism and liberalism, battles over the suppression of the privileges of the Catholic Church and the sale of its lands, the rise of nationalism, urbanisation and industrialisation, and growing social and class tensions. When compared with other European countries the balance of these developments stood out in three closely related ways: the survival of peripheral cultural identities and languages; repeated civil wars; and the intensity of the conflict between the Catholic Church and secularism and anti-clericalism.[8] All stemmed from the relative weakness of the state and what Juan Linz, a Spanish political scientist, called its lack of 'penetration' of the society through education and national values and symbols.[9] Nevertheless, recent historiography holds that beneath the politics of confrontation in nineteenth-century Spain, chaos and corruption there was more underlying progress than was commonly accepted. 'The old view of a failed and backward country has been swapped for another, which sees an authentic liberal revolution that entailed a deep and significant rupture with the old regime,' as Adrian Shubert, a Canadian historian of Spain, puts it.[10] Perhaps that was one reason why Franco said 'the nineteenth century, which we would have liked to erase from our history, is the denial of the Spanish spirit'.[11]

During the War of Independence the junta of officials and notables which opposed Napoleon, nominally on behalf of the imprisoned Fernando, called a Cortes for the first time since the seventeenth century. With 350 representatives from peninsular Spain and from Spanish America it met in Cádiz from 1810 to 1814. A narrow majority of its members were reformers and became known as 'liberals' – the first time the word was used as a political term. They approved a radical constitution in 1812. It was inspired both by the Bourbon enlightenment (the junta was initially headed by the elderly Floridablanca) and, ironically, some of the principles of the French Revolution. Its second article declared: 'The Spanish nation is free and independent, and cannot be the patrimony of any family or person.' And the third: 'Sovereignty resides essentially in the nation, and therefore it has the exclusive right to establish its fundamental laws.' The charter went on to say that Spain is a 'moderate [i.e. constitutional] monarchy' and that the power to make laws lay with 'the Cortes and the king'. It declared Spaniards to be Catholics and barred the practice of other faiths, but abolished the Inquisition, decreed freedom of the press, abolished many noble privileges and declared the liberalisation of farming, industry and trade. It defined the nation as 'the union of all Spaniards in both hemispheres', though that came too late to satisfy Spanish Americans. The constitution included provisions for the separation of powers and the election of a single-chamber parliament by indirect male suffrage (with some restrictions based on race, education and financial status).[12]

This document amounted to a determined assault on absolute monarchy and a ringing declaration of popular sovereignty, the most radical constitution of its day in Europe. But it was a charter of urban liberalism dictated by a small, enlightened minority for a largely rural, impoverished and conservative country. Most Spaniards were illiterate and eked out their existence either as small-scale farmers on often arid land or as seasonal farm labourers. The constitution's principles quickly became a battleground. Restored to his throne, Fernando VII decreed its abolition. He dispatched an army in a futile bid to prevent Spanish American independence. When another was being assembled in Cádiz in 1820, one of its commanders, Colonel Rafael de Riego, mutinied. He declared his adherence to the constitution and his opposition to the unpopular expedition. The army supported him, forcing Fernando to yield. It was the first of many *pronunciamientos*, as they were called – the normally bloodless officers' revolts that became a prime instrument of political change in Spain over the next century and more.[13] And it underlined the dependence of the liberal cause on the soldiers.

This first liberal triumph would prove short-lived: in what became another pattern of the Spanish nineteenth century the liberals fell out among themselves, dividing between moderates who favoured top-down reform, and radicals known as *exaltados* (hotheads) who favoured sweeping change from below by means of local juntas and militias. The restored Bourbon monarchy in France sent an army to support Fernando in his absolutist claims. This time there was no popular uprising.

A dozen captives stand on a beach, their arms or hands tied together. Some are being blindfolded by cowled monks. Several of the prisoners are dressed in the frock coats that mark them as gentry. Before their downcast, solemn faces lie four of their comrades, already executed by the squad of soldiers standing behind them. This vast, naturalistic canvas by Antonio Gisbert was commissioned for the Prado by a Liberal government in 1888. It has become a 'powerful liberal icon', according to Miguel Falomir, the museum's director. Though much less known abroad, it deserves to be bracketed with Goya's *Second of May* and *Third of May* and Picasso's *Guernica* in 'the gallery of great paintings dedicated to the history of Spain', argued Falomir.[14] It portrays the execution of General José María Torrijos and his comrades at Malaga where they had landed in 1831 in a vain attempt to overthrow Fernando's absolutist regime. Torrijos, aged 40, had fought with Wellington. Joining other Spanish liberals in exile in Britain, he and his cause were adopted by British Whigs, notably by a young Alfred Tennyson, the English post-Romantic poet, and the Apostles, a club of undergraduates at Cambridge University to which he belonged. The tall, red-haired figure standing next but two to Torrijos, eyes half closed, is Robert Boyd, a former British army officer who donated his fortune to Torrijos's expedition. A century before the Spanish Civil War, Spain's political conflicts inspired active solidarity abroad, especially in Britain.

After an 'ominous decade' (as it was called) of reactionary absolutism, the liberals returned to power in 1833 on Fernando's death, when his widow, María Cristina, turned to them to secure the right to the throne of her young daughter, Isabel, against the rival claim of her brother-in-law, Don Carlos. Supporters of Don Carlos soon took up arms in what became known as the First Carlist War (1833–40). It was a civil war on a similar scale to the far better-known conflict of 1936–39, with which it shared many characteristics but differed in outcome.[15] It left some 150,000 dead from a population of 13 million, proportionately not much less than the 300,000 from around 24.5 million a century later.[16] It pitted the liberal cities against the conservative, Catholic countryside. Carlism's social and military base was not only in the Basque Country and Navarre, but also in rural Catalonia and the remote Maestrazgo mountains between Aragon and Valencia. Its supporters were peasants, artisans, the clergy and the minor nobility. It stood for the defence of hierarchy, tradition, social order and a pre-liberal economy, for traditional local *fueros* (legal privileges) against a centralising state.[17]

The war lasted so long partly because of the effective guerrilla tactics of the Carlists, especially in the Basque mountains, and partly because María Cristina's governments lacked the resources to organise and equip an effective army. The correspondence of Baldomero Espartero, who became her army commander, is a litany of complaint at his lack of money and troops, which led him to adopt a cautious military strategy. He prevailed, but only after seven years. Espartero, the ninth son of a carter in a small town in La Mancha, became a national popular hero and would remain one for the rest of his long life, except to some in Barcelona, which he bombarded to crush a revolt against taxes and free trade.[18] Large numbers of troops were eventually mobilised by both sides. By 1835 the government had a force of 250,000, including some 22,000 foreign (mainly British) auxiliaries. A British naval blockade in the north prevented arms reaching the Carlists, whose armies by 1839 totalled 70,000.[19] Thanks partly to foreign support, the liberals prevailed. Under the Peace of Vergara of 1839 the bulk of the Carlist forces disarmed in return for a promise to keep a modified version of the Basque *fueros*. Espartero was magnanimous. He had earlier proclaimed:

> In civil wars there's no glory for the victors nor diminishment for the vanquished. Take note that when peace is reborn everything becomes muddled up; and that the register of sufferings and disasters, of triumphs and conquests are seen as the common patrimony of those who before fought on opposing sides.

Espartero's magnanimity suggests there was nothing inherently Spanish in Franco's reprisals against the defeated Republic in 1939.[20]

Carlism was one of several 'legitimist' movements in Europe after the Napoleonic Wars, which stood for absolute monarchy and the divine right of kings against creeping liberal advance and held that royal succession must always be by the male line and always by the eldest son. In France and Portugal legitimism ceased to pose a military threat after the 1830s, but retained a political presence. As late as 1873, 100 legitimists were elected to the French National Assembly, though out of a total of 650 deputies.[21] Yet in Spain Carlism became a deeply rooted military and insurrectional tradition in some parts of the country. During the Civil War of 1936–39 a Carlist militia raised mainly in Navarre fought for Franco on the Basque front. Carlism's durability owed much to the fact that Spain remained a largely rural society well into the twentieth century and to the ideological role of the Catholic Church. Its attachment to violent insurrection was perhaps a function of the relative weakness of the liberal state in a country where geography conspired against its monopoly of force.[22]

Yet the liberal state was making progress, albeit amid political instability. A sergeant's revolt at the palace of La Granja in 1836 obliged María Cristina to accept the 1812 constitution: although this would soon be modified, Spain would never again suffer absolute monarchy.[23] Two parties emerged from liberalism: the Moderates and the Progressives (the heirs to the *exaltados*). Their rivalry was one reason why Spain had thirty-two governments between 1843, when Isabel II was declared of age at just 13, and 1868. Five constitutions were enacted between 1834 and 1876. None until that of 1876 were consensual documents; rather, each one purported to erase its predecessor.

There were missed opportunities in this tangled tale. In 1836 Juan Álvarez Mendizábal, a Progressive prime minister and financier, tackled the Church's corporate power and wealth. He abolished the tithe, suppressed all small religious houses and in effect put most Church property up for sale. This was what the enlightenment reformers had hoped to do. Mendizábal was able to do so because of the crown's urgent need for money to pay for the Carlist War, and because public opinion had become increasingly anti-clerical since many priests and monks supported the Carlist cause. Historians disagree as to the extent to which Church lands, and the common lands of municipalities which were later also put up for sale, ended up in the hands of large secular landowners.[24]

The governments of the 1830s and 1840s laid many of the foundations of a modern state, picking up where the eighteenth-century reformers had laid off.[25] In 1833 Spain's territory was divided into forty-nine more or less equal provinces, inspired by the French departments. This new territorial organisation slowly eroded, as it was designed to do, attachment to the regions descended from the medieval kingdoms. The message was that Spain was a unified nation state in which all citizens and territories would be subject to the same laws. Even after the recreation of regions by the 1978 constitution, the provinces survive and are referents in everyday life. Conversely, some Catalan nationalists abhor the provinces. In 1844 a Moderate government created a professional police force, the Civil Guard. This had an impact, especially in tackling the brigandage and highway robbery that travellers had long complained of. But it was created as a military constabulary, initially reporting to the army. The rule that civil guards could not be stationed in their home region, intended to remove them from political influence, had the effect of making them seem like an occupying force. A professional civil service developed. Juan Bravo Murillo, the prime minister in 1850–52 whose motto was 'more administration and less politics', drew up civil service categories and career paths.[26] Recruitment was increasingly based on competitive exams (known as *oposiciones*) and merit. But some historians think the prime purpose of the civil service was to provide jobs for a growing middle class rather than public services for the masses.

A bigger missed opportunity came with a military-civilian uprising-cum-*pronunciamiento* (called the 'Glorious Revolution') in 1868, which overthrew Isabel II. The queen, who was still only 38 when ousted, had become reactionary, more interested in religion than politics; her reputation had suffered from financial and alleged sexual scandals; she intervened high-handedly even against her most loyal ministers, helping to undermine the parliamentary system that sustained her. She was 'always too young to take charge of the leadership' of such a conflicted country, as her biographer, Isabel Burdiel, has noted.[27] With revolutionary juntas, or committees, springing up in provincial cities, the army and much of the political elite turned against Isabel, who went into exile in Paris.

The principal leader of the Glorious Revolution was Juan Prim, a Catalan general who was a popular hero because of his success in an episode of colonial war in Morocco. He wanted a constitutional monarchy, just not a Bourbon one. So did a majority of the Constituent Cortes of 1869, the first to be elected under universal manhood suffrage. The 1869 constitution was a blueprint for a modern, democratic Spain, which included universal male suffrage, freedom of organisation and thus the right to form labour unions, and freedom of religion.[28] It ushered in important reforms, including civil marriage and a civil registry of births and deaths. Prim eventually offered the throne to Amadeo of Savoy, a son of King Victor Emmanuel of Italy. To modern eyes, this rent-a-monarchy looks bizarre, but it was not uncommon in that period. Thus, Otto Wittelsbach, a Bavarian prince, was king of Greece from 1832 to 1862, for example. In any event, Prim's gambit failed. The night before Amadeo arrived in Spain, Prim was shot in a Madrid street, by unknown enemies, and died three days later. Prim alone could hold together the diverse coalition of liberals and radicals that had made the revolution; conservatives did not accept the new regime or the foreign monarch. Amadeo lasted only two years before abdicating.

The Cortes voted to declare Spain a republic. But of what sort? Some wanted a unitary state like France. More favoured a decentralised federal republic. They included Francesc Pi y Margall, a Catalan who was the preeminent Republican leader and briefly president.

He quickly lost control of events amid sometimes violent disorder, as juntas declared local republics in the towns of the Levante and Andalucía in what became known as the Cantonalist revolution. The government also faced a new Carlist war and a rebellion in Cuba against slavery and for autonomy. Army discipline was collapsing, since the republic was pledged to abolish conscription. The republic lasted less than a year, in which it got through three presidents, all intellectuals, before a *pronunciamiento* installed a brief military government and then another restored the Bourbons in the person of Alfonso XII, Isabel's 17-year-old son, who was a cadet at Sandhurst.

Once again the idealised liberal country and the real one had diverged. The 1930s would repeat this story. The chaos of the First Republic gave federalism an indelibly bad name in Spain. That had serious consequences: it was why the framers of the 1978 constitution eschewed the formal federalism that might have avoided some contemporary tensions.

The Glorious Revolution set the battle lines between free-thinking democracy and conservativism in more or less authoritarian forms, a contest that embroiled the country for the next century. Both would soon come under pressure for more radical change from socialism and anarchism. The political system installed under the restored monarchy gave priority to stability over democratic representation. That would have diminishing returns. The underlying challenge the country faced was whether the system could evolve into a full democracy, capable of adapting to a fast-changing society and of incorporating new political forces. Ultimately it failed, despite the efforts of many well-meaning political leaders.

The architect of the new system was Antonio Cánovas del Castillo, a shrewd conservative politician from the former Moderate party. The new constitution of 1876, which would last until 1931, was pragmatic: it recognised Catholicism as the religion of state but allowed the practice of others. The system's political method was known as the *turno pacífico* – peaceful alternation in power, without *pronunciamientos* – between two broad-based parties, Cánovas's Conservatives and the Liberals, led initially by Praxedes Sagasta. Governments used electoral manipulation, arranged by the interior ministry, to provide themselves with a majority in the Cortes. For its critics the system entrenched an oligarchy and the power of local potentates in rural Spain, dubbed *caciques* (political bosses, a word of Caribbean origin). But it was more flexible than this suggests. Sagasta implemented many of the conquests of the 'Glorious Revolution', including universal manhood suffrage, freedom of association and worker organisation, and trial by jury. The state gradually took over functions previously carried out mainly by the Church or poverty-stricken local councils, such as health care and education. Restoration governments introduced social reforms, including factory acts on safety. In 1919, following a long strike in Barcelona, Spain became the first country in the world to legislate for the eight-hour day for all workers.

Caciquismo was really clientelism: the *cacique* was the intermediary between the state and a largely illiterate electorate, offering services and protection in return for votes, a system that was common to many European democracies at the time and still is in parts of Latin America. A bigger problem was that Restoration governments too often resorted to the security forces and repression in the face of agitation by organised workers or the desperation of the landless labourers of Andalucía who embraced a utopian anarchism. Anarchists wreaked their revenge, and helped to close off reformist paths. Inspired by Mikhail Bakunin, the Russian anarchist philosopher who preached 'propaganda of the deed', anarchist assassins would murder three Spanish prime ministers between 1897 and 1921. One was Cánovas himself, shot while taking the waters at a spa in the Basque Country. The other two were reforming prime ministers, José Canalejas, a Liberal, and Eduardo Dato, a Conservative. Canalejas, a potential Spanish version of David Lloyd

George, the British Liberal reformer, according to Raymond Carr, had tried in vain to tame a strike wave with a mixture of concessions and repression.[29]

Much of this was not particularly exceptional in Europe at that time. Italy after unification suffered from *caciquismo* and rigged elections, and from political violence in the form of half a century or so of undeclared civil war in the south. Spain's intellectual and political elites tended to compare their country obsessively with England, Bismarckian Germany or France, and there it often came up short. But not in every respect. Spain enjoyed more years of constitutional government in the nineteenth century than France, or indeed any other continental European country, for example.[30] France suffered political instability, too: it has had fifteen constitutions since 1789 to Spain's nine since 1812. The Spanish parliamentary *caciques* were not so different from the *notables* of the French Third Republic. In Italy, where suffrage was much more restricted until 1912, the period from the 1880s to the First World War saw 'transformism', in which governments became shapeless amalgams of nominal ideological opponents. In Portugal from the 1850s, as in Restoration Spain, elections tended to follow rather than precede a change of government, with the interior ministry organising the requisite parliamentary majority.

Contemporaries and later historians, especially Marxist ones, lamented the supposed lack of an industrial revolution in Spain. But the partial liberalisation of the economy, the replacement of corporate (Church and nobility) relations with capitalist ones, along with an opening to imports and foreign investment, especially in mining and railways, did prompt economic growth. Leandro Prados de la Escosura, an economic historian, has reconstructed a consistent set of national accounts dating back to 1850. They show that between 1850 and 1883 income per person in Spain grew at an annual average rate of 1.3%, faster than in France (1.1%) or Germany (1.2%), and almost as fast as in Victorian Britain (1.4%).[31] Growth slowed between the early 1880s and 1913. Prados de la Escosura hypothesises that this was because the Restoration governments were more protectionist, especially after the loss of the Cuban market in 1898. Growth picked up again during the First World War (in which Spain benefited from remaining neutral) and the 1920s before declining with the Great Depression, the Spanish Civil War and Franco's subsequent economic autarky. To sum up, in the words of Diego Palacios, a Spanish historian at the University of Stirling: 'slow growth, slow change and slow institutional development may depict Spain in the nineteenth century, but growth, change and institutional development did indeed happen'.[32] Nevertheless, in some crucial respects change and institutional development were too slow. By the 1930s the state was not quite developed enough, or the society quite democratic enough, to prevent the Civil War that irresponsible leaders and elites created (see chapter 5).

Cross the River Bidasoa from the border town of Irun in the Spanish Basque Country and you arrive immediately in Hendaye, a straggling town notorious as the site of a meeting in a railway carriage between Franco and Hitler in October 1940. Hendaye and the villages around it were long used as a refuge by ETA members and their sympathisers. Around a quarter of the town's population are Spanish Basques. Yet Euskara, the Basque tongue, is not an official language in Hendaye or anywhere in the department of Basses Pyrénées which comprises the French Basque Country, nor until recently was it taught in schools. That is the consequence of a determined and largely successful exercise in nation-building by the French state.

In 1863 about a quarter of the population of France did not speak the French language at all, according to an official statistical report. More than a tenth of the 4 million schoolchildren spoke no French, and 1.5 million of them couldn't write it.[33] These official figures are almost certainly underestimates. Even more than Spain in the same period, France was a patchwork of languages (such as Breton, Flemish,

Basque, Gascon, Catalan and various versions of its linguistic cousin, Occitan). Most of the non-French speakers were in rural areas in the west, south and centre of the country. Whereas Spain had enjoyed more or less stable borders since the sixteenth century, France was an agglomeration formed by conquest or annexation, right up to the incorporation of western Savoy in 1858 (leaving aside the battles over Alsace and Lorraine between France and Germany). In *Peasants into Frenchmen*, a classic text of modernisation theory, Eugen Weber argued that all this changed between 1870 and the First World War as a result of deliberate public policies by a state that had the resources to implement them. 'Undeveloped France was integrated into the modern world and the official culture – of Paris, of the cities,' in that period, wrote Weber, a Romanian-born historian. 'Traditions died and they were no longer replaced.'[34]

The 1789 Revolution in France bequeathed national unity as an integrating ideal. The Revolution 'completed the nation, which became one and indivisible', as Albert Soboul, a French historian, put it.[35] But this ideal only began to become consistent reality during the Third Republic, from 1870. Weber identifies three powerful agents of change and integration. The first was a government-financed crash programme of railway- and road-building, especially of all-weather secondary roads in rural areas. The railway network expanded from some 20,000 kilometres in 1879 to 65,000 kilometres in 1910. The second factor was schooling. In 1876 nearly 800,000 of the 4.5 million children of school age were not registered in any school, and many who were didn't attend. Girls were especially likely not to be at school. As education minister in the early 1880s Jules Ferry pushed through far-reaching reforms that made primary schooling compulsory, free and secular, and required all teaching to be in the French language. The government financed a massive school-building programme, improved teaching methods and introduced history and geography as classroom subjects. The third agent of change was military service. Introduced by Napoleon this had involved many get-outs for the better-off and was seen as a heavy tribute on the peasantry levied by an alien state. By the 1890s exemptions were curbed, conscripts were better treated and fed and the army came to be seen by the people as 'ours' not 'theirs'. Schools and the army alike taught their charges patriotism and *laïcité* (secularism). As Weber concludes: 'A Catholic God, particularist and only identified with the fatherland by revisionists after the turn of the [twentieth] century, was replaced by a secular God: the fatherland and its living symbols, the army and flag. Catechism was replaced by civics lessons.'[36]

The secular religion of French republicanism has proved lasting and generally popular. Shortly after he was elected president in 2017 Emmanuel Macron told an audience of young people that the French state 'built itself on the French language'.[37] Article 2 of the French constitution of 1958 states baldly that 'the language of the Republic shall be French' and no other languages have official status. Joseph Pérez, a French-born historian of Spain of Valencian descent, recounted that he grew up in France in the 1930s speaking the Valencian variant of Catalan as his mother tongue. He went to school: 'in the Jacobin schools, a small Spaniard or Portuguese entered and left as a Frenchman. . . . The Jacobin idea is to found a nation of citizens with the same rights; nobody said anything to me about being Spanish.'[38]

In recent decades the squashing of local languages, customs and particularisms has met some resistance, with the revival of Breton and, to a lesser extent, Occitan and (French) Basque nationalism, not to mention the cultural demands of some Muslim immigrants. In 2008 a constitutional revision recognised that 'regional languages contribute to the heritage of France'. It became possible for pupils to study a regional language as an optional subject, and in some cases these have been used for up to half of teaching. Few pupils take up this option: only 170,000 (out of 12 million) school students receive classes in a regional language and only a minority of them go to private schools, run by cultural associations, that offer 'immersion' in that language. In 2021 the National Assembly approved a law promoted by Paul Molac, a Breton nationalist, which would have allowed 'immersive teaching' of regional languages in public schools.[39] The law was opposed by Macron's government. Within weeks, the constitutional council struck down the clause regarding immersion. But the council said it was constitutional for local governments to finance the teaching of regional languages as a curriculum subject.[40]

Why doesn't Spain have the cultural uniformity of France? Since the time of the enlightenment part of the Spanish elite was deeply Francophile, known as *afrancesados*. Spanish governments in the nineteenth century did make nation-building efforts. But these were undermined by the poverty of the state and they tended to be too little, too late to overcome regionalisms.[41] In another missed opportunity, in a tax reform in 1845 a Moderate government surrendered control over the tax system to local boards of landowners and other notables. The result was that the rich undertaxed themselves and concealed wealth, while small farmers and consumption were overtaxed. The system was highly inefficient: between 1850 and 1890, for each peseta the Spanish government invested in tax and customs collection it harvested only six. In France, the equivalent figure was fourteen.

Governments recognised the importance of investment in transport links. They invited foreign capital to build railways. Bayonne, the capital of French Basqueland, was connected by train to Bordeaux and Paris by 1855; the line from Madrid to Irun, over far more difficult terrain, was completed by 1864. Railway construction speeded up further in the 1880s and 1890s, although lack of maintenance dogged an inefficient network. But roads and schooling lagged in Spain. The ministry of *fomento* (development), set up in 1845 to oversee transport and communications, spent only 9% of the national budget between 1850 and 1890 while France and the Netherlands spent around 15% of (bigger) budgets on transport. As late as 1910, 4,000 of the 9,200 towns in Spain lacked road or rail connection.[42] Governments had other priorities: more than half of the Spanish budget went on debt service and the army. In 1898 the state spent as much on the Church and on clerical salaries as it did on infrastructure, and five times more than it did on schooling.

Universal education had been decreed since the 1812 constitution, though it was not enshrined in legislation until 1857. This law made schooling compulsory for children aged from 6 to 9 years. But it tasked local councils with providing primary schools and they lacked resources. Provincial authorities were supposed to build a secondary school in each provincial capital. By the late nineteenth century half the schools envisaged by the law still didn't exist. Only 40% of children were in schools, and many of them were being taught by the Church.[43] The result was that by 1900 one Spaniard in two was illiterate, compared to one in six French people, or one in thirty Britons. In *The Forge*, his evocative memoir of his childhood, Arturo Barea tells a story of Mentrida, a village only 60 kilometres from Madrid, around 1910:

the school teacher had tried to hold daily evening classes for the young people, where they could learn to read and write, which hardly any of them knew how to do. But the priest was furious and the mayor forbade the classes. The school teacher stayed on for nothing except to teach the young children how to read. That was all he could do, because after they were seven to nine years old, the children were used to work in the fields.[44]

In Spain military service remained far from universal for more than twenty years after it had become so in France. Only the working classes served as soldiers, the army treated them poorly and conscription was hated. In 1909, in Barcelona, the embarkation of conscripts for the war in Morocco triggered a riot and a week of church burnings that Catholic propagandists subsequently called the *Semana Trágica* or

'Tragic Week'. This prompted a reform of military service by Canalejas in 1912.

The second big reason for the survival and resurgence of regional languages and feeling in Spain was the problem with which this chapter began: while in France regions that retained their particular languages and cultural identity the longest tended to be poor and remote, in Spain by the late nineteenth century they were the most economically dynamic parts of the country.

In just three hours on the calm, sunny morning of 3 July 1898, a Spanish battlefleet of four armoured cruisers and two destroyers was annihilated off Santiago de Cuba by a squadron of seven ships of the United States Navy. This doomed Spain to swift defeat in the Spanish-American war and the loss of Cuba, Puerto Rico and the Philippines. It was the extinction of the last remains of the empire that had dominated the world in the sixteenth century.[45] The *desastre* (disaster), as it was dubbed, was a crushing blow to Spanish self-esteem. It set off a bout of moody soul-searching and calls for the 'regeneration' of a country held to have been suffering centuries of decadence. Sagasta, the prime minister at the time, seemed to be the only realist, saying: 'We are a poor country, is it strange that we have been beaten?'[46]

'Regenerationism' would take different forms in Madrid, Barcelona and in the army. In Barcelona, as we have seen, the *desastre* gave a decisive boost to Catalan nationalism (see chapter 3). In Madrid a loose group of writers and intellectuals known as the Generation of 1898 (although in fact they spanned two generations) reflected on the causes of Spanish decline and backwardness, as they saw it, and came up with some contradictory remedies. Some were broadly liberal. They argued for a crash programme of public, secular education and for Spain to become more European. In the shock of defeat, much of this came to pass, with a reform that raised tax revenues and, at last, the creation of an education ministry in 1900. Others, who included Miguel de

Unamuno, a Basque philosopher and writer, thought that Spain should reconnect to its Catholic traditions. Joaquín Costa, an Aragonese historian and politician, not only called for more governmental effort in transport infrastructure and industrial development but also expressed contempt for the Restoration parliamentary regime (it was he who branded it *caciquismo*) and called for an 'iron surgeon' to pursue radical political renewal, not necessarily by democratic means. Many of the Generation of 1898 were associated with the Institución Libre de Enseñanza (Free Institution of Teaching), a project to spread rational, humanist education. It spawned a body to finance postgraduate study abroad (the Junta para Ampliación de los Estudios) led by Santiago Ramón y Cajal, a neurologist who won the Nobel Prize for medicine in 1906. These efforts were influential in training a liberal intellectual elite. They were matched on the conservative side by the Jesuits, who had founded the country's first private Catholic university at Deusto in Bilbao in 1886.[47]

The abiding sense of failure fuelling 'regenerationism' was most clearly expressed by José Ortega y Gasset, a writer and philosopher. Often referred to by Spaniards as a liberal, he was in many ways an elitist conservative. In vigorous prose in *España Invertebrada* ('Invertebrate Spain'), a hugely influential short polemic first published in 1922, he offered some sharp insights mixed with deep cultural pessimism and bad history, dressed up with pseudo-science.[48] He viewed the rise of separatisms in Catalonia and the Basque Country as part of a broader 'particularism' – a retreat from the common national interest into the local and the sectional – which he saw as the country's biggest problem. He detected a similar growth of particularism in Galicia, Asturias, Aragon and Valencia. He attributed its rise to the weakening of Castile. 'Castile had made Spain and Castile has unmade it.'[49] But he also blamed the lack of a common national project, especially after the loss of empire, and the historical weakness of the Spanish aristocracy and of its elites in general.

As for the army, Ortega argued, it had forgotten that it was part of Spanish society as a whole and pursued what it saw as its narrow corporate interest. The *desastre* soon spurred the generals to seek redemption in an opportunistic, brutal and unpopular war to expand the Spanish colony in northern Morocco. That merely exposed the army to another humiliation, the routing of 20,000 troops by a few thousand tribesmen at the Battle of Annual in 1921. Ortega went on: 'Morocco turned the dispersed soul of our army into a clenched fist, morally disposed to attack. From that moment the military group became a loaded shotgun without a target to shoot at.'[50] Wasn't it an inevitable consequence, he asked, that it fell upon the nation itself, in repressing a general strike in July 1917? It was not coincidental that Franco and many of his fellow coup leaders in 1936 had earlier fought in Morocco.

More broadly, the *desastre* and other turn-of-the-century political developments prompted ideological realignments, especially on the 'territorial question' of how Spain should be organised. On the one hand, Liberals' ideal of Spain had changed. Their support for local militias and juntas turned many Liberals and Republicans into decentralisers and federalists, though others continued to favour a strong centralised state in Jacobin mould. On the other hand, the army shed its nineteenth-century commitment to liberalism, while also returning to its pre-Restoration tradition of political intervention. The Church, weakened by Mendizábal, had gained renewed strength as part of a Catholic revival across Europe in the latter part of the nineteenth century. Conservatives and the Church hierarchy began to see in a strong central state the best guarantee of their interests, especially since the socialist and anarchist movements formed part of international organisations or networks. The army and other conservative forces adopted a defensive, identitarian nationalism that saw in Catalan and Basque nationalism a threat to national unity. 'The conservative world began to think that everything was in danger: religion, property, family and even the nation, that at the outset had been the creation of a liberal revolution against absolutism,' as Álvarez Junco puts it.[51] A first attempt at conservative centralisation came with Primo de Rivera's dictatorship. The Second Republic that followed tried to get to grips with orderly decentralisation.

In a celebrated parliamentary debate on the Catalan statute of 1932, Ortega y Gasset, who was elected as a deputy for a small Republican party, argued that Catalonia was a 'perpetual' problem that 'cannot be settled, it can only be lived with'. Manuel Azaña, the prime minister (later president) of the Republic, in a long reply to the debate in which – in an oratorical tour de force – he reviewed the sweep of Spanish history, began by noting that 'the policy of Madrid' towards Catalanism was to deny its existence instead of recognising it for what it was, the primordial problem of the organisation of the Spanish state. 'The reality is the fact of differentiated sentiments in the regions of the Peninsula,' he went on. 'We might prefer that in Spain a policy of assimilation, of unification had triumphed, it might be that to some it might seem that this would have been more worthwhile and that now all Spaniards might speak the same language.' However, he added to applause: 'To me this would have seemed to be an impoverishment of the spiritual wealth of Spain. But the fact is, like it or not, it hasn't happened.'[52]

This encapsulated the Republic's approach towards the 'territorial' question, expressed first in the Catalan statute (see chapter 3). The Basques' Catholic conservatism provoked little sympathy among Republicans and delayed a statute of autonomy for them. But it was approved by a referendum in 1933 (though it failed to command a majority of the vote in partly Carlist Álava). It was hastily put into effect when the PNV (Partido Nacionalista Vasco – Basque Nationalist Party) remained loyal to the Republic at the start of the Civil War. There was barely time to constitute the Basque provisional government before Franco's tanks rolled in. Towards the end of the nineteenth century Galicia, too, saw a revival of regionalist sentiment and of the *galego* language. A statute of autonomy for Galicia was approved in June 1936 but the outbreak of the Civil War prevented it being put into effect. Regionalist groups emerged in Andalucía, Valencia and Aragon as well.[53]

In victory, Franco imposed a rigid conservative centralisation, with the sole exceptions of Navarre and Álava: in deference to their loyalty to him he let them keep some of their fiscal privileges. He imposed Spanish nationalism in its new conservative and identitarian form. The public use of all regional languages was banned. All Spaniards were required to 'speak Christian' or 'the language of the empire' as the regime put it. But as Azaña had asserted, the denial of the existence of 'differentiated sentiments' did not make them disappear. Azaña's arguments triumphed posthumously in the 1978 constitution.

Carlton Hayes, an American historian who served as ambassador in Madrid during the Second World War, noted that the achievement of national consciousness everywhere was 'the history of the overcoming of centrifugal forces in the life of the nation by centripetal forces'.[54] In Spain the centrifugal forces were too strong to be overcome – but they were also too weak to prevail.[55] Xosé Manoel Núñez Seixas, a historian at the University of Santiago de Compostela, makes a similar point: 'Spain may be considered an unfulfilled nation state but it is also an imperfect multinational state, since the alternative national identities have not yet managed to impose their social hegemony within their territories.' He notes that 'mixed marriages, linguistic assimilation, multiple identities and hybridisation have been an almost constant feature of Spanish history'. That is the reality that the 1978 constitution, with its mixture of decentralisation and national unity, attempted to address.

CHAPTER 5

LET'S TALK ABOUT FRANCO

The massive stone cross atop a granite outcrop in a pine forest in the foothills of the Sierra de Guadarrama is visible from the outskirts of Madrid. Beneath it lie an open esplanade and a semicircular colonnade marking the entrance to an enormous stone vault, 250 metres long, dug into the mountainside. In its outer vestibule stand a pair of statues of exterminating angels carrying large swords. Everything about the Valley of the Fallen is intended to overawe, to inspire fear rather than sorrow or reconciliation. It is not a war memorial, but rather a monument to a victory, to General Francisco Franco's extermination of the 'reds' in the Spanish Civil War, in what he called his 'Crusade' (with a capital 'C'). In the decree of 1940 in which he ordered its building he stipulated: 'The dimension of our Crusade . . . cannot be perpetuated by the simple monuments with which it tends to be commemorated in towns and cities. . . . The stones that will be erected must have the grandeur of ancient monuments . . . so that future generations pay an admiring tribute to the heroes and martyrs of the Crusade.'[1] Franco's idea was that the Valley would be the burial place of his troops and supporters. But despite using, in part, the forced labour of prisoners, it took eighteen years to build. When it was complete many nationalist families didn't want to move their relatives' remains, and mayors sent some Republican dead as well. Perhaps 34,000 people are buried there, of whom 21,423 have been identified. Many bones are irretrievably jumbled up.

After dying in his bed in 1975 Franco was buried at the Valley, in haste and without much thought. But his presence there, in one of only two named tombs on either side of the altar (the other is that of José Antonio Primo de Rivera, son of the former dictator and the founder of the Spanish Falange, the fascist party) came to be widely seen as an aberration. Apart from anything else, Franco didn't die in the war. Above all, 'a dictator can't have a state tomb in a consolidated democracy like Spain's', as Carmen Calvo, Pedro Sánchez's deputy prime minister, rightly said. In October 2019, in an operation organised by Sánchez's government and attended by twenty-two of the dictator's descendants, Franco's coffin was dug up. In scenes broadcast live on television it was then carried by the family, first to a hearse and then a helicopter which took it for reburial at a quiet public cemetery at El Pardo, in a military cantonment on the outskirts of the capital where Franco's wife was already interred. Sánchez was carrying out a resolution of the Spanish parliament and a promise he made on becoming prime minister. It took more than a year to overcome legal objections from Franco's family – who wanted to rebury him, prominently, in the crypt of Madrid's cathedral – and the threatened disobedience of the Benedictine prior who administered the basilica and monastery at the Valley. The Spanish Catholic hierarchy and the Vatican slapped down the prior; the Supreme Court ruled unanimously that the government could rebury Franco at El Pardo.

'It's a great victory for Spanish democracy,' Sánchez said of the court ruling that allowed the government to go ahead with the exhumation. Slightly more Spaniards agreed with him than disagreed, even if the timing of the operation, a fortnight before a general election, looked to some like a campaign stunt. Only Vox actively opposed what it called a 'profanation' of Franco's tomb. The PP complained that it opened old wounds, but said it would rather discuss the future.

More than two years after Franco's departure from the Valley, the government had not decided what to do with the place. The Socialist parliamentary group wanted to turn it into a 'museum of memory'. Emilio Silva, the president of an association for the recovery of historical memory, and many historians say this museum should explain the Valley's own history and propaganda uses. Many think it should be desacralised and the Benedictines evicted. Others would like it to be left as an untended ruin. They include Nicolás Sánchez-Albornoz, a historian who was assigned to work at the Valley after he was arrested for political activism when a student in 1947. With the help of his political group he escaped after four months. 'They shouldn't spend a centavo on maintaining the Valley,' he said. 'Let nature do its work.'[2]

It is often claimed that Spain has been uniquely inhibited in dealing with the legacy of its past. In fact, several other European countries have struggled to reach agreement on what to do with places associated with their dictators, and have taken time to do so.[3] Modern Spain is not in thrall to Franco's ghost, at least not obviously so: the dictator's small number of active sympathisers exercise little or no influence on politics or the state (at least if one excludes Vox, which rarely refers to Franco explicitly). Most Spaniards alive today have no memory of him. Having been omnipresent for almost four decades, he disappeared from public discourse and debate with surprising speed. A poll in *El País* newspaper twenty-five years after his death found that 42% were 'indifferent' to Franco, 38% had 'negative feelings' towards him and 17% 'positive feelings'. While 59% said his regime was 'definitely in the past', 33% said 'it has some influence', but only 5% thought it was 'still a significant influence'.[4]

If Franco has recently again figured more prominently in political discourse, that is partly because this suits the propaganda of Podemos and Catalan separatism. Nevertheless, the dead dictator still casts a shadow. The lack of unanimity over the exhumation showed that the country has yet to agree on the past – and perhaps it never can. Spain has many museums, but none of its twentieth-century history. Many on the left point out that it has no equivalent of the anti-fascist memorials in Germany or Italy. But the contrast is misleading, as this chapter will explain. And one might argue that there is no more powerful public memorial possible to the victims of Franco and fascism than Picasso's *Guernica*, the artist's great denunciation of the horror and pain of war. Painted for the pavilion of the beleaguered Spanish Republic at the Paris international exhibition of 1937, it has hung since 1981 in the Reina Sofía museum in Madrid, with its context fully explained. Yes, there is unfinished business from the dictatorship – but quite how much is a matter of bitter political dispute. It is an issue about which sweeping statements are often wrong.

When democracy came to Spain in the late 1970s it was not imposed by conquering foreign armies, as in Germany or Italy after the Second World War. Rather, it arrived through agreements between moderate supporters of the dictatorship and a realistic democratic opposition (see chapter 1). There was a rupture with the past, codified in the 1978 constitution, but a less radical one than, for example, in neighbouring Portugal, with its revolution of 1974. One pillar of Spain's democratic transition was the amnesty law and a broad understanding not to use the past as a political weapon – arrangements often misleadingly dubbed a 'pact of forgetting'. Given how deep and raw the conflicts of the past were, that was wise. These accords did not preclude the swift dismantling of *franquismo*. But the amnesty did mean that no *franquista* official or soldier was put on trial for their actions.

This largely seamless transition was widely hailed as a success. But younger generations and some on the left worry that Spain never addressed the crimes of its past and some of the deeper scars. They think it should. The move to do so began with Zapatero, who represented a new generation with no direct memory of the Civil War and little of the dictatorship. Zapatero's paternal grandfather was an army captain in León who was executed in August 1936 for refusing to join Franco's rebellion (his maternal grandfather, whom he knew, fought for Franco, which he played down). Zapatero believed in the politics of wedge issues: if his government's law of 'historical memory' of 2007, timid though it was, was bitterly opposed by the PP that was surely part of its political purpose. There were also other reasons for the law. The attempt by Baltasar Garzón, a Spanish judge, to charge and extradite General Augusto Pinochet, Chile's dictator, under a claimed universal jurisdiction for crimes against humanity, exposed Spain to the accusation of hypocrisy. And a number of civil society groups had begun to press for what they called 'historical memory'.

The Historical Memory Law attempted to correct an anomaly: Franco's regime had honoured its own dead but ignored or persecuted Republican victims. The law declared Franco's military tribunals and their verdicts illegitimate; prohibited the relatively few remaining public monuments that recognised Franco and his allies; required the Church to remove plaques in homage to the 'fallen for God and Spain' in the 'Crusade'; prohibited any *franquista* commemorations at the Valley of the Fallen; and called for the Valley to become a memorial to all victims of the war. It offered government money for the opening of the unmarked graves into which many of the victims of political repression on both sides were thrown.[5] In a democracy people clearly have a right to know where their relatives are buried, especially if they were victims of the state, though some historians questioned whether a law was needed to do what the government should have done anyway. When the PP returned to power in 2011 amid the economic slump it cut funding for the Historical Memory Law. But some local governments and civil society associations continued to finance and organise exhumations.

One day in November 2018 I took the AVE to Valencia and arrived amid a deluge that made the short taxi ride to the suburb of Paterna almost impossible. But we made it to the small municipal cemetery. It is surrounded by high brick walls with burial niches; palms and cypresses are dotted among the graves. Just off the central pathway a blue and white tarpaulin protected a 2-metre-deep hole from the rain. It was one of many unmarked mass graves scattered among the flower-decked formal tombs. That morning Alejandro Vila, an archaeologist, and his team had exhumed a skeleton from the hole, the 266th since they began work at the cemetery eight months before. In an office at the entrance sets of bones were carefully arranged on trays. The team sampled their DNA for matching with that of surviving relatives.

Valencia was one of the last bastions of the doomed Republic. After their military triumph Franco's forces unleashed a reign of terror. Military tribunals conducted summary trials not just of Republican fighters and members of left-wing parties but of civilians who were accused of sympathising with what had been the legal government. 'It was a political purge,' said Vila. At Paterna alone more than 2,000 civilians were summarily shot and their bodies dumped. 'We know nearly all of their names, though we don't know if all of them are there in the cemetery,' said Rosa Pérez, a United Left (Communist) representative in the Valencia *diputació* (provincial council) who is in charge of historical memory. The *diputació* is paying for the dig. Relatives of the victims, many of them now the grandchildren, take a close interest. 'Many come almost daily,' said Vila. 'They feel relieved. There was a long night of silence. They feel a burden removed.' Some families want to take the remains back to their towns. More just want confirmation and to be able to put up a memorial plaque in the cemetery. Some don't want their relatives to be exhumed, according to Pérez. In all, perhaps 100,000 or more people were buried in such graves around the country. Between 2000 and 2019 784 graves were opened and the remains of 9,600 people exhumed. According to a government adviser only about another 20,000 are still recoverable.[6]

Nearly all the public memorabilia of the dictatorship has disappeared, with the exception of the odd street name or memorial in small villages or towns. As time passes remaining anomalies are being rectified. In 2015 Manuela Carmena, a labour lawyer who had narrowly escaped the massacre of her office colleagues by far-right gunmen during the transition, was elected mayor of Madrid for a left-wing coalition. She set up a broad-based committee of historians which recommended changing fifty-two street names, a move that was approved by all parties except the PP, which abstained. In 2020 a judge required the Franco family to hand over to the nation, without compensation, the Pazo de Meirás, a country house in Galicia which had been 'donated' to the dictator in 1938 by sympathisers, but as the summer residence of the head of state rather than as private property. The house had been built by Emilia Pardo Bazán, a nineteenth-century writer and feminist. The court found that Franco had illegally appropriated the property in 1941 with a forged document of purchase.[7] The family still conserve a town house in A Coruña which was similarly 'donated'. And several of Franco's wartime generals have prominent tombs in cathedrals.

In 2020 Carmen Calvo unveiled a draft law of 'democratic memory' that would go much further than the 2007 law. It was a mixed bag. It reiterated the government's commitment to finding the remains of victims. The law would also annul the verdicts of Franco's military tribunals (rather than merely denying their legitimacy) and withdraw titles and medals awarded by the dictatorship. It proposed the ejection of the Benedictines from the Valley of the Fallen, and its redesignation as a civilian cemetery with an explanation of its history. Other provisions were more questionable. It would give the government the power to shut down groups that 'exalt' or 'apologise for' the dictatorship, such as the Francisco Franco foundation. This is a private archive run from an obscure Madrid flat, which attracts a small number of nostalgics. To turn it into a martyr for freedom of expression seemed unwise. Two other parts of the bill were the most troubling. One would require schools to incorporate 'democratic memory' into the history curriculum. That looks like the government establishing official history and deciding who was good and who was bad. Second, the bill proposed setting up a special prosecutor to investigate human rights abuses from 1936 to 1978. Not only was this largely futile since most perpetrators were dead, but it also came close to overturning the amnesty law by the back door.

Powerful constituencies, including UN lawyers, some human rights groups, Podemos and some Socialists want to unpick the amnesty and thus the transition. One reason is that it contravened what is now called 'transitional justice'.[8] This holds that peace agreements must include provisions to hold accountable those guilty of large-scale human rights violations through prosecutions and/or truth commissions. It favours reparations to victims and official efforts to preserve the memory of past abuse. This is well-intentioned and in some cases has been at least partially effective, especially with truth commissions set up soon after democratic transitions (such as in Argentina, Chile, El Salvador and South Africa).

In the autumn of 2021 Esquerra and EH Bildu (which incorporates supporters of ETA) proposed an amendment to the democratic memory bill to repeal parts of the amnesty. In response the Socialists and Podemos tabled another amendment to their own bill which would interpret the amnesty law to recognise that international humanitarian law now holds that crimes against humanity cannot be amnestied nor subjected to time limits. Calvo had left the government but her replacement, Félix Bolaños, admitted that this change would have no practical effect, since the law cannot be retrospective and anyway almost all *franquista* officials are dead. This episode suggested that the debate about history had degenerated into tactical gesture politics.

Desirable though they all are, truth, justice and reconciliation form an impossible trinity. Arguably, Spain's transition to democracy was successful precisely because it did not incorporate transitional justice, which might well have delayed it, made it more violent or prevented it altogether. The amnesty law and other legislation during the transition did allow for reparation. More than 700,000 people benefited, receiving a total of more than €21 billion in compensation or pensions over the next forty years. They included families of those executed during the war or afterwards, Republican soldiers and their families, those imprisoned for political reasons during the dictatorship, and civil servants of the Republic and their families.[9] Calvo's law was also attempting to fit the messy and complex history of the Civil War and its aftermath into a simplistic template which owes as much to contemporary political battles as to the past. Familiar though that history may be to some, it is relevant to review it.

The Spanish Civil War has generally been seen by outsiders – who were responsible for writing its history while Franco was still alive – as a heroic anti-fascist struggle that was the prelude to the Second World War. This was certainly one dimension of it. But it also featured 'red terror', some of it spontaneous and some directed by the Comintern, as Orwell and others reported. The war carried further meanings for Spaniards. In its origins it was an internal conflict, the continuation of the battles of the nineteenth century with the stakes raised by totalitarian ideologies, modern armaments and outside intervention. It erupted in the context of deepening political tensions between a modernising urban society and a backward rural one, between unitary Spanish nationalism and regional identities, between Catholics and anti-clericals, between civilian democrats and military praetorianism (see chapter 4). It was also in part a class war that set landlords, industrialists and sections of the middle class against organised worker and peasant movements. The war was not inevitable, as portraying it as the prologue to the world war might suggest. Chance, contingency and the actions of individuals played a role too.

Even while the Generation of 1898 was fretting, Spain had changed much in the first three decades of the twentieth century. Partly because the country didn't enter the First World War, it enjoyed a 'silver age' – as it was later dubbed – of economic progress and cultural ebullition. The population of the main cities doubled between 1900 and 1930. A growing and more diverse middle class occupied the opulent art nouveau residential buildings in the new 'expansions' of many cities, while a new working class of rural migrants gathered in slums on the periphery. The result was a society that 'offered the most violent contrasts' of modernisation and backwardness as Manuel Azaña would write in 1939. 'In some urban centres, a high standard of living, adapted to all the customs of contemporary civilisations, and a few kilometres away villages that seemed still to be in the 15th century.'[10] At least half of Spaniards had ceased to be illiterate and, for the first time, less than half of them worked in agriculture. But in a total population of 24 million there were still up to 2 million small-scale farmers in the north and 1.5 million landless labourers working on large estates in Andalucía, Extremadura and La Mancha.

Azaña, a bookish, shy man with an unworldly air and thick spectacles, was, in Paul Preston's words, 'the personification of the Second Republic'.[11] He was a lawyer, intellectual, senior civil servant and writer before entering politics as a liberal republican. He was prime minister from 1931 to 1933, as well as war minister, and then president of the Republic from 1936 to 1939. He was an outstanding orator, both in parliament and in outdoor mass meetings. He was a democrat, a man of laws and of absolute personal honesty and integrity. He was perhaps the greatest Spanish liberal. His core belief was that the essence of the *patria* (the nation) was the equality of citizens before the law, and not exclusionary definitions of racial or religious identity. He believed, too, that politics should be governed by reason and votes. He remained loyal to the Republic to the end, even while knowing it was doomed (he died in 1940 in exile in Montauban in France). All this made him an object of particular hatred and venom on the right.

Azaña was also vain, lacking in empathy and could be rigid. Like the statesmen of Spain's eighteenth-century enlightenment he tended to overstate the extent to which laws could change realities. His political judgement was sometimes faulty. He was lulled into a false sense of security by the ease with which the monarchy collapsed in 1931. He and others called this a 'revolution', but it involved no fundamental change in the structures of power. Arguably, the Republic tried to change too much too quickly. Azaña consistently underestimated the extent to which the country remained split down the middle politically, as well as the threat to the Republic posed first by the Catholic right and then by plotters in the army.[12]

The Republic began in 1931 under the auspices of the centre-left with a drive, led by Azaña, to tackle the unfinished business from the nineteenth century: to curb the Catholic Church's influence, reform the army and address the social and regional conflicts that Primo de Rivera's dictatorship (see chapter 3) had tried to smother but had not extinguished. Azaña complained that, despite Mendizábal's reforms, the Church had regained political influence during the Restoration monarchy. 'Instead of seizing property, it seized the consciences of the propertied and thus made itself master of both conscience and property.'[13] A new constitution separated Church and state, turned the Church into a civil association subject to law, cut clerical salaries, forbade religious orders from teaching and removed the crucifix from public schools. It was a determined attempt to impose French-style *laïcité*. 'Spain is no longer Catholic,' Azaña said. That was a statement of juridical fact that sounded to his opponents like a provocation. The constitutional curbs on the Church prompted some centrists to leave the government coalition. Thanks to the advocacy of Clara Campoamor, a feminist lawyer elected as a Radical deputy, the constitution also included not just divorce and the legal recognition of children born outside marriage but also votes for women. That followed a fierce debate in which some on the left opposed female suffrage because they thought women would be too influenced by Catholic priests, while many on the right opposed on traditionally sexist grounds.

In his role as war minister Azaña vowed to 'republicanise' the army. He trimmed the top-heavy officer corps with early retirements. He shut down the military academy in Zaragoza, of which Franco had been the director since 1928 and which had been dominated by *africanista* officers, as those who served in the colonial war in Morocco were known. Azaña tried to institute greater civilian control over army promotions, and promoted officers known to sympathise with the Republic.[14] These measures were appropriate for a democracy but would be bitterly resented by many in the army who saw Azaña as their enemy. Many military officers were also opposed to the statute of autonomy for Catalonia approved in 1932.

The Republic was born in a difficult international context. Like the rest of Europe, Spain was hit by the Great Depression: between 1929 and 1935 the economy contracted by almost 10%, investment fell by around 35%, exports declined by a quarter, unemployment rose and the budget fell into deficit. The government lacked the funds to finance its reforms. An agrarian statute envisaged expropriation of large estates with compensation. Both this and a labour reform aroused the alarm of proprietors without satisfying peasants and workers. The anarchists began a campaign of strikes against the government.

Some leaders on both sides of the political divide began to question democracy, rhetorically at least. José María Gil Robles, of the Confederación Española de Derechas Autónomas (CEDA), a new and fast-growing Catholic right-wing party, admired the authoritarian and corporatist *Estado Novo* (new state) installed by Antonio Salazar in Portugal in 1933. 'What does it matter if it costs us bloodshed?' Gil Robles said during the 1933 election campaign. 'Democracy is not an end for us, but rather a means to go on to conquer a new state. When the moment comes, the parliament will submit or we will repress it,' he said.[15] In the same election campaign Francisco Largo Caballero, the leader of the left-wing of the Socialist party, threatened: 'if you want we will make the revolution violently. . . . We are in an all-out Civil War. Let's not be blind, comrades.'[16]

(This was almost three years before the Civil War began.) With the left divided because Largo Caballero refused to continue the Socialists' coalition with more centrist Republicans, the right swept to power in the election. There were moderates, too, in both CEDA and the Socialist party. But when CEDA entered the government in October 1934 the left responded with a call for revolution. The UGT, the Socialist union confederation, called a general strike. The miners of Asturias rose in an armed insurrection, imposing a revolutionary social order for a fortnight. They murdered thirty-four priests or seminarians. The government dispatched Franco and 18,000 troops to suppress the rising. He did, at a cost of 1,100 dead among the insurgents, 300 among the troops and 30,000 arrests.

Azaña always thought that the unity of the Republican parties and the Socialists was fundamental to the success and survival of the Republic. He forged a Popular Front including both the Socialists and the small Communist Party and narrowly won an election in February 1936. An atmosphere of mounting polarisation was further inflamed by tit-for-tat murders: when a Socialist lieutenant in the Assault Guards, a police force created by the Republic, was murdered by Falangist gunmen, in retaliation his comrades killed José Calvo Sotelo, the monarchist parliamentary leader. That was the trigger for the military coup which a group of generals had already planned. Their leader, General Emilio Mola, intended a violent putsch that would see political and union leaders arrested and the installation of a military dictatorship in the mould of Primo de Rivera's regime. Military officers who did not join the rising would be executed.

But the coup, launched on 17–18 July only half succeeded. A majority of senior generals and a large minority of their troops stayed loyal to the Republic, as did most of the navy and the air force. In some cities, including Madrid, the workers' organisations rose, prompting garrisons to hesitate. The government hesitated, too, to arm the workers, though it soon would. Coup attempt had become civil war, revolution and counter-revolution. By early August Spain was divided into two zones according to the loyalties of military commanders and the balance of forces in different cities and regions. The nationalist rebels had parts of Andalucía and most inland areas north of Madrid with the exception of a coastal strip from the Basque Country to Asturias; the Republic controlled the rest.

The nationalists won, after almost three years of total war, for two main reasons. First, they received swifter and more effective foreign support than the Republic. Hitler and Mussolini sent squadrons of transport planes to convey Franco's Army of Africa, including the Foreign Legion and battle-hardened Moroccan mercenaries, to the mainland. That was a crucial intervention: without it the coup would probably have failed and the war might never have happened. They followed that up with equipment and the German Condor Legion, which in bombing the Basque towns of Durango and Guernica committed war crimes (as denounced by Picasso). Denied help from the British and French governments by their policy of non-intervention, the Republic did get Soviet aid, especially tanks and the International Brigades organised by the Comintern. This served to prolong the war, not to win it.[17]

The second reason was that the nationalists enjoyed unity of command and purpose. In the Republican zone, arming the workers empowered myriad left-wing militias who were often more interested in making revolution than war. The Republic would eventually organise a disciplined army because of the growing influence of the Communists and the dedication of loyal regular officers. They included General José Miaja, who commanded the defence of Madrid, and General Vicente Rojo, who rose to be the chief of the Republican general staff. That army resisted. It had initial tactical successes in important battles (such as Brunete and Teruel in 1937 and the Ebro in 1938) but was unable to turn them into victories mainly because of poor communications and inferior junior officers.

The Spanish Civil War quickly acquired mythical status. By one count, at least 40,000 books had been published about it by 2007, and plenty more have appeared since. According to Enrique Moradiellos, a Spanish historian, two myths have emerged around the war: the myth of the Civil War as an epic and heroic conflict between good and evil, to be praised and remembered; and the myth of a tragic collective madness that should be deplored and forgotten.[18] Modern historiography suggests a more nuanced view. Spaniards experienced the war as a desperate fratricidal conflict that divided families, neighbours and colleagues. On both sides during the war there were heroes and villains, idealists and opportunists, acts of cruelty and acts of kindness. Families were sometimes split, with brothers fighting on opposite sides, either out of conviction or more often because of where the outbreak of war found them. Both armies had recourse to forced recruitment.

The politics were more complicated than the first myth allows. Moradiellos argues that the Second Republic saw a 'triangular fight' in which three forces confronted each other: republican democratic reformism, fascistic authoritarian reaction and internationalist socialist revolution. The split between democrats and revolutionaries that had weakened the governments of the centre-left continued on the Republican side during the war. It ran down the middle of the Socialist party. Largo Caballero, the vain, incompetent but powerful president of the UGT, the Socialist trade union federation, gloried in the sobriquet of 'the Spanish Lenin' bestowed upon him by the correspondent of *Pravda*, the Soviet newspaper. In the spring of 1936 he had fatally weakened the pre-war government by his sectarian refusal to allow Socialist ministers and by blocking the appointment as prime minister of Indalecio Prieto, the tough and capable leader of the party's moderate wing and his great rival.[19] Had the Republic won with Soviet aid, Spain would almost certainly have suffered a Communist regime, just as Eastern Europe did after 1945.

This dismayed Manuel Chaves Nogales, the journalist from Seville who had reported with such insight from Catalonia (see chapter 3).

He defined himself as 'a liberal petit-bourgeois' and 'citizen of a democratic and parliamentary republic', both anti-fascist and anti-revolutionary by temperament. He was told before the war started that a fascist group planned to kill him, while anarchists and Communists thought he was 'perfectly shootable'. When the war broke out the workers' committee of *Ahora*, the newspaper he edited in Madrid, ejected the owner and took control. Chaves worked amicably with them. He left the capital in November 1936, the day that the Republican government and Largo Caballero, who had become prime minister in August, fled Franco's siege for Valencia. He saw that as the end of the parliamentary republic in which he believed. In early 1937, in exile in Paris, he published a collection of extraordinarily vivid reports of episodes of the early months of the war. In the preface he wrote that whichever side won the result would be 'a dictatorial government that with arms in hand will force Spaniards to work desperately and suffer hunger without a murmur for 20 years until we have overcome the war'.[20] How right he turned out to be.

The democratic reformists lost doubly. Some like Azaña, or Juan Negrín, the Socialist prime minister from May 1937 to March 1939, loyally served the Republic to the end. Many others, liberals, democrats and moderate Socialists, saw no option but to take the path of exile even before the war was over. They included people like Clara Campoamor, Ortega y Gasset and many other intellectuals and writers. One was Arturo Barea, a committed Socialist who had worked in the Republic's censorship office during the siege of Madrid. Shell-shocked from the bombings by Franco's forces, he fell foul of the Communist Party's mistrust of him and of Ilsa Kulcsar, an Austrian independent Marxist whom Barea met during the war and subsequently married. They reluctantly took refuge first in France and then in Britain. *The Forging of a Rebel*, Barea's extraordinarily vivid autobiographical trilogy about his childhood in Lavapies, a working-class barrio of Madrid, his service in the war in Morocco and then his eye-witness account of the

Civil War, was not published in Spain until 1978. Chaves, too, found refuge in Britain. Long forgotten in Spain, he has been rediscovered and his work republished only in the past decade.

The Republican government enjoyed democratic legitimacy of origin, and Franco's rebellion had none. Franco's project was authoritarian, repressive, obscurantist and utterly reactionary, a rebellion against the modern world. Azaña stayed at his post, despite his many misgivings about the revolutionaries on the Republican side, because of his fundamental rejection of Franco's rising. In a speech in Valencia in 1937 he said:

> Even if all the evils which are held against the Republic were true, war wasn't necessary. It was useless as a remedy against those evils. It made all of them worse, and added those that came from so much destruction.[21]

But the Republicans' conduct was far from spotless. Just as Franco and the Falange did in their part of Spain, left-wing activists imposed a reign of terror in their zone. It used to be said that the repression in Republican Spain was more spontaneous, the work of out-of-control militias. Although there was much of that, recent studies have established that it involved a far more organised elimination of political opponents.[22]

Estimates of the death toll in the Civil War and its aftermath vary wildly. Recent calculations by Spanish historians suggest that around 300,000 to 350,000 people died in the war, of whom 175,000 were killed at the front or in bombardments. Of these, three-fifths died on the Republican side. Another 155,000 were victims of repression, of whom around 100,000 in *franquista* areas and the rest in the Republican zone. A further 20,000 were executed by the Franco regime in the first six years after the war ended. Around 350,000 people died of disease and hunger during the conflict. At least 170,000 went into exile permanently.[23] As in the Carlist wars, prisoners were often shot out of hand, at least in the early weeks of the conflict. And as in any war, there were cases of rape and sexual violence against women. Franco's military tribunals did commute many death sentences against Republicans; more prisoners were pardoned than executed, which shows that there was no 'Spanish holocaust'. But the dictator's aim was certainly to crush 'the Reds'. Not for him the magnanimity in victory of Espartero in the First Carlist War. Rather, he erased the name of Principe de Vergara (as Espartero had been ennobled) from a long avenue in Madrid and replaced it with that of General Mola.

Life and death were a lottery for civilians, especially in the early months of the war, and for Republicans, in its aftermath. The most notorious murder was that of Federico García Lorca, the poet and playwright, in August 1936; he was seized from his house outside Granada by three men, including a former CEDA deputy and a Falangist landowner. When Colonel Juan Yague's column of the Army of Africa took Badajoz in August 1936, some 1,200 disarmed militia and civilians were herded into the bullring and shot. Women and children fleeing Malaga ahead of the nationalists were strafed on the road to Almería by Franco's air force and shelled from the sea. At the start of the siege of Madrid, on the orders of Santiago Carrillo, a young commissar who would go on to lead the Spanish Communist Party, some 2,000 prisoners, including army officers and civilians, were taken from prison and shot in the area of Paracuellos del Jarama, a village that today overlooks Madrid's Barajas airport. Leopoldo Alas, the rector of the University of Asturias and a member of Azaña's Republican Left party, was shot by a *franquista* firing squad in Oviedo; one of its members, who was a former student of the rector's, was shot too, after refusing to fire. Melquiades Álvarez, a friend of Alas, fellow law professor at Oviedo University and a conservative republican, was arrested and then killed by leftist militiamen in Madrid in August 1936 because he looked 'bourgeois'. News of his murder led Azaña, who had joined Álvarez's Reformist Party in 1913, to say he wanted to resign.[24] Gregorio Marañon, who is the chair of Madrid's opera house and whose paternal grandfather was a famous Spanish doctor and liberal, has told the story of his maternal grandmother, who belonged to a liberal family which had suffered exile, persecution and assassination at the hands of absolutist governments in the nineteenth century. In August 1936, aged 70, she was dragged out of her house by Republican militiamen and shot against the cemetery wall of Aravaca, on the outskirts of Madrid.[25] Joan Peset i Aleixandre was a bacteriologist and lawyer who had been rector of the University of Valencia and then an MP for Azaña's party. During the war he had worked in military hospitals and had tried to prevent killings by anarchists. When Valencia fell he was accused, without evidence, by three envious professional rivals of ordering killings. A military tribunal found him guilty of rebellion and sentenced him to death but recommended commutation. After the Falange presented to the tribunal a lecture Peset had given in which he condemned the 1936 coup, it activated the death sentence. He was shot in the cemetery in Paterna in 1941.[26]

Was Franco a fascist? Should he be bracketed with Hitler and Mussolini? Unlike those two, Franco was a career military officer. He was born into a lower middle-class naval family in the Galician port of El Ferrol.[27] 'I am a soldier,' was how he defined himself. His ideology was that of many officers of the Army of Africa: a fierce Spanish nationalism which saw the Catholic religion as integral to the country's past glory. For him, the causes of the country's decline were liberalism, freemasonry (a particular obsession), Communism and Catalan and Basque nationalism, all to be fought uncompromisingly. He was suspicious of the outside world. Rather than Hitler or Mussolini (who were both overthrown by foreign invasion), he bears comparison to the reactionary military dictators of Eastern Europe between the world wars and those of Latin America or Salazar in Portugal (1933–70).

In Morocco, where he served for ten years, Franco showed himself to be a brave, dedicated but cold-blooded officer, surviving a serious combat wound. He had enjoyed a swift rise, promoted to brigadier-general aged just 33 in 1926. Like General Augusto Pinochet of Chile, he abused power to accumulate personal wealth, in his case in the form of property and land, the appropriation of public donations and the extraction of bribes. According to Paul Preston, he died with a fortune worth €400 million (in 2015 values). He was also extraordinarily cunning and ruthless, with a supremely developed instinct for his own survival and the weaknesses of rivals. He turned the *gallego* trait of inscrutability into an art form. He used his command of the Army of Africa at the start of the war, and his negotiation of aid from Germany and Italy, to place himself swiftly at the head of the rebellion. At two days of talks at an airfield near Salamanca in September 1936 he secured the backing of his fellow generals, many of whom were his seniors in the military hierarchy. They agreed to him becoming Generalissimo of the armed forces and head of government for the duration of the war.[28] Many of the generals hoped for and expected a swift post-war restoration of the monarchy. Franco turned this conditional mandate into one of the twentieth century's longest-lasting personal dictatorships. That was the result of good fortune as well as skill. Several potential rivals departed the scene: generals Sanjurjo and Mola, more senior rebels, died in air crashes; the start of the Civil War found José Antonio Primo de Rivera on the Republican side of the divide, where he was imprisoned and executed.

Franco headed a broad right-wing coalition that ranged from Fascists and Carlists to moderate Catholics. As Preston has noted, he was masterly at the manipulation and control of the different 'families' within the regime, playing them off against each other and forcing their complicity by involving them in corruption. Like Argentina's Juan Perón, who helped Spain economically in the late 1940s and chose Franco's Madrid as his place of exile from 1955 to 1973, Franco was adept at leaving each group the impression that he agreed with them. He also 'had the gift of being convinced by his own lies', as Preston puts it.[29] Franco's regime was based on three institutional pillars: the army, the Church and the 'Movement', formed in 1937 when he forcibly merged all existing right-wing parties into a single official party of the state, under the unwieldy name of the Falange Española Tradicionalista y de las Juntas de Ofensiva Nacional Sindicalista or FET y de las JONS. Founded in 1933, the Falange itself was small at the outbreak of war. At first the Movement had many of the outward trappings of the Falange but over time it became less ideological, a machine for rewarding the regime's supporters with jobs or sinecures. By the 1960s a fourth institutional pillar emerged in the form of a professional, meritocratic bureaucracy.

Franco was a fascist of convenience rather than conviction, placing Falangists in prominent positions during the Second World War when they were useful to him and then pushing them aside. He owed his victory in part to the Axis powers, and thought they would win the Second World War. He knew that Spain was too weak, economically and militarily, to join the war. But he sent a force of 'volunteers', the Blue Division, to fight on the Russian front and hoped to scoop up Gibraltar from what he assumed would be an Allied defeat.[30] The suspicious nationalist and anti-liberal in Franco liked the Falange's economic policy of autarky and state control. The Falange's lasting imprint was corporatism, the Mussolini scheme of vertical 'syndicates' which conciliated the interests of workers and business, or subordinated the former to the latter. But fascism was not Franco's essence, as Azaña grasped early on. In 1937 he wrote in his journal:

There are or might be in Spain all the fascists you want. But there will not be a fascist regime. If force triumphs against the Republic, we would fall back under the power of a traditional ecclesiastical and military dictatorship. No matter how many slogans are translated and how many mottos are used. Swords, cassocks, military parades and homages to the Virgin of Pilar. The country can offer nothing else.[31]

As the Second World War ended, Franco swiftly distanced himself from the Axis. Almost overnight, the regime's ideology began to stress Catholicism, in the Spanish conservative tradition dating back to the nineteenth century or even to the Counter-Reformation. A photo of the Pope replaced those of Hitler and Mussolini on Franco's writing table. He named Alberto Martín-Artajo, the head of Catholic Action, a lay organisation, as foreign minister, a post he held from 1945 to 1957. Martín-Artajo was misled into believing his job was to work for a return of Catholic monarchism. Franco's propagandists falsely claimed that he had helped to save the Allies by stalling Hitler's supposed pressure for Spain to join the war (in fact, Hitler told Ciano, Mussolini's foreign minister, in 1940 that Spanish intervention 'would cost more than it is worth').[32] The dictator now presented himself as an anti-Communist cold warrior, 'the sentry of the West'. This was enough to secure a defence treaty with the United States, which was invited to set up military bases in Spain, and a Concordat with the Vatican.

By 1950 repression had begun to ease, but living standards were lower than in 1930. The pursuit of ultra-protectionist autarky brought the economy close to bankruptcy. That prompted a new phase in the regime. Luis Carrero-Blanco, the colourless naval officer who was Franco's long-serving chief of staff and would become his de facto prime minister, drafted in a team of talented economists, several of them from Opus Dei, a Catholic lay organisation. They implemented a 'stabilisation plan' in 1959 that opened the economy to the outside world. Helped by foreign investment, the start of mass tourism to Spain and remittances from hundreds of thousands of Spaniards who had emigrated in search of work, over the next decade and a half the economy grew at an annual average rate of close to 7%. A large middle class came into being. That brought Franco wider public support. The civil service started to recruit its members on merit, including the children of Republicans.

As his health deteriorated, Franco withdrew into semi-isolation in his last years. Henry Kissinger reported that when he and President Richard Nixon visited El Pardo in 1970 for talks, Franco soon fell asleep. In 1969 he had named Juan Carlos, Alfonso XIII's grandson, as his successor. Some in the regime hoped that after Franco's death things would continue as they were. He himself had claimed that he was leaving matters 'tied down, and well tied down'. Any chance of that disappeared in 1973 when ETA killed Admiral Carrero-Blanco, with a bomb that blew his car high into the air after he had left morning mass at a church on Calle Serrano in Madrid. That prompted a final burst of repression – the police would carry on torturing to the end. But after Franco died the moderates in the regime swiftly gained the upper hand over the hardliners.

In 1938, in his last public speech, from the balcony of Barcelona's city hall on the second anniversary of the uprising, Azaña warned that if future generations 'on some occasions feel that their blood boils with rage and once again the Spanish temper grows furious, with intolerance, hatred and an appetite for destruction, think of the dead and learn their lesson . . . *paz, piedad y perdón* (peace, mercy and pardon).' That was the spirit of mutual forgiveness and tolerance in which the transition was carried out. In many ways Spain's current parliamentary monarchy represents the values of Azaña and the Republic.

Was there a 'pact of forgetting', and if so was it a bad thing? The term is at least a misnomer. Rather, Spanish democracy can be seen as a pact which encouraged remembering: a poll in 2008 found that 74% said that when they were young their family said 'little or nothing' about the Civil War and for 70% the same applied to the Franco regime.[33] But since the 1970s Spanish society has 'remembered' the

Civil War and the dictatorship in a flood of publications, research, exhibitions, films and commemorations. Javier Cercas, a contemporary novelist who has written movingly of the Civil War, has said that there was a pact of remembering in another sense: everyone was conscious of the horrors of the past and determined to avoid repeating them.[34] The sweeping amnesty approved in the transition was a demand of the left, not of the right. It had been the policy of the Communist Party since 1956 and the Socialists for even longer. There was much to be said for agreeing not to use the past as a political weapon, given how bitterly divisive it was.

'Historical memory', the banner of those who denounce a pact of forgetting, is an oxymoron. Memory is not history. It is individual and it is fragile.[35] Any attempt to turn it into a collective state-sponsored product, as Sánchez's government seemed to be trying to do, is an attempt to rewrite history for political ends. 'Memory only seeks to rescue the past in order to serve the present and the future,' as Jacques LeGoff, a French historian, has put it.[36] History, in contrast, should be an attempt to grapple as objectively as possible with the facts and complexities of the past.

Those who make the case for 'historical memory' have two arguments. One is that public remembering recognises and eases the sufferings of victims. The other is that the nurturing of 'historical memory' will prevent a repetition of past atrocities. But the first issue is what and how to remember, who should be celebrated and who condemned in a putative exercise of 'democratic memory'. As this chapter has shown both the Civil War and the Franco regime were less straightforward than myths allow. There was civil war, not genocide. Almost half the country had voted for the right in 1936. Foreign governments eventually recognised Franco. In the same poll in 2008 almost 60% agreed that Franco had done both bad and good things.[37]

The starting point for this discussion must be that the Republican administration in 1936 was unquestionably the legitimate government of Spain, and that the nationalist generals staged an illegal coup attempt. Go further, and there are shades of grey. Cercas has pointed out that while the Republic had right on its side politically, it did not enjoy a monopoly of moral reason or virtue. 'Just as there are scoundrels who support good causes, there are people who in good faith back the wrong side. To judge them now is too easy.'[38] Not all of those on the Republican side were democrats and not all of those on the nationalist side were not; and those who were democrats weren't necessarily continuously so. Prieto, whose questionable role in the uprising of October 1934 was the only blemish on an otherwise impeccably democratic political career, wrote to Negrín in 1939 with self-critical awareness: 'Few Spaniards of the current generation will be free of blame for the infinite misfortune into which they have plunged the fatherland. Of those of us who have been active in politics, no-one.'[39]

Pedro Sánchez, visiting Chile in 2018, stated that: 'we have to set up a truth commission to agree a national version of what happened in the Civil War and the Franco dictatorship.' He added that the commission should be 'the most plural possible' and should 'incorporate all the historical perspectives on the Civil War' so that 'from there we can definitively close all the wounds'. It sounds wholly reasonable. More than fifty truth commissions have been set up around the world since the 1980s. Their primary function is to establish what happened, and to allow victims to tell their stories if they want to. That can be especially valuable in the immediate aftermath of a conflict. Some proponents claim that time is no barrier. President Macron in 2021 decided to set up a commission into France's colonial war against Algerian independence of 1954 to 1962. 'France has been in denial for a very long time,' said Benjamin Stora, the historian who will direct it.[40] That followed a similar decision in Belgium, where a commission is looking at the country's appalling record as the colonial power in the Congo.

Yet, in the case of Spain, the work of historians and researchers means that little about the Civil War and the dictatorship remains unknown. Any gaps would best be filled by reforming the official secrets act to give researchers access to military archives, something successive governments have promised but failed to do, a failure that smacks more of bureaucratic inertia than conspiracy. And eighty-five years after the start of the Civil War it is the descendants, rather than the victims, who would give testimony to a truth commission. Some Republican families certainly long felt that their suffering was not recognised. It wasn't during the dictatorship, but it is now. It is highly questionable, too, whether a single 'national version' of the past can ever be established. Remembrance and reconciliation are especially painful and difficult after civil wars, as General Charles de Gaulle pointed out towards the end of his life: 'All wars are bad. . . . But civil wars, in which in both camps there are brothers, are unpardonable, because peace is not born when the war ends.'

'We should pose questions more than answers,' Santos Juliá, one of Spain's most distinguished historians, who died in 2019, told me.[41] To close, rather than open, wounds, the 'democratic memory' law would have to be negotiated with the PP. The government showed no intention of doing that. And a truth commission would have to be an exercise in self-criticism and mutual recognition and forgiveness by both right and left. In 2002 the PP did bring itself to condemn the coup of 1936.[42] But conscious that many of its older voters grew up *franquistas*, it is uncomfortable about delving too deep into the past. And the left continues to mythologise the Republicans.

Everything about the proposals for a truth commission and the proposed law of democratic memory suggested that history was once again being used as a political weapon. In fact, this trend resumed around the turn of the century. 'That didn't happen in the transition,' said Juliá. 'Nobody asked where was your father in the Civil War.' Twenty years later politicians began to derive political identity from the doings of their grandfathers. Podemos, in particular, has used anti-*franquismo* as a political discourse. But both sides of the political divide

1. Diego Velázquez's great painting, *Las Meninas* (The Ladies in Waiting), 'plays with our sense of certainty about what we see when we look'.

2. Voting for the constitution in 1978, which ended four decades of dictatorship.

3. Lieutenant-Colonel Tejero, leading a squadron of Civil Guards, burst into the Congress in a coup attempt in 1981, the defeat of which secured democracy.

4. Supporters of Catalan independence throng Barcelona at the Diada (national day) demonstration in 2012 which marked the start of the separatist *procès*.

5. Catalan and Spanish flags on balconies in Barcelona in 2017. The declaration of independence that wasn't revived dormant Spanish nationalism.

6. The Benedictine monastery of Montserrat was the cradle of a revival in Catalan nationalism in the 1950s and 1960s.

7. Francisco Goya's *The 3rd of May 1808 in Madrid*, or *Los Fusilamientos* (The Executions): with the popular uprising against Napoleon's forces, ordinary people became the protagonists of Spanish history.

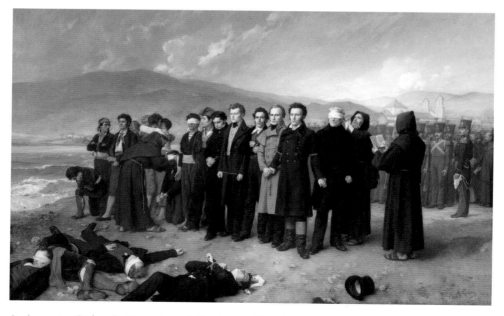

8. Antonio Gisbert's *Execution of Torrijos and his Companions on the Beach at Málaga*, an icon of the liberal struggles of Spain's nineteenth century. In 2021, for the first time the Prado hung it next to Goya's *Los Fusilamientos*.

9. Manuel Azaña, the prime minister and then president of the Republic in the 1930s, filled bullrings and football stadiums for mass meetings.

10. The Spanish Civil War of 1936–9 involved both a battle between democracy and dictatorship and an attempted social revolution led by anarchist militias such as these in Barcelona.

11. General Francisco Franco saluting his victorious nationalist troops at the end of the Civil War.

12. The exhumation of one of tens of thousands of victims of the Civil War and post-war repression who were thrown into unmarked graves.

13. Frank Gehry's Guggenheim Museum in Bilbao became a globally known poster child for urban renewal in the Basque Country's former industrial capital.

14. The bursting of a housing bubble in 2008 threw Spain into an economic slump and left tens of thousands of empty apartments such as these at Seseña near Madrid.

15. With remarkable speed Spanish society has thrown off social conservatism and embraced feminism.

16. Large swathes of rural Spain have emptied out, with villages inhabited only by the elderly.

17. For many commentators, Spanish politics, with its *crispación* or confrontation for its own sake, began to resemble Goya's *Duel with Cudgels*.

18. Pedro Sánchez, prime minister from 2018, was the great survivor of Spanish politics.

19. In 2022 Alberto Núñez Feijóo, the experienced president of Galicia, took over as the national leader of the conservative People's Party.

20. Pablo Iglesias, here with Ada Colau, the mayor of Barcelona, tried to be the great disruptor of Spanish politics, but resigned his formal posts in 2021.

17. For many commentators, Spanish politics, with its *crispación* or confrontation for its own sake, began to resemble Goya's *Duel with Cudgels*.

18. Pedro Sánchez, prime minister from 2018, was the great survivor of Spanish politics.

19. In 2022 Alberto Núñez Feijóo, the experienced president of Galicia, took over as the national leader of the conservative People's Party.

20. Pablo Iglesias, here with Ada Colau, the mayor of Barcelona, tried to be the great disruptor of Spanish politics, but resigned his formal posts in 2021.

21. Santiago Abascal exploited fears over Catalan separatism and immigration and turned Vox into Spain's version of the European populist-nationalist hard right.

22. The future of the monarchy lies with King Felipe and Queen Letizia and their daughters.

23. Every day, high-speed trains streak across what used to be a large country from Madrid's Atocha station.

24. For better or worse, partying and sun have become symbols of the Spanish way of life.

have recently played politics with history. After the publication of the draft 'democratic memory' law, Madrid's city council, in the hands of the PP, decided to tear down a plaque to Largo Caballero which had been approved unanimously in 1981 (though both he and Prieto still have prominent statues in Madrid).

The second argument by defenders of 'historical memory' and transitional justice is that a failure to confront the past leads to a weaker or flawed democracy still impregnated with authoritarian streaks. In a celebrated phrase George Santayana, a Spanish philosopher who spent much of his life in the United States and Italy, argued: 'Those who cannot remember the past are condemned to repeat it.' This is wrong. As David Rieff has argued in a thoughtful and erudite critique of 'historical memory':

> far too often collective historical memory as understood and deployed by communities, peoples and nations – which . . . is always selective, more often than not self-serving, and historically anything but unimpeachable – has led to war rather than peace, to rancour and *ressentiment* (which increasingly appears to be the defining emotion of our age) rather than reconciliation, and to the determination to exact revenge rather than commit to the hard work of forgiveness.[43]

This certainly applies in the Balkans: for Serb nationalists defeat at the Battle of the Black Mountain in 1389 plays a similar role to 1714 for their Catalan equivalents. It applies, too, in Northern Ireland, and in the commemorations of the Confederacy in the southern United States from which a line leads to the current attempts to restrict the right of black Americans to vote. As Rieff concludes: 'we do not have to deny the value of memory to insist that the historical record . . . does not justify the moral free pass that remembrance is usually accorded today.'[44] According to Carmen Calvo, 'we don't have the right to forget, we have the obligation to remember.'[45] Again, this is wrong. There is no absolute moral obligation to remember, and proponents of 'historical memory' have no claim to moral superiority. These are questions for individuals, not the state, to decide as they see fit.

The practical question is whether Franco's ghost still exercises influence over Spanish society and over the institutions of its democracy. And the answer is: very little. There are one or two bars – out of many tens of thousands – which are shrines to his memory. But his overt supporters are a small hard core, numbering no more than a few thousand. It took a few years for the Civil Guard to adopt democratic practices. Democracy brought a new national police force, alongside the guard. Like the police forces, the judiciary is predominantly conservative – as these institutions tend to be in many countries – but today none of its members was appointed by Franco. The armed forces lost their political veto when Suárez legalised the Communist Party against their opposition, and with the failure of the 1981 coup attempt. Entry into NATO and participation in peacekeeping missions has brought about the democratic modernisation of the army that Azaña yearned for.

The events of the past few years have prompted faint rumblings of discontent in the security forces. Some were alarmed by the threat to the unity of Spain posed by Catalan separatism. There were murmurings when Pablo Iglesias and Podemos, an openly Republican party whose loyalty to the constitution was initially equivocal, entered the government. The government's deals with Bildu and Esquerra for the 2021 budget produced particular fury on the right. The army was annoyed, too, that Sánchez agreed with the Basque Nationalist Party to hand over an important barracks in San Sebastián to the city council for urban development. In November 2020 this disquiet surfaced when a hundred or so retired officers signed an open letter to King Felipe in which they complained that the 'social-communist government, supported by philo-ETA people and separatists' was threatening national unity. Some 270 retired officers – out of a total of around 20,000 – signed another letter, organised by the head of the Francisco

Franco Foundation, claiming that 'the unity of Spain and constitutional order' were at grave risk. A leaked WhatsApp chat group
contained at least one posturing comment invoking Franco.

General Miguel Ángel Villaroya, the chief of the general staff, issued
a statement criticising the letters and the chat group, and insisted that
those involved didn't represent the armed forces. Prosecutors investigated but concluded that the WhatsApp group involved purely private
communications with no intention that they be made public.[46] These
events were soon put in perspective in April 2021 in France, where a
score of retired generals and around 1,200 other former service personnel
signed an open letter to a right-wing magazine. They complained of the
'disintegration' of France at the hands of anti-racists and Islamists 'who
are contemptuous of our country, its traditions and its culture', and
warned that military intervention might be necessary. The army identified eighteen serving soldiers among the signatories. A study found that
in the first round of the 2017 election 41% of military personnel and
54% of police voted for Marine Le Pen, the far-right candidate,
compared with 16% of electorate as a whole. But the army commander
insisted that, as in Spain, the great majority of service personnel respected
their duty of political neutrality.[47] Germany, too, has recently seen signs
of far-right sympathies in the army. In October 2020 Horst Seehorfer,
the interior minister, reported that there had been 1,400 cases of
suspected far-right extremism among the police, the army and the intelligence services. The following year the army dissolved a company of the
special forces because of its ties to the extreme right.[48] So it is hard to see
Spain's military malcontents as a consequence of a supposedly flawed
democratic transition. Rather than Franco, they seemed to be more in
tune with Vox, which is just one among a dozen or so hard-right parties
that have emerged across Europe in this century.

For the first thirty years or more of the democratic period, Spanish
nationalism was in abeyance, discredited by the authoritarian form it

had taken under Franco. After the PP got into power in 1996 the most Aznar did was to install a gigantic Spanish flag in the Plaza Colón, in the heart of bourgeois Madrid, which then started to become a rallying point for demonstrations by the right. As right-wing national-populist parties sprung up elsewhere, many commentators remarked on the absence of one in Spain, often attributing this to Franco's toxic legacy. In fact, it was only a matter of time, and the required circumstances, for this to change.

What roused Spanish nationalism from its long hibernation was above all the separatist *procés* in Catalonia. In the autumn of 2017, Spanish flags appeared on balconies across the country. And Vox emerged from obscurity. The party was founded in 2013 by PP leaders in Catalonia and the Basque Country, who broke away in fury at what they saw as Rajoy's pusillanimous response to those territories' nationalisms. Its founding leaders included Santiago Abascal, whose family had suffered repeated attacks and harassment by ETA sympathisers; Javier Ortega Smith, a lawyer with *franquista* and military connections; Iván Espinosa de los Monteros, an aristocratic property developer; and his wife, Rocío Monasterio, an architect of Spanish-Cuban descent. Vox's breakthrough came in the Andalucian regional election in 2018, when it won 11% of the vote and 12 of the 109 seats in the regional assembly.

There were three factors behind its growth, Espinosa de los Monteros told me. 'Catalonia has given us visibility,' he said. The second was a defence of traditions, such as hunting and bullfighting, against political correctness and feminism. In Freudian terms, Vox represented the Spanish male id. It refused to accept that gender violence was an issue, falsely claiming that women killed men just as much as men killed women. And the third factor was that WhatsApp and other social networks allowed the party to bypass the traditional media. As Catalan separatism receded somewhat, Vox increasingly emphasised illegal immigration. In the campaign for a Madrid regional election in May

2021, it stigmatised immigrants who were unaccompanied minors, exaggerating their numbers and their cost to the state.

One evening in April 2019 I went along to the Plaza Colón to listen to Vox's final rally in the campaign for the election that would see its entry into national politics. Perhaps 15,000 people attended, filling most of the raised section of the square, beneath the vast Spanish flag and in front of the brutalist monument to Columbus's voyage to America. All four of Vox's founding leaders spoke. Their pitch was simple: the uncompromising defence of the unity of Spain, the upholding of traditional conservative moral values ('those of your father and grandfather' as Abascal put it) and a rejection of illegal immigration, in that order. There was no mention of Franco. Talking to several of those who came to listen, the message was always the same. They were former PP voters who saw the party as weak and corrupt. They liked Vox because 'it defends the family, life and the nation', as Ricardo Rojo, an administrative worker in the Madrid municipal government told me. Only once, on a big occasion, did Abascal make reference to Franco, and that was indirectly. He claimed in a parliamentary debate on a censure motion he tabled in October 2020 that Sánchez's administration was 'the worst government in 80 years'. In this muddled speech he defended Donald Trump, aligning with his 'anti-globalism', attacked the 'Soviet pretensions' of the EU (even as it proposed to give Spain €140 billion in emergency aid) and the 'theme park' of regional autonomy. All the other parties in the Congress of Deputies, including the PP, voted against the motion. In a depressing exercise of historical stupidity, in their parliamentary clashes and in the Madrid regional election campaign of 2021, both Vox and Podemos deployed the rhetoric of the Civil War, of 'reds' and 'blues'. Fortunately, it seemed that most Spaniards were not swayed by this.

Clearly Vox draws on some of the same traditions of national Catholicism as Franco did, and which pre-dated him. But it is hard to see its emergence as a consequence of any alleged failure of the transition. After all, a far-right party (Chega) has recently emerged in Portugal. Vox grew swiftly, achieving 15% of the vote and fifty-two seats in the November 2019 election, making it Spain's third-strongest party. Researchers have found that those who vote for Vox tend to be men who lean to the right and who are unhappy with the functioning of democracy. Significantly, they tend to be younger than average, as is true for Chega as well. 'Iberian populist radical right supporters are not older people who are nostalgic about the authoritarian regimes of the past, but are instead predominantly a new generation of people attracted by the radical right,' according to a recent study.[49] Vox voters appear to be broadly satisfied with the work of previous PP governments. This implies that many former PP voters now sympathise with Vox and could return. In other words, an effective leader of the PP might be able to curb Vox's growth.

While one of Vox's leaders had contact with Steve Bannon, Trump's former adviser, the party itself identifies most closely with the Catholic nationalist government of Poland. Abascal has also held friendly meetings with Viktor Orban of Hungary and Giorgia Meloni of Fratelli d'Italia, the descendant of Mussolini's party. Vox did not favour the nationalist corporatist economics of France's Marine Le Pen. 'We are liberal on economics and conservative on moral questions,' Iván Espinosa de los Monteros, one of its leaders, told me in 2019. It later made some attempt to move away from its neoliberal, low-tax economic policy towards a kind of nativist welfarism. Across Europe in the past decade, right-wing national-populist movements have exploited discontent at economic stagnation and the sense of dislocation prompted by mass immigration, globalisation and the financial crash of 2008. Rather than Franco, disquiet about those issues and Catalan separatism are the sources of Vox's support. Spain needs to address them, as later chapters will make clear.

But first there is another recent matter which relates to historical memory: the long campaign of terror by ETA which blighted the

Basque Country in the name of nationalism. In a parliamentary exchange in 2020, Cuca Gamarra, the PP's parliamentary spokeswoman, criticised the government's selective approach to historical memory by referring to its having negotiated support for its budget from EH Bildu, which includes sympathisers of ETA: 'How come you think it's sensible to rake up the embers of 70 years ago while with unworthy pacts you trample on the memory of the victims of ETA?' To which Carmen Calvo replied: 'Why do you need to bring ETA constantly into Spanish politics?'[50] The answer is that ETA's terror is much more recent than Franco's. It has been another aspect of Spanish exceptionalism, even if it is now at last receding.

CHAPTER 6

THE BASQUE PARADOX AND
GALEGUISMO

A bookshop called Lagun, meaning 'friend' or 'companion' in the Basque language, opened in 1968 in Plaza Constitución in the heart of the old quarter of San Sebastián. Lagun's owners were Socialists, and were fined by Franco's dictatorship for closing the shop to support a strike. But it was ETA that would make their venture almost impossible. The terrorist group and its sympathisers, who call themselves the *abertzale* (patriotic) left-wing, considered the old quarter to be their territory. 'They didn't like our presence there,' Ignacio Latierro, the co-owner of Lagun told me in 2018. From the mid-1980s they first began to spray paint Lagun's windows and then break them repeatedly. The owners responded by placing wooden screens on the windows. 'It was like Fort Apache,' said Mr Latierro. Sympathetic citizens rallied to their support. 'For a fortnight we sold books like never before.' Then in January 1996 the *abertzales* sacked the shop, burning its stock of books in the square. It carried on operating, under police guard. ETA shot the husband of Mr Latierro's business partner, leaving him gravely wounded. In 2001 Lagun moved a few blocks away to a site in the city's main shopping district where it has survived into calmer times after ETA gave up violence in 2011. 'It was the bookshop with the most bodyguards in the world,' Mr Latierro went on. The hostility of both ETA and the Franco regime was 'for the same fundamental reasons: we weren't prepared to do what they wanted'.

It is a paradox that the only serious violent challenge to Spanish democracy came in the Basque Country. With a total population of just 2.2 million, it is one of the most prosperous and developed parts of Spain. Since the transition, it has enjoyed the most wide-ranging autonomy of any region in the EU. The Basque government not only runs public services, its own police force (known as the Ertzaintza) and a public television station but also collects its own taxes. In an arrangement known as the *concierto económico*, it hands over a small slice of revenue to the central government to pay for the few remaining services this provides. The result is that in the Basque Country and Navarre, which enjoys a similar privilege, public spending per person is higher than in any other Spanish region. It is a paradox, too, that an organisation like ETA that claimed to be a radically left-wing opponent of the Franco regime should end up practising the closest thing to fascism the country has seen in the past forty years. It was 'the last trace of *franquismo*', Alfredo Pérez Rubalcaba, who as Zapatero's interior minister did much to bring it to an end, told me in 2008. ETA's murders of political opponents in combination with the violent intimidation of the *abertzales*, in their attacks on Lagun and in the wider practice of what they called *kale borroka* (struggle in the streets), all in the name of nationalism, closely resembled the actions of the *squadristi*, the paramilitary activists and thugs who paved the way for Mussolini's rise to power in Italy in the 1920s. Or as Eduardo Madina, a former Socialist member of the Congress of Deputies from Bilbao, put it: 'These few people, here, who didn't tolerate anything that wasn't their ideas . . . turned the Basques into the last corner of the country that resisted democracy.'[1]

After declaring two truces, one in 1998 and the other in 2006, both of which it soon broke, ETA at last announced 'a definitive end' to its violence in 2011 and its disbanding in 2018. Its successor political alliance, EH Bildu, is now engaged in a 'battle for the narrative' as Arnaldo Otegi, its leader who was an ETA member, has said.[2] In other words, it is attempting to rewrite the recent history of the Basque Country.

Basque nationalism has many similarities with its Catalan equivalent, in its identitarian defence of a separate language and culture, its sense of victimhood, its historical links to the Catholic Church and the frequent internal divisions among its followers. But there are also differences. Basque nationalism only emerged right at the end of the nineteenth century, and only achieved broad support in the current democratic period. It constitutes 'a truly spectacular triumph of the invention of an identity and of a tradition', according to Álvarez Junco.[3] That identity is based partly on a fertile collection of myths developed from the fifteenth to the seventeenth century. They include such fables as that the Basque language was brought to the area by Tubal, the grandson of the biblical Noah, that the Basques were the first Europeans and that Noah himself had written their *fueros* (legal privileges). Much is made of the fact that Basques tend to have a different blood group than other Spaniards. 'Ultimately, what is striking is not the enigma of the [Basque] past in itself, but the existence of a people bewitched by the ethnographic spell which has been cast over that enigma,' according to Joseba Zulaika, a Basque anthropologist.[4]

The notion that Basques form a separate race is questionable. A study published in 2021 found that they show genetic differences from other Spaniards but these differences seem to be relatively recent, dating from the end of the Iron Age (around 2,500 years ago),[5] and they are greater in the core Basque-speaking areas than in the Basque periphery. The researchers found that Basques and other Spaniards all descend from the same Stone Age migrants from Europe's eastern steppes. It appears that the ancient Iberians, too, spoke a non-Indo-European language. The differentiation only began when the Romans turned up in

Iberia. Contrary to some myths, they did conquer the Basques but few seemed to have settled in the core areas. The Arab-Berber invaders scarcely got there at all. Impenetrable mountains and an incomprehensible language discouraged genetic mingling, the researchers surmised.

It was this geographical isolation that formed the Basques. The Basque Country is very different from the lands to its south, though not so much from Cantabria and Asturias to the west. It is a place of steep, forested mountains and tight valleys, wedged between the Pyrenees, the Cantabrian chain and the Bay of Biscay. That was why Euskara, the Basque language, clung on in rural areas. It is one of only four surviving non-Indo-European languages in Europe, along with Finnish, Estonian and Magyar. The bedrock of Basque society was the solid stone farmhouse, the *baserri* in Euskara, that can still be seen today and is similar to the Catalan *masia*. The region developed its own folklore and culture. This includes a tradition of choral singing and poetry recital, as well as sports such as pelota or *Jai-Alai*, akin to squash, in addition to stone-carrying, caber-tossing and rowing in thirteen-oared open fishing boats called *traineras*. Basque cooking is more elaborate than its austere Castilian equivalent. Not only is the region studded with Michelin-starred restaurants but Basque eateries can be found across Spain. The powerful Basque bourgeoisie have long been patrons of the arts. The Bilbao Fine Art Museum has one of the finest collections outside Madrid. Two internationally renowned Basque sculptors, Eduardo Chillida and Jorge Oteiza, led an artistic revival in the region in the later decades of the dictatorship.

Basque nationalists seek to create their own state spanning the three Spanish Basque provinces, Navarre and three Basque districts around Bayonne that make up part of the French department of Pyrénées-Atlantiques. Like Catalonia, the Basque Country has never previously been an independent nation state. The feudal lordship of Vizcaya was incorporated into Castile around 1100; the other Spanish Basque provinces, Álava and Guipúzcoa, had followed by 1200, while across the Pyrenees the French Basque districts were part of Gascony. Navarre, parts of which are culturally Basque but others not, was an independent kingdom until it was absorbed by Castile in 1515. For centuries Basque identity was not anti-Spanish; rather, by some accounts at least, the Basques saw themselves as the most authentic Spaniards of all.[6] And that is how many Spaniards saw them. In the many demonstrations against terrorism in cities across Spain, the chant was often *Vascos sí, ETA no* (Basques, yes; ETA, no). Sancho Garcés III, the king of Navarre from 1004 to 1035, briefly united all the Basque lands, but only because he gained control of the kingdom of León which held the coastal areas at the time. Significantly he styled himself 'King of the Spains'.[7] A fierce Christianity took root in the Basque Country. Before Queen Isabella expelled the Jews from the rest of Castile in 1492, the Basque lords had done the same in the name of 'purity of blood'. Inácio de Loyola, the founder of the Jesuits, was from Guipúzcoa. As seafarers, colonists and royal officials, the Basques played a leading role in Spanish America, and Basque surnames are still common today in countries such as Mexico, Colombia and Peru.

Under their medieval *fueros*, each Basque province and many towns enjoyed autonomy over laws, a reduced level of taxation and exemption from military service. These privileges were accepted by successive monarchs. Because the Basques had backed the Bourbon cause in the War of the Spanish Succession the *fueros* survived the Nueva Planta, and only came into question in the nineteenth century. Under the Peace of Vergara, which ended the First Carlist War, the *fueros* were incorporated into the Spanish constitution and the customs barrier moved to Spain's border with France, ending what had been a kind of free-trade area. In the telling of history by some Basque nationalists, 1839 and the end of the *fueros* play a similar role to 1714 for their Catalan peers. The *fueros* were an anachronism in a liberal state that was attempting to build a homogeneous nation. A law of the Restoration monarchy in 1876 scrapped them altogether, replacing them with an economic arrangement – the *concierto económico* – under which the Basque provinces continued to collect their own taxes but shared the revenues with the central government. Only Navarre retained a *fuero*, recognition of its history as an independent kingdom that had merged with Castile.

Not coincidentally, Basque nationalism emerged just when the iron and steel works of Vizcaya became the second great pole of the Spanish industrial revolution after Catalan textiles. Along with the ironworks, shipbuilding flourished in Bilbao and metallurgical businesses, many of them family-owned, in Guipúzcoa. A powerful Basque bourgeoisie, in Bilbao especially, came to dominate much of Spanish finance and business. The factories and shipyards drew in migrants from elsewhere in Spain. Bilbao and the other Basque cities were Spanish-speaking strongholds of liberalism and socialism while San Sebastián became an elegant summer resort for the Spanish monarchs and the European aristocracy.

This dilution of a supposedly 'pure' Basque race alarmed Sabino Arana, an eccentric and reactionary writer from a Carlist family who founded the PNV in 1895. His ideology and conception of Basque identity were based on a fundamentalist Catholicism and a racist hostility to other Spaniards whom he dubbed *maketos*. That echoed the anti-Semitic concern with the 'purity of the blood' of the Spanish Inquisition. He saw women as subordinate to men. Arana and his brother invented a name for the Basque provinces (Euskadi) and a flag, the red, green and white *ikurriña*, whose design they copied from the Union Jack. Arana called for independence. In contrast to Catalonia, he based this claim on race rather than language. Euskara, a clutch of dialects whose use was largely confined to rural areas, was only codified into a single language in 1968. The great Basque writers – such as Miguel de Unamuno and Pio Baroja – preferred to write in Castilian Spanish. Only in the current democratic period has Euskara, which is now energetically promoted by the Basque regional government, started to acquire a literature. Arana invented many new words in Euskara, including versions of Spanish Christian names. One neologism was *jeltzalea*, meaning a supporter of his slogan *Jaungoikoa Eta Lege Zarra* ('God and the old laws'). In Euskara he called his party Eusko Alderdi Jeltzalea. Its official initials today are EAJ-PNV.

The PNV gained early support in the countryside and especially among the urban lower middle class, which felt squeezed between the cosmopolitan financial elite and the largely immigrant workforce. At first the heirs to Carlism looked on the PNV with suspicion as a rival. But the party put down roots, through social clubs called *batzoki*, unions and hill-walking clubs. Towards the end of his life, ill and in prison, Arana had moderated his demand for independence into one for autonomy. His legacy to the movement he created was thus ambivalent, and enabled the PNV to attract supporters of both.[8] Many of its subsequent leaders have combined an emotional commitment to independence with a hard-headed appreciation of the benefits of autonomy within Spain. After Arana's early death the PNV became increasingly pragmatic. In the Civil War of the 1930s the PNV and the main Basque cities backed the Republic, while 80,000 Carlist volunteers from Navarre and Álava fought for Franco. What swayed coastal Basque loyalty to the Republic was the grant of a home-rule statute in 1936. José Antonio Aguirre, a PNV leader who was a far more attractive figure than Arana, became the first *lehendakari* or president of the regional government. Aged just 32, he was the mayor of Getxo, a bourgeois suburb of Bilbao, a former footballer for Athletic Bilbao and the heir to a family chocolate factory.[9] Politically he was a moderate centrist. It is Aguirre's portrait that hangs today in the vestibule of the PNV's imposing headquarters in Bilbao.

In victory, Franco was vengeful towards the Basques. He took it as a particular betrayal that the conservative, Catholic PNV should have backed the Republic. In contrast, because they had supported him, Álava was allowed to keep its *concierto económico* and Navarre its *fuero* and

Euskara was tolerated there, in the only exceptions to Franco's unitary regime. But Vizcaya and Guipúzcoa, the 'traitorous provinces' as he called them, were singled out for punishment in a decree published after their capitulation: their *concierto económico* was abolished and the public use of Euskara banned, as with Catalan. This collective punishment would eventually prompt a violent reaction.

The two souls of Basque nationalism surfaced again when part of the PNV's youth wing broke away in 1959 to form Euskadi Ta Askatasuna (Basque Homeland and Liberty', ETA). By then the PNV had evolved into a staid pro-European Christian Democrat party, most of whose leaders wanted autonomy rather than independence. ETA wanted to take on the dictatorship more actively. It defined itself as 'a revolutionary Basque organisation for national liberation'. Its worldview combined ultra-nationalism, authoritarian Marxism-Leninism and Catholic mysticism. 'It began as a national cause, became a revolutionary cause and ended as pure, hard terrorism,' was how Andoni Ortuzar, the current president of the PNV, described ETA's trajectory.[10] Though its founders were students and urban professionals it quickly put down roots in the small towns inland from San Sebastián and Bilbao, partly through a network of *herriko tabernas* (people's taverns). It revived the Carlist tradition of insurrection.[11] Another legacy of the Carlist tradition was that many Catholic priests in the Basque Country were nationalists and some supported ETA more or less explicitly. They included José María Setién, the bishop of San Sebastián from 1979 to 2000, who refused to hold funerals for victims of ETA in his cathedral. ETA would later attract support from a new left of feminists and ecologists. Most of its members were from the middle class, and many of its victims were civil guards from poor, rural Spain. 'It was a class struggle in reverse,' as José Antonio Pérez, a historian at the University of the Basque Country, put it.[12]

ETA began with propaganda actions, such as placing the banned *ikurriña* on church towers and bombing *franquista* monuments.[13] In

1968 it murdered a hated police commissioner in Irun. This was designed to provoke Franco. He duly responded by declaring a state of siege in the Basque provinces, with the police shooting some suspects, carrying out mass arrests and torturing detainees. In 1970 the regime put fifteen ETA members, including two priests, on trial before a military court in Burgos for the murder of the commissioner. Five were sentenced to death. That prompted an international outcry which caused the dictatorship to commute the sentences to long prison terms. Then, in 1973, in a carefully planned operation ETA detonated high explosives under the car of Admiral Carrero-Blanco. The murder of the man whom Franco was counting on to continue the dictatorship after his death brought ETA popularity among many Spaniards. Had it abandoned what it called its armed struggle with the transition to democracy, history would judge it very differently.

But it didn't. ETA was part of a wave of urban guerrilla or terrorist groups that emerged in Europe in the 1960s, such as the IRA in Northern Ireland, the Red Army Faction in Germany and the Red Brigades in Italy. Alone among them it took its violent campaign into the twenty-first century. In all, ETA would be responsible for 853 murders and its shootings and bombs injured 2,632.[14] It forced thousands to flee the region.[15] More than 90% of its 853 killings, of which 357 were of members of the security forces, occurred after the death of Franco, despite the amnesty that freed its prisoners and despite the arrival of democracy. In 1978, the year of the constitution, it killed sixty-five; in 1979, when the Basque statute of self-government was approved, it killed eighty-six.[16] The group resorted to indiscriminate terror, in a war against Spanish society as well as the state. A car bomb at a hypermarket in Barcelona in 1987 killed twenty-one people and injured forty-five; another, six months later, outside the barracks of the Civil Guard in Zaragoza killed eleven, including five children, and wounded eighty-eight. In the 1980s, in what it called, in a sinister Orwellian term, the 'socialisation of suffering', ETA began to murder local councillors from the Socialists and the PP in the Basque Country. It kidnapped eighty-six people in all, to raise funds and to spread fear. An academic study estimated that ETA raised €106 million through kidnapping, €21 million from extortion and €19 million from robberies. The group kidnapped fifty-five businessmen, of whom four were murdered, five freed by the police and thirteen released after being shot in the legs as a punishment. The rest paid a ransom. Much of the *kale borroka* street violence against shops was linked to extortion.[17] In ETA's fanatical worldview violence became a self-sustaining end in itself, and it killed several of its own members or former members who dared to dissent.

The transition to democracy coincided with harder economic times in the Basque Country. Its heavy industry had become uncompetitive. In 1971 Vizcaya had the highest income per head of any Spanish province, followed by Guipúzcoa and Álava in second and third place. The ten years after 1975 saw no economic growth in the region, and unemployment surged from 1.8% to 23.6% as a painful economic adjustment took place.[18] But ETA's main ally was the brutal police repression in the aftermath of Carrero-Blanco's death. Police excesses continued in the early years of democracy. It was a serious blot that during Felipe González's first government some members of the police organised a death squad called the Grupos Antiterroristas de Liberación (GAL). This killed twenty-seven ETA members and suspects between 1983 and 1987. Another thirty-five were killed by other far-right paramilitary groups. This was partly an enraged response to ETA's killings of army and police generals which were designed to provoke a coup. Behind the GAL also lay frustration that French governments tolerated the use of their territory across the border as a safe haven for ETA.

GAL was not only illegitimate, it was disastrously counter-productive. As a result of the repression up to a fifth of the Basque population felt alienated from Spain's young democracy. Rather than terrorism, the *abertzales* proclaimed that ETA's violence was a defensive response against the violence of an essentially undemocratic state and that it was a consequence of an unresolved political conflict between the Basques and (the rest of) Spain. False and far-fetched though this narrative was, it was lapped up to varying degrees by some foreign observers. It is expressed, for example, in Mark Kurlansky's *The Basque History of the World*, a bestseller that combines credulity towards many nationalist fables, the presentation of the Basques as comic-book heroes akin to Asterix, and a nauseating moral equivalence between terrorism and a democratic state, whatever its imperfections.[19] Not only was there a huge disproportion between the scale and duration of the GAL's murders and those of ETA, but a police general and a Socialist interior minister were jailed for their involvement in the death squad, and it was swiftly shut down.

In summary, the police violence was an aberration which was punished; ETA's violence was a political project and a tool to seek power. The conflict was not between the Basque people and the Spanish state but involved a minority of Basques who refused to accept the will of the majority and the rules of democracy. Unlike in Northern Ireland, 'there were never two sides here', José Antonio Pérez, the historian, told me. 'There was never a political party or a social group that supported police crimes.' He and other historians also question the *abertzale* narrative that the police continued to practise systematic torture against ETA suspects long after Franco was dead. An investigation by the Basque government into allegations of torture reported that there were 4,000 cases between the 1960s and today. But many of these claims were made years later. 'There is no proof except in a few cases,' he says.

In the 1980s and 1990s ETA created a society dominated by fear. By one calculation, over 40,000 Basques were under threat, and many had to live for years with bodyguards shadowing their every move. In what is a relatively small, claustrophobic society, the menace came from neighbours, former classmates or work colleagues. That made it especially chilling. It might begin with spray-painted threats, such as the sign of a target, on front doors. In a book published in 2021 Eduardo Madina, the Socialist politician, and Borja Sémper, who became the president of the PP in Guipúzcoa, talked of those years. Born within a day of each other in 1976, both were lucky to be still alive. In 1997 the Civil Guard arrested an ETA team, led by Iratxe Sorzabal, which was poised to shoot Sémper in the neck at the law faculty in San Sebastián where he was studying. The gunwoman had desisted at the last moment because she thought he had a bodyguard, though on that occasion he didn't. In 2002 a bomb detonated under Madina's car while he was driving to work. He lost a leg but survived, he thinks mainly because his height (he is 6 feet 3 inches) meant that the blast missed his upper body.[20]

Fernando Aramburu, a Basque writer who lives in Germany, offered a powerful and authentic fictional account of those years in *Patria* (Homeland), a novel that has sold more than a million copies in Spain and was turned into a Netflix series. Set in Hernani, a town a few miles inland from San Sebastián, it tells the story of two couples who were neighbours and close friends. Txato sets up a successful haulage company. He helps his poorer pals, Joxian and Miren, who is so close to Txato's wife, Bittori, as to seem like a sister. Then Miren's middle son, Joxe Mari, joins ETA, having become entangled in the *abertzale* world through his drinking buddies in the *herriko tabernas*. Txato becomes a target of extortion. The first time he pays up. Then he refuses. After all, he reasons, his father was wounded fighting Franco on the Basque front during the Civil War, and: 'I'm from here, I speak Basque, I don't get involved in politics, I create jobs. . . . Don't they say they're defending the Basque people. Well, if I'm not the Basque people, who is?' Overnight Txato and Bittori's lifelong friends turn their backs on them, and Txato is ostracised from his Sunday morning cycling fraternity. He is murdered. Joxe Mari is captured, tortured and jailed, and eventually repents.[21]

In the end three things brought about ETA's defeat. The first and most important was better policing, and cooperation from the French government. In 1992 French police arrested the entire ETA leadership in Bidart, just across the border. The Civil Guard repeatedly tracked down its successors. Militarily, ETA was beaten by the early 2000s. The second was that global opinion hardened against 'armed struggle' and terrorism after the attacks of 11 September 2001 in the United States and of 11 March 2004 in Madrid. Third, after decades of looking the other way, either out of fear or indifference, Basque society at last began to turn against the gunmen. The trigger was two atrocities in the summer of 1997. First the Civil Guard stumbled upon a home-made dungeon where José Antonio Ortega Lara, a prison officer, had been held as a hostage for eighteen months. He was emaciated and close to death. Ten days later ETA kidnapped Miguel Ángel Blanco, a 29-year-old PP councillor in the small inland town of Ermua, almost halfway between Bilbao and San Sebastián. They gave Aznar's government forty-eight hours to move all ETA prisoners to jails in the Basque Country, though they knew that no Spanish government could or did give in to such threats. Blanco was taken to a forest less than an hour away and killed with two bullets to his head, having been forced to kneel.[22] But in those forty-eight hours massive demonstrations demanding his release took place across Spain, including the Basque Country.

Blanco's murder was a turning point. ETA came to realise that it had lost the tacit consent of a broad swathe of Basque society. Through Herri Batasuna (HB, Popular Unity), the party of the *abertzales* which it directed, ETA sought and obtained an agreement with the PNV. Under the Pact of Lizarra, signed ahead of a Basque regional election in 1998, both parties agreed to seek independence and break off coop-eration with the PP and the Socialists while ETA declared a truce. The PNV party president, Xabier Arzalluz, a former Jesuit priest and the *éminence grise* of the Basque government, had previously collaborated with both González and Aznar in return for the transfer of powers. But he showed a sinuous ability to play several games at once. He declared that 'the Basque people don't fit in this constitution'. The Basque parliament approved a reform of the autonomy statute that would have included 'the right to decide' on independence and a relationship of 'free association' with the rest of Spain. It was overwhelmingly rejected in the Spanish parliament in 2005 (by 303 to 29, all of whom were peripheral nationalists). ETA's truce was long over by then. In 2000 it murdered twenty-three people, including the general secretary of the Basque Socialist Party.

In response Aznar's government proposed to the Socialists that they agree a law to ban HB. Some Socialists were initially reluctant to back a move that many abroad saw as illiberal. But Zapatero had proposed a pact with the PP aiming to take terrorism out of the arena of partisan competition and quickly agreed to it. That was the right judgement. The law was later upheld by the European Court of Human Rights. It forced the *abertzales* to choose between 'guns or votes' as Rubalcaba, Zapatero's interior minister, put it. They would eventually choose votes: Arnaldo Otegi, an ETA operative who was HB's general secretary, began to press his remaining armed comrades to make peace. Another truce came in 2004. Although this was broken in 2006 when ETA blew up two newly arrived Ecuadorean migrants in the car park at Barajas airport in Madrid, the group was a spent force.

Moderates had taken control of the PNV. Zapatero's government pursued ETA's remnants implacably while organising arm's-length talks. It agreed gradually to move the 300 or so ETA prisoners, who had been deliberately dispersed around the country, to jails in the Basque Country, but made no political concessions. Aznar's government had staged direct talks with ETA after the 1998 truce, but that did not stop the PP criticising Zapatero. In 2011 three hooded ETA members, including Sorzabal, who had tried to kill Sémper, declared an indefinite cessation of violence. This time it lasted. Sortu, the successor to HB, had amended its statutes to include a rejection of violence and was legalised in time for the 2012 election, in which it stood as part of EH Bildu, a new *abertzale* coalition. In 2018 ETA at last announced its disbandment. To promote their narrative of an underlying political conflict, the *abertzales* tried to dress this up as the result of a 'peace process' with a motley group of international observers attending a ceremony across the border in France. Rajoy's government took no part in this but nor did it obstruct it. Rubalcaba wrote: 'The only truth is that Spanish democracy suffered a lot, it's true, but in the end it vanquished the terrorists, who didn't achieve any of their political objectives.'[23]

The Euskadi of 2018 was a very different place from the Basque Country of half a century earlier, when ETA had begun its violent campaign. Whatever its political ambiguities the PNV, which has run the Basque regional administration for all but three years since its inception in 1980, has provided generally clean and effective government, and piloted an economic transformation. That was exemplified by Bilbao, which changed from being a heavily polluted rustbelt city to a globally known poster-child for urban renewal. Its emblem was the Guggenheim Museum, designed by Frank Gehry, an American architect, and opened in 1997. It is a remarkable building, its titanium exterior mimicking the folds and creases of the hills behind or, seen from the opposite bank of the River Nervión, resembling a ship about to take sail. Creating what was then the first overseas franchise of the New York museum required heavy public investment (perhaps US$170 million) and continuing public subsidy. The decision to do this owed much to the PNV's political control at all levels of government: region, province and city hall.[24] The Guggenheim was, above all, a bold statement about the future of the Basque region. It changed the sociology of the city, attracting cultural tourism, as Miguel Zugaza told me. The director of the Bilbao Fine Arts Museum from 1996 to 2002, he returned there in 2017 after a successful stint running the Prado and felt the 'Guggenheim effect'. When he left, his museum got 150,000 tourists a year; when he returned it got double that, many of them foreign tourists.

In the Guggenheim's wake the city hired other starchitects to design new bridges (by Santiago Calatrava), new metro stations (Norman Foster) and a new airport terminal (Calatrava again). It opened up the previously decaying left bank of the river as a pedestrian *paseo*. Yet, as important as Bilbao's facelift was to the region's economic renaissance, so too were the Basque government's effective industrial and training policies. 'The industrial and business vocation of the 1970s is still here, but industry is much more modern and competitive now,' according to Pedro Azpiazu, its economic councillor. Though services make up more than half of the Basque economy, industry still accounts for over a fifth of its GDP. Including Navarre, the region houses half of Spain's car industry, a quarter of its aeronautical industry and 80% of machine-tool making.[25]

In the early 1990s the Basque government adopted an industrial strategy aimed at promoting business clusters, focusing on technology, the car industry, aeronautics and biosciences. One of its fruits is the Automotive Intelligence Centre, outside Bilbao. A private-sector project with help from the *diputación* of Vizcaya, it is a research and innovation hub that houses thirty-one companies, ranging from local to multinational, and provides 800 jobs. It has its own training academy. Mercedes has a big plant nearby in Vitoria and Volkswagen in Pamplona. Many of the 300 car parts makers in the region are the Basque equivalent of the German *mittelstand* of mid-sized family-owned manufacturers. Behind Bilbao's airport the regional government and the *diputación* set up the Vizcaya Science and Technology park, with 200 high-tech companies and Spain's second-biggest business incubator (after one in Barcelona). Iñigo Angulo-Barturen, the founder of a biotech start-up housed there, praised the political commitment of the region's authorities to business development, and the availability of qualified staff. Vocational training, a weakness in

Spain in general, works well in the Basque Country. There are some 25,000 students in training centres in the car industry alone, mostly in dual schemes involving government and businesses, which combine instruction with work experience.

All these new businesses allowed the region to regain a top spot in income per head in Spain, behind only Madrid and above the EU average. Of course the *concierto económico* and the resulting generous funding of the public sector helped. But on the whole public money was well spent in the Basque Country. Given the PNV's long stint in power it is perhaps surprising that there have been only isolated cases of corruption reported in the region. That may owe something not only to Jesuit morality, but also to the smallness of the political and business worlds in Euskadi. 'Government is very close to the people,' according to Iñigo Urkullu, the *lehendakari* since 2012. 'We can almost say everyone knows everyone else.'[26] It may also help that the practice of the PNV is to separate the job of head of the party from that of head of the regional government.

The PNV is the most impressive political machine in Spain. Its current leaders, with Ortuzar running the party and Urkullu the regional government, are shrewd realists. Their political objective is a new statute that would embody the sharing of sovereignty with Spain rather than independence. 'We are not starting from scratch, we have spent forty years building institutions,' Ortuzar told me when I sat down with him for an hour at the party headquarters in Bilbao in 2018. 'There's nobody in Europe closer to being a nation [state] without being one.' But, he went on: 'The Basque national cause is not incompatible with Spain. A nation doesn't have to have a state, not in Europe today.' What he would like, he said, is a confederation but he quickly added 'we are conscious that this doesn't exist, not even in Switzerland'. This circumspection reflects public opinion. The regional government has succeeded in reviving Euskara. Most children in public schools are taught in it, and for about 40% of the population it is their habitual language. But that hasn't translated into wanting to break away from Spain. Polls suggest that two-thirds of the population of Euskadi feels itself to be both Basque and Spanish and fewer than a quarter favour independence.[27] It is hard not to conclude that the current situation of radical autonomy represents the best of all possible worlds for the Basques.

'The remaining task before us is to avoid that the defeated impose their false narrative,' Rubalcaba wrote when ETA disbanded. In June 2021 King Felipe, Pedro Sánchez and Urkullu opened a memorial centre to the victims of terrorism housed in the imposing former branch office of the Bank of Spain in Vitoria, the regional capital. A public foundation attached to Spain's interior ministry but with the support of the Basque government, the centre is in memory of the victims of all terrorisms, including Islamist attacks. But 60% of the victims were those of ETA. It includes a reconstruction of the dungeon where Lara Ortega, the prison official, was held hostage. Its aims are to honour and remember the victims, to provide a truthful narrative of what happened and to spread information about this among young people. 'We are professional historians, trying to reconstruct a historically rigorous account,' according to Raúl López Romo, who is in charge of its exhibitions. The idea of a conflict between two sides is propaganda to whitewash the image of ETA, he went on, while admitting that it is present in Basque society and abroad.

Take Hernani, the town of 18,000 people with a medieval centre and several industrial estates portrayed in *Patria*. It remains an *abertzale* stronghold. As ETA announced its disbandment in 2018 I visited Hernani and spoke to Koro Etxeberria, the deputy mayor from EH Bildu. 'The conflict still exists, though in different parameters,' she insisted. She hadn't taken part in it, but 'the armed struggle was to get rights that have been usurped. . . . Here repression by the forces of the state was brutal.' Others felt excluded from Hernani. The local secretary of the Socialist party spent a decade without going to the centre of town. He is greeted now, but not talked to. 'There are places you don't go,' Latierro, of the Lagun bookshop, said. 'In the 1950s and 1960s my generation went to Hernani to dance there on Sundays in the square. I have only been back there twice in the past 20 years.'

On the same visit I crossed the border to Hendaye to speak to Agus Hernan, a leader of the Foro Social, an umbrella group of *abertzale* social movements. He argued for the idea of 'inclusive memory', by which he meant that there were two sides with equally valid narratives. 'Our idea is that we all have to live together and that means listening to all accounts.' In a score of towns across the Basque Country there were initiatives by mayors to set up conversations between victims and those responsible. But for many victims this was hard. 'Reconciliation is an empty word,' said Consuelo Ordoñez, a leader of a victims association. 'I don't have to be reconciled with my brother's killer.' Her brother, Gregorio Ordoñez, was the PP deputy mayor of San Sebastián, shot in the neck by ETA in 1995 as he sat in a bar with two party colleagues. 'Basque society is still kidnapped. The majority don't want to talk.'

In 2021 Otegi went further than ever before in apologising for ETA's violence, saying to victims: 'We want to tell them that we feel their pain and to state that it should never have come about. Nobody can derive satisfaction from this happening. It shouldn't have gone on for so long.'[28] For some victims' groups this was a step in the right direction, since it dropped Otegi's previous distinction between the relatives of civilian victims, to whom he apologised, and those from the police. Others said it still fell short of a clear condemnation of terrorism. They also wanted the prisoners to help with unsolved crimes and an end to the welcome ceremonies for freed prisoners who returned home.

For many, the political acceptance of EH Bildu by the Socialists came too soon. Because of the tight parliamentary arithmetic, Sánchez's government negotiated the approval of its budget in both 2020 and 2021 with the *abertzales*, along with other groups. The Socialists also relied on the support of Bildu to form a regional government in Navarre. 'We Socialists now see Bildu as a normal party,' declared Jesús Egùiguren, a former president of the Basque wing of his party who had held talks with Otegi during Zapatero's government.[29] This contrasted with the *cordon sanitaire* other parties continued to place around Sinn Féin in the Irish Republic two decades after the Good Friday Agreement ended the IRA's violence. Yet the PP's refusal to accept that ETA's dissolution was an important change for the Basque Country also carried costs. On taking over from Rajoy Pablo Casado replaced the leadership of the PP's Basque branch with hardline conservatives. They seemed out of touch with Basque society as it had evolved rapidly over the previous decade. Polls showed that many younger Basques had little knowledge or memory of ETA's crimes. In a regional election in 2020, although the PNV retained power in coalition with the Socialists, the big winner was EH Bildu, with 28% of the vote, which consolidated its position as the second-largest party. Admittedly its gains were mainly at the expense of Podemos, and the turn-out of 51% was depressed by the pandemic. The PP won only 7% of the vote, down from 21% in 2001. It looked as if EH Bildu might, before too long, form part of a Basque government, which would bring new difficulties for Spain.

Travel some 500 kilometres west from Bilbao and you come to Galicia, the third of Spain's historic 'nationalities', in the constitution's term. It too has a pronounced regional identity. It is a land of mists, forests and long Atlantic *rías* (inlets); of pilgrim routes to the vast medieval cathedral of Santiago de Compostela; remote from almost everywhere, its people are famous for their caginess. Like Catalonia and the Basque Country it has its own language – *galego*, which to the outsider sounds like a mixture of Spanish, Portuguese and autochthonous elements, and which has a literature dating back to the twelfth century. It has a long history of human settlement, originally by Celtic peoples, and it has clear borders. Like Catalonia and the Basque Country, the Arab-

Berber presence was light and brief. For a period in the tenth and eleventh centuries it was an independent kingdom, although centred on León, before being absorbed dynastically by Castile. It has characteristic folklore, such as the bagpipes, and legends derived from a plethora of ancient Celtic fortresses known as *castros*. In the mid-nineteenth century Galicia saw a cultural movement known as the *rexurdimento*, inspired by the Catalan *Renaixença*.[30]

Nevertheless, its story is very different from that of Catalonia or the Basque Country. Political nationalism came late to Galicia, perhaps because it was long one of the poorest parts of the Iberian Peninsula, a land of emigration rather than immigration. The first nationalist organisations were founded during the First World War and the first nationalist party, the Galeguista, in 1931. Its members were mainly from the urban middle class in what was then an overwhelmingly rural region. Galician representatives in the Cortes were negotiating a statute of autonomy when the Civil War broke out in 1936. Franco's coup was successful in Galicia. The dictatorship's repression meant that the seed of nationalism would not flower again until the 1960s, and then mainly in cultural form such as the renewed public use of the *galego* language. Unlike in Catalonia or Euskadi, nationalist parties did not play a leading role in negotiating Galicia's autonomy statute of 1981. Represented since the 1990s mainly by the Galician Nationalist Bloc (BNG) the nationalists have never obtained more than 30% of the vote in regional elections, and more often 15% to 25%. Rather, it has been conservatives who have successfully overseen a strong regional identity in Galicia.

Manuel Fraga, Franco's former information minister and a founder of what is today the PP, was the regional president in Galicia from 1989 to 2005. After a brief Socialist-led interlude, the PP has ruled again since 2009 under the leadership of Alberto Núñez Feijóo until 2022. Polls find half of respondents saying they feel equally *galego* and Spanish, while only around 15% think of themselves as having a separate national identity. 'We're not on the psychiatrist's couch asking who we are,' Feijóo told me when I talked to him in his office on a hill opposite the cathedral in Santiago. Like Fraga before him, Feijóo practises *galeguismo*. 'We have defended Galicia as a place that has its language, culture and particularities,' he said. 'We are the party of the home, the land.' In what he calls 'cordial bilingualism' teaching in school is half in *galego* and half in Spanish, though the BNG complains that in practice *galego* gets shorter shrift. Nevertheless, Feijóo argues that his *galeguismo* has halted nationalism. It also prevented Vox from making headway. Autonomy has served not to create nationalists in Galicia but to strengthen the region's double identity, according to Xosé Manoel Núñez Seixas, the historian at the University of Santiago de Compostela. '*Galegos* feel very *galego*. But they don't see a contradiction in that with being part of Spain.'

It is a regionalism that wants to get ahead rather than break away, and to defend its interests by having a strong influence in Madrid. This is a formula that has largely worked. Since democracy arrived, Galicia has progressed from its poverty to enjoying an income only slightly below the national average, becoming the Spanish region with the fastest economic growth in this century. In other words, it was a textbook example of 'levelling up'. Its success owed much to political stability and a cohesive society. Unlike Catalonia and the Basque Country, where primogeniture kept the *masia* and the *baserri* intact, Galician tradition was to divide farms among all children. That led not only to rural poverty and emigration but also to a culture that values private property, the *leira* (homestead) and hard work. Its economy has diversified. It boasts Europe's largest fishing industry, shipbuilding, dairying and timber. Its white wine from the Albariño grape has become an international brand. Galicia also has two industrial mainstays. Inditex, based near A Coruña has grown from being a single draper's shop to the world's biggest provider of fast fashion through Zara and its other chains. Second, the vast Citroën plant near Vigo anchors 30,000 car industry jobs. The regional government has invested European funds in motorways. It is still six hours to Madrid by car but it used to take twice as long. Another motorway runs along Spain's north coast to the French border. A third connects Galicia with Porto, in northern Portugal, in what has become a seamless economic region. After many delays, in December 2021 the last section of the AVE high-speed railway to Madrid was completed, slashing journey times.

Having caught up, Galicia's challenge is to continue to progress socio-economically. Critics of Feijóo complained that he failed to halt an exodus of talent, as young professionals seek opportunities abroad. 'The economic model gives priority to cement over knowledge,' Núñez Seixas argued. Galicia spends little on research and development (R+D) compared with the Basque Country. It has three airports where one would suffice; many *galegos* cross the border to Porto, which has a wider range of international flights. Economic dynamism in the coastal strip from A Coruña to Vigo contrasts with the hollowing out of the interior. Half a century ago more than 800,000 people in Galicia were involved in farming.[31] Now only 45,000 are. In the emptier countryside forest fires are common. Galicians are ageing. The regional government is trying to encourage immigration. Ana Pontón, who revived the BNG in the regional election in 2020, highlights these problems and argues that their solution lies in 'the right to decide' on independence, or at least a Basque-style *concierto económico*. But there is little sign that most *galegos* are likely to agree.

The PP in Galicia is much more moderate and pragmatic than its national incarnation was under Pablo Casado, whom Feijóo replaced in April 2022 (see chapter 9). Feijóo is a manager rather than an ideologue. His critics saw him as a *cacique*. But that may have merely reflected the power and prominence that regional governments have acquired across Spain. Alongside the three historic nationalities the *estado autonómico* has created a mosaic of more or less strong regional identities, some initially artificial. That is both a strength and a weakness, a point to which we will return.

CHAPTER 7

THE FADING OF THE SPANISH DREAM

Linares is a dense, compact town of 58,000 people in the province of Jaén, near the gateway to Andalucía from Spain's central plateau. It has been successively a centre of lead mining, a railway hub and the site of a large factory making Santana jeeps. Today it is a town with a reputation for having the highest unemployment rate in Spain, at 33%. The Santana factory, which employed more than 2,000 people in its heyday, closed in 2011. High-speed trains to Seville and Granada bypass Linares. So do tourists heading for nearby Úbeda and Baeza with their ancient churches and renaissance palaces of honeyed stone.

A large Corte Inglés department store in the main square of Linares closed in March 2021 and stands decaying like a rotten tooth. Inditex, the fast-fashion giant, recently closed most of its shops in the town too. 'Many young people are neither studying nor training,' Manuel Gámez of a civic pressure group told me when I visited Linares in June 2021. In economic terms, 'the whole province of Jaén is a *páramo* (wasteland),' he said. Indeed, Jaén is known mainly for its 'green sea' of endless olive trees that produce a fifth of the world's olive oil. We were talking in Gámez's furniture shop, which received only one customer during our hour-long conversation. The business was in its third generation, but 'my children won't be able to live from it', he said.

Linares briefly drew national attention four months earlier when an altercation at a bar terrace involving two off-duty policemen triggered a street brawl which ended with fourteen arrested and twenty police lightly hurt. The national media portrayed a town at breaking point.[1] That was an exaggeration. Linares's reputation is overdone, insisted Raúl Caro-Accino, the mayor. Formerly the director of the local chamber of commerce he was an independent, elected for Ciudadanos in a town that long voted Socialist. He pointed out that the store closures were the result of national business decisions related to the take-off in internet commerce during the pandemic. He enthused about technology businesses in industrial estates on the outskirts of the town. He took me to see one called Sicnova that makes customised steel parts using 3D printing. Evolutio, a cloud-services subsidiary of British Telecom, planned to set up a research centre in Linares. These businesses were drawn by the presence in the town of the technology faculty of the University of Jaén and its business incubator. The unemployment rate was in line with other places in southern and western Spain, the mayor insisted. 'We have a problem of unqualified labour,' he admitted.

What that meant was long-term unemployment for many people in Linares, and a self-fulfilling sense of failure and lack of opportunity. 'I've been looking for work for months,' said Carlos Márquez, aged 21, who was laid off from a job selling mobile phones in a hypermarket before the pandemic. 'There's nothing in Linares. I would have to go somewhere else.' Some blame themselves for failing to get qualifications. 'I was unemployed for ages, I didn't study, I was lazy,' said Antonia Delgado as she walked along the Pasaje del Comercio, the main shopping street, with her son. She had just got a month's work looking after old people, but wasn't optimistic. 'There are no opportunities. Things were bad and are now worse with the pandemic. This place is dead.'

Spain's economy stands out in Europe mainly for its chronic high unemployment, especially among women, young people, men over 50 and those with few skills and little education. A large chunk of the unemployed have been so for more than a year, or even two. This is the main reason why inequality and poverty rose above the European average after the great recession of 2007–9 (in Spain's case, 2008–13). It is a waste of human potential and a policy failure. One might expect this to be more of a scandal than it is, especially with left-wing governments in office since 2018. But this social problem is 'quite invisible', according to Xavier Coller, a sociologist at Pablo de Olavide university in Seville.[2] That is partly because while the jobless are poor they are 'not dying of hunger', he said. Those who don't qualify for unemployment insurance receive €400 per month from the government. Some are immigrants. The unemployed are often thought to profit from the black economy, especially in Andalucía. This may be equal to around 17.5% of Spain's GDP, though that is close to the EU average.[3] A second feature of the economy is a kind of dualism exemplified by Linares, with a modern, internationalised segment coexisting with a large mass of small, unproductive family businesses. A third, more positive, feature is the Spanish economy's ability to grow fast and reinvent itself, at least partially.

Until the slump of 2008 to 2013, each generation of Spaniards since the 1960s had lived better than their parents and the middle class steadily expanded. Many achieved – or could at least aspire to – the Spanish dream of owning a flat and a car, and taking a month's summer holiday. In many cases they spent that holiday at a second home, either at the beach or in the *pueblo*, the rural village whence their parents or grandparents had migrated to the city. This dream is now fading under the impact of two deep slumps in a decade. A poll of 18–34-year-olds for *El País* newspaper, published in July 2021, found that 75% thought they would be worse off than their parents while only 12% thought they would be better off. This generation has reached adulthood not just in a stop–start economy but also in a dysfunctional labour market in which *precariedad* (precariousness, or lack of stability) and temporary contracts are the norm. Its plight was summed up in *Feria*, a surprise bestseller by Ana Iris Simón, a previously unknown writer born in 1991. In a video that went viral she challenged Pedro Sánchez, complaining: 'I've been made redundant three times, and my temporary contract expired two days after I was due to give birth for the first time. I have neither a car nor a mortgage because I can't afford them.'[4] Her parents were postal workers from La Mancha, and lifelong Communists. Her memoir began: 'I envy the life my parents had at my age.' As she highlighted, the implicit social contract between generations is fraying. While the welfare state looks after older Spaniards, younger generations get short shrift and face uncertain prospects. This – and not nationalisms or historical memory – is the biggest problem facing the country. And it doesn't get anything like the attention it should.

What has gone wrong? In both the 2008–13 recession and in the pandemic slump of 2020–21 Spain was hit worse than most of the rest of Europe. In different ways, both recessions highlighted structural weaknesses in the economy. Yet in between the country enjoyed a vigorous recovery, and the contrast between what happened in each of these recessions points to potentially encouraging underlying changes. But remaking the social contract will require far-reaching reforms. And there is little sign that the politicians can find sufficient consensus to enact them.

Between 1995 and 2007 Spain's economy grew at an average rate of 3.5% a year, well above the EU average of 2.2%. Unemployment, which had rocketed upwards with the economic restructuring and oil shocks of the 1970s, at last fell steadily during this long expansion, reaching a floor of 8% in 2007. Yet the growth was unbalanced, unsustainably skewed towards the construction and housebuilding boom. It was also inefficient. A later study for the Bank of Spain by a team of economists found that productivity declined during this period while it increased in the EU as a whole.[5] In other words, the growth all came from adding workers – this was when immigration took off and younger women joined the workforce at a faster rate than in the past – and capital, helped by the cheapness of credit as Spain joined the euro. The ratio of total credit to GDP tripled between 1994 and 2007. Much of this money was in effect wasted, and not just the billions which went on white elephants. There seem to have been several reasons for this inefficiency in allocating resources. One was that some of the growth was in industries that depended on government regulation, such as banking and energy as well as construction and infrastructure. The authors of the study refer drily to the 'important macroeconomic costs of cronyism'. Another reason was that newer and more efficient firms seemed to find it harder to get bank credit. As a result, there was insufficient competition to drive efficiency. At the top Spanish business often resembled a cosy, male oligarchy. Chief executives of publicly quoted companies behaved as if they were owners rather than the hired help of shareholders. They stayed for ever. Francisco González glued himself in as the CEO of BBVA, one of the big three banks, from 2000 to 2018. He was forced out only when he was charged with maladministration, after the bank's management hired José Manuel Villarejo, a rogue former police commander, to spy on the boss of a construction company which attempted to organise a takeover bid for BBVA. González, who pleaded his innocence, faced further charges of using the bank for private purposes. Two other long-standing bosses, Antonio Brufau of Repsol, an oil and gas company, and Isidre Fainé of La Caixa, another big bank, were investigated over their firms' use of Villarejo though charges against them were dropped for lack of evidence. Ignacio Sánchez Galán has run Iberdrola, a large electricity company, since 2001.

The flaws of Spanish crony capitalism were exposed by the bursting of the housing and credit bubbles in 2008. Between that year and 2013, Spain lost 9% of its GDP in real terms, private consumption fell by 14% and unemployment surged again, to 27% by early 2013.[6] Young people were hit especially hard: the average income of those under 35 fell by a quarter between 2008 and 2014, while youth unemployment (i.e. among those aged 15 to 24) peaked at a searing 57% in 2013. Almost 230,000 companies perished, according to an estimate by the Círculo de Empresarios, a business think-tank. Perhaps 1 million young Spaniards, as well as some of the recent immigrants, left the country in search of work.[7] The scars took years to heal. It was not until mid-2017 that the economy surpassed its level of 2008.

There were still places where it hadn't. Take, for example, Talavera de la Reina, an hour and forty minutes south-west of Madrid on a slow train. The site of a battle during the Peninsular War it was long known for its blue and yellow hand-painted tiles and pottery. When I visited in 2017, it had become notorious for unemployment, just as Linares became in the pandemic slump. Although its population had shrunk by 5,000 (to 85,000) since 2012, its jobless rate was still around 35%. During the housing boom Talavera had thrived, as many people worked in building materials firms sited along the Tagus valley or commuted to the Madrid suburbs to work on construction sites. Those jobs disappeared and had not come back. On the wall of the bullring someone had spray-painted, in English, 'Make Talavera Great Again' (it was not long after Donald Trump's election victory under the slogan 'Make America Great Again'). There seemed to be only the faintest of chance of that. Its pottery had fallen out of fashion. Its moribund textile industry had failed to modernise. The exhibition centre, normally used for livestock marts, was hosting a two-day 'Job and Enterprise Fair', but only about 100 jobs were on offer. 'Talavera needs to change its economic structure,' explained Joaquín Echaverría of the local chamber of commerce.

That was true for Spain as a whole, and to an extent it has happened. The skeleton of a new and more competitive economy emerged from the wreckage of the housing bust. As well as the economic blackspots there were plenty of less remarked bright spots. In 2017 I visited a research centre tucked away in Abrera, in the Llobregat valley west of Barcelona, amid a jumble of old wine-producing villages and box-like modern factories and warehouses. The centre was one of a dozen owned by Gestamp, a firm from Burgos that in just two decades became one of the world's leading makers of bodywork, doors and bonnets for the global car industry. With more than 100 plants in 23 countries and revenues in 2019 of €9.1 billion, Gestamp is a specialist in hot stamping. This process makes parts six times more resistant than if they are cold-stamped, allowing cars to be safer, lighter and less polluting. What was once mere metal-bashing had become a high-tech operation. 'We are working on cars that will only go into production in five or six years' time,' explained Juan José Matarranz, one of over sixty scientists and engineers at the Abrera centre. This work included differential heating of parts for shock absorption and smart doors that close automatically when they detect an obstacle. Alongside, in a factory equipped with robots, laser-cutters and high-temperature forges, Gestamp churned out parts for shipment to Ford and Audi in the United States as well as for SEAT's large car plant down the road at Martorell.

Spain has become Europe's second-biggest producer and exporter of cars, after Germany. The industry represents 8.5% of GDP and provides 19% of exports and some 2 million jobs, most of them of good quality. In June 2021 Pedro Sánchez and King Felipe went to SEAT's plant at Martorell to announce that the first big project on which the government planned to use European post-pandemic aid was a bet on electric mobility. This would involve €4.3 billion in public investment, partly to set up a nationwide charging network and offer subsidies to trade in diesel and petrol cars.[8]

When recovery at last began in 2014 it was led by exports, which reached 33% of GDP by 2017, up from 23% in 2009. More than 150,000 Spanish companies exported in 2016, half as many again as in 2007. As well as cars, Spain also makes trains and parts of Airbus jets. It excels, in modern formats, at traditional nineteenth-century industries. As noted, Inditex, is the world's leading retailer of fast fashion. One of its dozen clusters of factories and suppliers worldwide remains in Spain, producing clothes worth €1.2 billion in 2018.[9] Many top-quality, hand-stitched women's shoes are made in Mallorca. The country has a broad-based food and drink industry. It supplies Europe with much of its fruit and vegetables. Its many excellent wines are starting to command higher prices abroad. Iberian ham, from pigs reared outdoors which gorge on acorns, is a luxury product whose exports are growing. New exports included chemicals, pharmaceuticals, machinery and professional services. In many cases, in textbook fashion, firms looked to sell abroad because the recession cut demand for their products at home. One study found that this explained almost 75% of the increase in exports between 2009 and 2013.[10] Another talked of a Spanish 'export miracle'.[11]

One addition to the ranks of exporters was ASTI Mobile Robotics, based in a large, featureless shed beside the motorway between the Castilian towns of Burgos and Lerma. Inside, on the main shop floor, when I visited in 2018, a score of workers armed with iPads were testing driverless contraptions mounted on red or orange steel frames. The robots, or automatic guided vehicles, they were designing, building and controlling with customised software operated in factories and warehouses in sixteen countries, delivering parts to production lines. They were the brainchild of Veronica Pascual, a young aeronautical engineer who took over her parents' small conveyor-belt maker when it ran into trouble. She turned it into a mid-sized multinational with 300 workers and sales growing by 30% each year since 2015. As a research-intensive high-tech company with global ambitions, growing fast and run by a woman, ASTI was everything that Spanish business traditionally was not. But commanding the capital and resources to achieve global scale in a high-tech business is tough. In 2021 Pascual sold the business to ABB, a giant Swiss-Swedish engineering company, though she was to have a senior role in its robotics division.[12]

Companies like ASTI have sprung up across the country, led by a new generation of entrepreneurs, many of them educated abroad and more internationally minded than their parents. In Barcelona, Madrid and the Basque Country, start-ups in technology and biomedicine flourished, some linked to universities. The first Spanish 'unicorns' (a privately owned start-up whose market value exceeded US$1 billion) included eDreams, a Barcelona-based online travel agency; Cabify, based in Madrid and a rival to Uber; and Glovo, a meal delivery outfit.

Tourism also boomed (before the pandemic brought it to a halt), though that was partly because of terrorist incidents in rival destinations, such as Tunisia, Egypt and Turkey. Most of it remained the traditional low-cost sun and *sangría* holidays on the *costas*. But a growing segment was year-round cultural tourism as cities across the country sought to replicate Bilbao's 'Guggenheim effect'. Some merely wasted money on starchitects, but several succeeded sooner or later. Malaga was once a dull place skirted by tourists heading for the Costa del Sol. Under the leadership of the mayor since 2000, Francisco de la Torre, it acquired a cluster of art museums, including outposts of the Russian state museum and Paris's Pompidou Centre, and became a tourist destination in its own right. Santander, along the coast from Bilbao, was pursuing a similar course to its neighbour. Valencia's €1.3 billion splurge on the City of Arts and Sciences, a complex of fantasy buildings including an opera house, aquarium and several museums, started to pay off at last, as tourist numbers rose. The proportion of foreign tourists who came to Spain mostly for cultural reasons was still only 15% of the total but was rising fast, from 8 million in 2012 to 12.9 million in 2017.[13]

Recovery was helped by favourable external conditions, including low interest rates and oil prices (Spain imports much of its energy). But it was also aided by Rajoy's economic reforms. The clean-up of the *cajas* and the banking system meant that credit began to flow again. The bank rescues had cost €66 billion, according to an estimate by the Bank of Spain, but at least they seemed to have worked. In the pandemic slump the banks proved not to be a source of worry, though regulators kept a weather eye on them. The collapse of Banco Popular, a mid-sized lender, in 2017 was a delayed reaction from the housing bust rather than the start of a new wave of insolvency. The banking industry went through a wave of necessary shrinkage, cost-cutting and mergers, of which the most notable was the absorption of Bankia by La Caixa. Between 2008 and 2020 the banks closed almost half of their branches and laid off 37% of their workers. Even so, Spain still had more bank branches per head than anywhere in the EU, except France.[14]

The labour reform helped firms to compete. The Spanish economy proved to be more flexible than those of France or Italy, reckoned José Luis Escrivá, the director of a new independent fiscal authority appointed by Congress, who went on to become social security minister in Sánchez's government. He compared 2017 with 1999, a cyclically neutral year, and pointed out many differences. A current account deficit of 3.3% of GDP had changed to a surplus of close to 2%. Before the great recession, inflation and labour costs in Spain were uncomfortably high. Since then unit labour costs had fallen well below the eurozone average and inflation was lower than in Germany. The labour reform of 2012 contributed to rapid job creation as the economy picked up. Fátima Báñez, the labour minister who introduced it, said that it set in motion 'a new employment culture in Spain, of flexisecurity'. She claimed it had helped to generate more than 3 million jobs in the recovery, and meant that the Spanish economy no longer had to grow faster than 2.5% per year before employment expanded.[15] The main macroeconomic weakness was that the public debt and the fiscal deficit were both much higher as a result of the recession.

But the structure of the economy was only partially changed, and the policy environment in which businesses operated was only half-reformed. At the top, big Spanish companies were still disproportionately to be found in regulated industries, clustering in Madrid in a nexus of politics and the media. They included banks, utilities and construction firms. The biggest expanded into Latin America in the 1990s and into the UK and Europe in the following decade before, in many cases, retrenching. There is a Spanish *mittelstand* of mid-sized, often family-owned, manufacturers, especially in Catalonia, the Basque Country, Navarre, north-east Castile and Valencia. And then there is the vast mass of low-productivity small and micro businesses. Under 1% of Spanish firms have more than fifty workers, compared with 3% in Germany and 1.8% in Britain, according to the Círculo de Empresarios. Moving up the scale was hard. That was partly because the rules discouraged it: once a firm had fifty workers or sales of over €6 million a year it had to set up a union committee, comply with additional regulations and pay higher taxes. There was a case for phasing in such requirements as firms grew, and raising the floor at which they came into effect. Companies like Gestamp and ASTI, which invested heavily in innovation and R+D, were exceptional. Public spending on R+D was slashed during the great recession. In 2019 it totalled only around 1.3% of GDP, half the average in the OECD (Organisation for Economic Co-operation and Development) group of mainly rich countries.

Spain enjoys world-class communications infrastructure, as seen in its high-speed trains, motorway network and modern ports and airports (although railway connections for freight and in rural areas are weak). It has the most extensive fibre-optic network for high-speed data transmission in Europe. But the burden of ineffective government regulation is heavy. The piles of pointless red tape for which Latin America is notorious were largely invented in Spain and are alive and well there. In the World Economic Forum's Competitiveness Index in 2019 Spain ranked an impressive seventh out of 141 countries for infrastructure. It was placed in a lowly 114th position for the burden of government regulation, well below countries such as Guatemala and Paraguay for example.[16]

Spain is a country dominated by lawyers and engineers. Its elite civil servants belong to a corps called *Abogados del Estado* (state lawyers). For help in filing your tax return, you go to a tax lawyer rather than an accountant. The country has suffered regulatory inflation for decades. The norms approved each year have multiplied around tenfold since 1978.[17] Most of that has involved regulations from regional governments and parliaments, although municipal ordinances have increased too. Studies found that the proliferation of regulations appeared to be a deterrent to the expansion of firms outside their home town or region. They also suggested a lack of trust between state and citizens. Bureaucratic sloth has deep roots. It was lampooned in a satirical article published in 1833 by Mariano José de Larra, a Romantic writer, entitled 'Vuelva usted mañana' or 'Come back tomorrow'. Spaniards overwhelmingly view the EU, with its single market, favourably. But decentralisation has erected mounting barriers within their national market: business permits for one region are not automatically valid in others. The Rajoy government made an effort to restore a single market in Spain but it was half-hearted and foundered on resistance from Catalonia and the Basque Country, and the desire of other regions to assert their powers. At the same time, the judicial system was understaffed and slow moving. Resolving civil and commercial cases took around a year on average, a time period that is rising.

After the economy grew at an annual rate of over 3% from 2015 to 2017 the pace of recovery then began to slow, to just 2% in 2019. Spain needed further reforms. Sánchez's first government was too weak to take ambitious measures. It faced a balancing act between cutting the deficit, restoring social spending and raising business taxes. 'We've spent years being told that the crisis was over. The time has come for

Spaniards to feel it,' declared María Jesús Montero, Sánchez's finance minister, as she unveiled a draft budget for 2019, agreed with Podemos, that modestly raised social spending while raising some taxes. In the event Sánchez was unable to get the budget through parliament, a failure which precipitated 2019's twin elections. But the government raised the minimum wage by a total of 35% between 2019 and 2022. Given the low level of many wages that was politically justified; though there was much debate as to its impact on jobs, it seemed to have been neutral. But business was suspicious, especially after Podemos entered government in January 2020. The coalition agreement promised rises in income tax on high earners and on corporate taxes to finance increases in social benefits. Sánchez was not an ideological radical. He largely kept economic policy away from the hands of Podemos and in those of Nadia Calviño, the economy minister, a moderate social democrat trusted by both business and Brussels, where she had been the European Commission's budget director. But Podemos's anti-capitalist rhetoric and the frequent political noise generated by tensions between the coalition's two factions did little to encourage economic confidence.

One evening at the end of February 2020 I found myself chatting with a senior government official at a drinks party, and asked him how he saw the economic outlook. He foresaw a slight dip in growth in 2020 and then a tranquil horizon. At that moment Covid-19 was raging through northern Italy. Within three weeks it would force the government to impose a drastic shutdown of the economy. The economic impact of the pandemic was severe. GDP contracted by 10.8% in 2020, compared with the euro-area average of 6.5%. And Spain was slower to recover than the rest of Europe. Forecasters originally reckoned that the economy would not match its pre-pandemic output until 2023, later pushed back to 2024. But data for employment, exports and tax revenues painted a less pessimistic picture.

One big reason for the seemingly slow recovery was the weight of tourism and the hospitality industry in the economy. These activities, of course, were the most directly affected by lockdowns, border closures and restrictions on gatherings. In 2019 Spain had received 84 million foreign visitors, second in the world behind France. Tourism accounted for 12% of GDP and 13% of jobs. Another fifth of the economy is comprised by commerce, transport and hospitality, though there is some overlap in these calculations. In 2020 fewer than 20 million foreign tourists made it to Spanish beaches or cathedrals. It was 'the most catastrophic summer in 50 years', declared José Luis Zoreda of Exceltur, the industry lobby.[18] The Canaries and Balearics, where tourism made up over a third of the economy, were especially hard hit. Beyond tourism, many small businesses lacked the resources to stay alive. In 2021 disruptions to supply chains hit the car industry in particular. And then Russia's invasion of Ukraine further darkened the economic outlook. After energy prices rose in 2021, inflation headed for 9% in 2022. Rising interest rates meant that some thought the economy might flirt with recession.

There were two mitigating factors. In contrast to the 2008–13 slump the government was able to provide emergency support. That was because the political and social costs of austerity imposed during and after the great recession had forced a radical change of mind among European policymakers. The European Central Bank offered limitless credit to governments at zero cost while the European Commission waived its rules on fiscal stringency. The Spanish government offered credit guarantees to businesses totalling some €80 billion. And it paid most of the salaries of furloughed workers who numbered 3.4 million at the peak in May 2020. By mid-2021 all but 360,000 were back at work. Unemployment rose (to 15.6% in the second quarter of 2021), but then fell again to 13.7% a year later, lower than its 2019 level. 'This is the first recession in which the fall in employment and tax revenues has been less than that of GDP,' Calviño, the economy minister, told me. 'We've managed to ensure that jobs haven't been destroyed, nor family incomes, nor tax revenues.'[19]

Critics accused the government of being too slow and parsimonious with direct cash support to businesses, as Germany offered for example. That was partly because even in the new lax policy climate Spain had less fiscal margin than others. Both the Rajoy and Sánchez governments had slowed the pace of deficit reduction. Despite the strong economic recovery of 2014–19, Spain entered the pandemic having posted a fiscal deficit of 2.9% of GDP in 2019 and with public debt equal to 96% of GDP, both among the highest in the eurozone at that time.[20] Calviño insisted the government's measures had been effective in preparing the basis for recovery: 'In other countries there were announcements of bigger programmes but the reality was in line with Spain.' All told, government support totalled around 20% of GDP, according to the OECD.

The second boost was that Spain was due to receive from 2021 to 2023 a total of some €70 billion in grants from the EU's Next Generation recovery scheme, and was eligible for a similar amount of soft loans. In line with the European Commission's guidelines, much of this would go on big projects, such as that for electric mobility and others aimed at creating a greener, more digital economy. But there will be plenty of money, too, for overhauling the public administration, vocational training and for active labour market policies to help the unemployed find jobs. On paper, it is a matchless opportunity to tackle Spain's chronic problems of joblessness and low productivity.

Will it be seized? There were complaints from the opposition and the regions that the government had drawn up its plans for spending the EU funds with insufficient consultation or participation in decision making. But officials insisted they had to move quickly and create a coherent national plan, and in the event this satisfied the European Commission. There was a tension between the EU's desire that the aid should achieve a structural transformation of Europe's economies and the need of many Spanish businesses for continued counter-cyclical spending. That was something the government was ill-placed to provide, with public debt having risen to around 120% of GDP by 2021. The government faced a tricky decision as to when and how fast to start cutting spending and/or raising taxes. There were fears of a chain of bankruptcies once support was withdrawn. 'You can't go and talk to many of my colleagues now about sustainability or digitalisation, but rather about how to get to the end of the month,' said Gabriel Escarrer, the chief executive of Meliã, Spain's biggest hotel chain, in August 2020. Conditions for many companies had eased somewhat eighteen months later but were still fragile.

The aid was tied to promises of reforms, especially of the labour market and pensions. The European Commission, the OECD and other experts reckoned Spain needed to make its labour market still more flexible while tackling the abuse of temporary contracts. They also thought the country needed to adjust the pension system to longer life expectancy, either by delaying retirement ages or capping benefits, and to reform education, training and skills. On many of these issues the government was caught between pressure from the European Commission on one side, and from the unions and Podemos on the other. On paper, the coalition was committed to counter-reform of both the labour market and pensions. The coalition agreement stated: 'We will repeal the labour reform. We will restore the labour rights stripped by the 2012 labour reform' (Sánchez had previously talked only of changing the 'worst' aspects of it).[21] The unions objected, in particular, to clauses which ended the automatic rolling over of existing contracts if negotiations were stalled and which gave priority to firm-level agreements over sectoral ones. These measures reduced their leverage. They were not much used in practice. But their existence meant the unions had to be more prudent in bargaining. The 2012 reform meant that firms could adjust to a deterioration in trading conditions by cutting, or not raising, wages, rather than through lay-offs as in the past. It was not coincidental that jobs were created at a faster rate in the post-2013 recovery than in previous ones.[22] The 2012 reform also introduced furlough schemes, which proved vital during the pandemic. It did not end the duality in the labour market, in which 25% of workers were on temporary contracts, some as short as a week, and in practice denied rights. But nor did it create this problem. Temporary contracts were introduced by Felipe González's government in the 1980s as a response to a rise in unemployment. They had expanded ever since, as a means to dodge the burdensome regulations attached to permanent contracts.

Yolanda Díaz, the labour minister in the coalition government, wanted not just to repeal the 2012 reform, thus making permanent contracts even more inflexible, but also to abolish nearly all temporary contracts by fiat. A Communist and the daughter of a trade union leader, Díaz was appointed by Podemos. When Pablo Iglesias resigned from the government, he chose her to replace him in his role as deputy prime minister. She was a more conciliatory figure than he, and she attracted sympathy from many who otherwise had little time for Podemos. She said that what 'doesn't let me sleep' was the imperative that 'we don't come out of this crisis more unequal than we entered it'.[23]

That was indeed important: income inequality was relatively high by European standards before the pandemic, although less so if housing costs are taken into account, in a society in which most people are owner-occupiers who have paid off their mortgages. In 2018 the income of the top 20% was six times higher than the bottom 20%, compared with an EU average of five times.[24] But much of the increase in income inequality was recent, the consequence of high unemployment and low salaries, and the best cure was faster growth. The problem was that Díaz's proposals would have rigged a system that already favoured insiders even further against the jobless, and thus would have done little to reduce inequality. They 'would lead to the most restrictive and rigid labour-market regime in Europe in the country with the second-highest unemployment rate and the highest youth unemployment rate,' according to Marcel Jansen, a labour economist at the Universidad Autónoma in Madrid.[25] They risked destroying jobs rather than creating them.

Díaz's proposal was not backed by Calviño, the leader of the government's reformist wing. European aid strengthened her position – Sánchez promoted her to first deputy prime minister in a reshuffle in July 2021. The funds could be cut off if Spain approved blatantly job-destroying measures. In the end, although Díaz spun the agreement struck between unions, business and government in December 2021 as a great victory, while Casado and the PP damned it as a counter-reform, in reality far from repealing the 2012 reform it consolidated it. Its main, and welcome, novelty was to curb the abuse of temporary contracts, limiting them in most cases to ninety days a year and discouraging their use by linking them to higher social security contributions. It restored the indefinite rolling over of collective agreements until a new one was reached (something the Supreme Court had required) and the pre-eminence of sectoral agreements for wage-bargaining but not in working conditions. It retained the 'flexisecurity' elements of the 2012 reform and blessed them with a tripartite agreement. It was the coalition's most important piece of legislation. Yet it was approved in the Congress by just one vote (and that cast by mistake by a PP deputy), as both the PP and the government's nationalist allies baulked.

Although the outcome was much better than many feared, reformers would have liked more. Many labour-market experts believed that to encourage hiring Spain needed to make permanent contracts less onerous for employers while endowing workers with an individual fund for use if they are out of work. Under this system, adopted in Austria, firms would pay a monthly sum to the worker's individual account instead of having to pay a large lump sum in severance pay if the worker is laid off. The worker takes the fund with them if they move jobs. This scheme protects the worker rather than the job. It could be combined with other measures to discourage temporary contracts, and to equalise the rights and obligations of different kinds of contracts. Sánchez had signed up to this reform in the abortive pact he forged with Ciudadanos in 2016, but then backed away from it.

To be serious about tackling unemployment the government needed, in addition, to overhaul radically the public employment service and what economists call 'active labour-market policies', or measures to help the unemployed get back to work. Spain spends some €6.5 billion a year on these. Though in relation to the number of unemployed that is less than in many other European countries, nevertheless it gets a very poor return for the money. The central government pays, but responsibility for the public employment service and active labour-market policies is decentralised to the regions. The employment service varies widely in quality, but in general is understaffed and bureaucratic. In 2016 there was one caseworker for more than 250 unemployed clients and anyway caseworkers had to devote much time to administration.[26] The Rajoy government introduced reforms, such as profiling of the long-term unemployed and the allocation of funds to regions according to quantitative indicators of how effective they were at getting people into jobs. This was scrapped when Sánchez came to office, and then reinstated under European pressure in 2021. Much more radical reform is required. In a 2017 report AIREF, the independent fiscal watchdog, noted that only 2% of those in jobs say they got them through a public employment office. It called for the integration of unemployment benefit, active labour-market policies and social policies into a single system that quickly profiles the unemployed to see whether they need training or just benefits.[27]

Despite high unemployment, businesses complained that it was hard to find workers. A study of the quality of education and the skills level of the workforce in the twenty-one developed economies in the OECD found that Spain ranked at the bottom.[28] The country had two specific skills problems. 'Skill levels in Spain are like an hourglass,' says Jansen. The proportion of graduates at the top is in line with the European average; at the bottom is a bulge of people with few or no qualification. There is only a slender middle of well-trained technicians. Only 23% of the population has non-university further education, compared with an EU average of 43%. And at the bottom, some 13% of pupils left school at 16 without any qualification. That figure had fallen from 30% at the turn of the century, but it was still above the EU average of 10%.

During the construction boom this high drop-out rate was partly because of the lure of easy money for youngsters with no qualifications. Tobias Buck, who covered Spain for the *Financial Times*, recorded in his book *After the Fall*, about the post-2008 bust, a conversation with David Pérez, a worker at a factory making metal window frames at Cebolla, a town up the Tagus valley from Talavera. He had left school at 16 and was soon earning up to €2,500 a month. A university professor, by contrast, might get only €1,300. 'We earned so much money. The only people who didn't have a BMW were the ones who didn't want one,' said Pérez, who was by then unemployed after the factory closed in 2012.[29] Many people like him have been thrown on the scrapheap of long-term unemployment at a relatively young age. Schools did not do enough to encourage them to stay.

In the last quarter of the twentieth century, Spanish education improved in some ways and became more universal, but that progress largely halted in this century. School rolls were swollen by immigration while austerity meant a cut in education budgets. Public spending on schools fell from €53 billion in 2010 to €44 billion in 2019, although there were 10% more students. But money was far from the only problem. The organisation of education contrasted with the health service, which, despite limitations exposed by the pandemic, was generally reckoned to be efficient and of good quality. Luis Garicano, the leading economist in Ciudadanos, noted that while hospitals had professional managers and doctors had flexible contracts, head teachers had little autonomy and schools were not subjected to proper evaluation.[30]

Teaching in Spanish schools was often archaic, based on rote learning. The curriculum had too many subjects, and with an overly academic bias (secondary school students are taught philosophy, for example). Students who struggled were required to repeat a year, which educationalists criticised as demoralising: in 2018, 29% of 15-year-olds had had to repeat at least one year of schooling, compared with an average in the OECD countries of 11.3%. Given the country's income level, Spanish students fared more poorly than they should have in international tests. In the 2018 PISA tests of proficiency of 15-year-olds in maths and science Spain performed slightly below the average for OECD countries.[31] As always there were big regional variations: in the 2015 PISA test in maths, Navarre, and Castile and León, performed as well as Canada, while Andalucía and the Canary Islands were similar to Greece.

Social segregation in schooling is increasing. Basic education is free and compulsory by law since the transition. But around a quarter of pupils attend what are called *escuelas concertadas* – schools that are privately operated, almost wholly by Church bodies. They are supposed to follow the same entrance criteria as state schools and to charge only for additional facilities (such as libraries or swimming pools). In practice that deters many poorer parents.

A new education law drawn up by Sánchez's government tried to address some of these problems. It made grade repetition less automatic. It set out a reform of teaching methods in which encouraging children to reason would be more important than memorising. But it abolished external evaluation based on published school results. It aimed, too, gently to restrain the expansion of *escuelas concertadas*. It was the eighth education law since 1977. Education has been a political football, kicked between the Socialists and the PP. Each law has repealed aspects of its predecessor, and none of the laws have been agreed by consensus. The debate is polarised between the Socialists' concern for equality and the PP's championing of freedom of choice, and between the right's defence of religious instruction and the left's interest in 'civic education' which its opponents see as a political agenda. Spain would do well to look at Portugal, which produces better educational outcomes with less money. It has raised the school-leaving age to 18, reformed teacher training and introduced rigorous evaluation of schools.

Spanish universities have flaws, too. They are notoriously endogamous, with a preference for appointing professors who studied at the university in question and a deep reluctance to welcome foreign academics. They produce too many humanities graduates and not enough scientists. They have resisted external evaluation. Most have little tradition in research and that penalises them in international rankings. They lost 20% of their public funding and suffered a hiring freeze between 2009 and 2015. Nevertheless, most do a creditable job of teaching. In the Academic Ranking of World Universities for 2021, a list compiled in Shanghai, only the University of Barcelona ranked in the world top 200. But thirty-eight out of forty-seven public universities and the University of Navarre, a private institution linked to Opus Dei and strong in medicine, placed in the top 1,000.[32] The relatively lacklustre universities contrasted with outstanding privately run business schools, with four in the top twenty-five in Europe, according to the *Financial Times* ranking for 2021.

The poor relations were vocational education and training. They tended to be looked down upon. They were split between the education ministry and the labour ministry. Some of the education courses seemed to be effective but there were not enough of them. In 2018 I visited a further education college in Heliópolis in Seville, and sat in on a class of fifteen students on a two-year course to train as head waiters. Dressed in black trousers, white shirts and black-and-white striped ties they stood around a table set with spirits and liqueurs. Normally they would be in their teens, but this group ranged in age from 19 to 42. Most were confident they would get a job locally. 'There is always more demand than places,' said Ildefonso Rodríguez, the college's director. 'The problem is those who don't get there.'

'Training for work', the labour ministry segment, functioned well in the Basque Country and to an extent in Catalonia and Madrid, but poorly elsewhere. In Andalucía, which most needed it, vocational training was shut down for five years because of a corruption scandal under the Socialist regional administration. Courses used to be run jointly by unions and bosses' organisations, with no evaluation of quality. At the insistence of Ciudadanos, Rajoy's government introduced a voucher scheme that allowed jobless people to choose private training providers, but many regional governments blocked this in practice. Fátima Báñez, Rajoy's capable labour minister, also introduced German-style dual training schemes, in which pupils mix classroom study with practical experience in companies. But it is hard to involve the mass of small businesses in this. The Sánchez government's education law included the transfer of parts of 'training for work' to the education ministry. The government also approved a vocational training law, which aimed to generalise the dual model and incorporate new subjects. It also promised to provide 200,000 extra places.

As Spaniards live ever longer, the country's pension system has come under strain. Towards the end of its term, Zapatero's government had raised the legal retirement age from 65 to 67 and increased the number of years of contributions taken into account when calculating the pension from 15 to 25, both with gradual effect. Under the pressure of the financial crisis, in 2013 Rajoy's government approved a more radical reform of pensions, which capped the annual increase in their value at 0.25%. It also introduced a 'sustainability factor' under which every five years pensions would be slightly reduced to take into account the increase in life expectancy. This was due to take effect in 2019. The reason was that increased longevity threatened the basic principle of the pay-as-you-go public pension system, under which pensions are paid from the contributions of today's workers whose retirement will in turn be paid for by tomorrow's workers. The account of the Social Security Institute (INSS), which administers the system, fell into deficit and it exhausted its reserves. As spending on pensions rose by €7 billion each year, by 2019 the system's deficit was €18.4 billion.

Pensioners did relatively well during the slump because Spain suffered price deflation and they still got their 0.25% increase. Between 2011 and 2014, the average income of over-65s in real terms rose by 5% even as that of younger people plunged. Pensioners began to play a key role in sustaining younger members of extended families. But they lost income as prices began to rise again. The Rajoy reform became the target of regular and persistent demonstrations by pensioners across the country. Conscious that older people are a larger cohort than the young, and that more of them tend to vote, the politicians panicked. Pensions are the subject of one of the few surviving cross-party negotiations, known as the Pact of Toledo. The parties, including the PP, agreed to tear up Rajoy's reform. The introduction of the sustainability factor was suspended. Sánchez's government reduced the INSS's deficit by an accounting trick, transferring parental pay to the general budget (even so, the deficit was almost €12 billion in 2021). In June 2021 the prime minister organised a ceremony at the Moncloa with union and business leaders to celebrate an agreement formally to reintroduce the indexation of pensions to inflation and to scrap the sustainability factor. This was to be replaced with a 'mechanism of inter-generational equity', which turned out mainly to involve an increase of 0.6% in employer contributions and incentives to delay retirement, from which business dissented. It amounted to a counter-reform. It was followed immediately by a surge in inflation: the result was that the government budgeted for an increase in pensions of over

8% in 2023, more than in most other European countries and more than wages were rising.[33]

Scrapping indexation as Rajoy did had proved politically unsustainable. The problem was that the politicians didn't want to face up to demographic and actuarial realities. Whatever the legal retirement age, in practice Spaniards left the labour force at an average age of 62 and were likely to live for another twenty years at least. Their pensions were relatively generous at 96% of average earnings, well above the average in the OECD countries. It was true that contributions were relatively high. Pensions already gobbled up a rising share of public spending. Spain's total spending on pensions of 10.9% of GDP in 2019 was above the OECD average of 8% but below that of other big Western European economies. The problem was that the numbers were due to get sharply worse because the baby boom happened later in Spain – between the late 1950s and the 1970s – than elsewhere in Western Europe.

Demographic calculations suggested that by 2050 there would be 78 pensioners for every 100 people of working-age population, compared with an average of 53 in the OECD countries.[34] Today's 10 million pensioners would increase to 15 million. Restoring indexation added 1% of GDP per decade to the pension bill, reckoned Pablo Hernández de Cos, the governor of the Bank of Spain. And that was before the sudden rise in inflation. According to the OECD, the intergenerational equity mechanism will raise only 0.2% of GDP while scrapping the sustainability factor would increase pension outlays by 1% of GDP. So the reform would not be enough to make the system sustainable. Future governments will undoubtedly have to do more.

It was almost impossible to have a rational discussion about pensions. Escrivá, the social security minister, proposed further increase in the years of contribution used when calculating pensions from the last twenty-five years of work to the last thirty-five, which would reduce new pensions by around 5%. But he was shot down. On the day of the

Moncloa ceremony Escrivá said bluntly that the baby-boomer genera-tion will have to choose between lower pensions or working longer. Again he retreated under a storm of criticism. But he was right.

The pension issue illustrates the hard choices on taxation and spending that Spain, like many countries, faces more broadly, especially in the wake of the pandemic. The country has a fairly small welfare state by Western European standards. The Franco regime chose to spend on state companies. While expanding education, health care and social protection, democratic governments also gave relative priority to spending on infrastructure. The weight of pensions in public spending is one reason why this is less redistributive than in some other coun-tries. The Spanish welfare state mainly redistributes from the haves to the haves. The pandemic shone a spotlight on holes in it. Even before the virus struck 12.4% of Spaniards had an income below 40% of the median (€1,050 per month) and were thus officially classed as being in 'severe poverty' compared with 6.9% in the EU as a whole. When the government locked down the country in the spring of 2020, in Madrid's poorer southern neighbourhoods *colas del hambre* (hunger queues, as they were dubbed) formed for food handouts provided by the Church and community groups. Caritas, the Catholic charity, reported a surge in demand for its help, including from people who had never been in touch with it before.[35]

In response the government introduced a new national minimum income. Drawn up by Escrivá, this was targeted, not universal as Podemos wanted. It paid up to €1,015 per month to families and €461.50 to individuals in 'severe poverty'. Previously social assistance was the purview of the regions and, as always, varied widely. The rich Basque Country was generous; poorer Andalucía not. 'Something that was designed to reduce inequality had the opposite effect,' Escrivá told me.[36] To offer an incentive to seek work, the new payment will be tapered gradually if earned income increases. He estimated the total cost of the scheme at about €3 billion, or 0.24% of GDP. It was broadly welcomed – only Vox voted against it. But it was only a qualified success. The public administration was slow to process applications. A year after the scheme was approved 276,000 households were receiving the minimum income. Escrivá had thought that 850,000 would qualify but many of these apparently didn't apply. In the summer of 2021, 190,000 people still depended on the Madrid Food Bank, a charity. The state also faced demands to spend more on young people and families more generally. Because of the slump, the inter-generational social contract frayed. While pensioners were protected, younger Spaniards struggled (see next chapter).

On top of these social demands, the government will have to address the fiscal deficit. Under the pressure of the pandemic, it swelled to 11% of GDP in 2020 before falling to 6.8% in 2021. As long as interest rates remained low and the European authorities permissive, a gradual reduction of the deficit would be manageable. But the emergence of inflation in 2021 signalled that the era of cheap money was drawing to a close, and faster deficit-cutting might be necessary. While stressing that stimulus should not be withdrawn before recovery was complete, Hernández de Cos, the governor of the Bank of Spain, repeatedly called for a broad, cross-party agreement on Spain's fiscal course. There was little sign of that.

There were political choices to be made on the balance of tax and spending. Tax revenues, plus social security contributions, were equal to 35% of GDP in 2019. That was less than in France, Italy and Germany, but broadly in line with Portugal or the United Kingdom. The headline rates of income and corporate taxes were comparable to the rest of the EU. But there were too many exemptions and loopholes. The nominal rate of corporate income tax was 25% but in 2017 Spain's largest companies paid an average effective tax rate of 17%.[37] Professionals find ways to avoid taxes. Many doctors insisted that private patients pay them in cash, for example. The VAT rate was

21% but the tax brought in less than the European average, mainly because tourism and some other activities paid a reduced rate of 10%. And environmental and 'sin' taxes (e.g. on alcohol) were lower than average.[38]

Certainly there were strong arguments for the government spending more on things such as childcare, education and skills. The left argued that the government should gradually raise taxes to take them to the EU average of around 40% of GDP. There is scope for some increases in taxes. On the other hand, polls showed that taxes were increasingly unpopular. Much public spending was poorly directed. The country could get much better value from its existing spending if this were subjected to more effective evaluation and oversight. The trick will be to raise taxes without hurting economic growth. Many of the government's changes involved increasing the costs and regulatory burden facing business, albeit modestly. In mid-2022, Sánchez veered left, announcing windfall taxes on the revenues (not profits) of energy companies and the bigger banks. The European Central Bank found fault with the bank tax but the prime minister ignored its warning. He began to criticise Spanish business. It remained to be seen whether all this would have an impact on business investment.

Spain has increased its income per person, in purchasing-power parity terms, by 50% in the past thirty years. But it is no longer converging with the EU's richest members. In 2007 Zapatero hailed Spain's achievement of an income per person of 105% of the EU average and its *sorpasso* (overtaking) of Italy, with 103%. But those figures were later corrected. Spain was at 103% of the EU average income and Italy 107%. Then the great recession took its toll. In 2019 Spain's income per person was 91% of the average and Italy's 96%.[39] Unless the politicians can reach agreements, Spain risks stagnation. Make the right choices, and the Spanish dream can revive.

CHAPTER 8

SCANDINAVIA IN THE SUN?

In February 1971 Richard Nixon sent General Vernon Walters, a soldier turned diplomat and spy, to Madrid to visit Franco to find out what might happen after he died. Walters told the American president that this was a subject nobody in Spain dared discuss. In the Pardo palace, in some trepidation and to flatter the elderly dictator, Walters told him that Nixon was interested in his views on the situation in the western Mediterranean. Franco replied, in Walters' account: 'What really interests your president is what will happen in Spain after my death, no?' His answer was that he had created some institutions, that Juan Carlos would take over as king and that 'Spain will go a long way down the road that you people, the English and the French, want: democracy, pornography, drugs and so forth. There will be a lot of crazy things but none of them will be fatal for Spain.' Walters asked him how he could be sure of that. 'Because I left something that I didn't find on taking over the government of this country 40 years ago.' Walters thought he would refer to the armed forces. But Franco said: 'The Spanish middle class. Tell your president to trust the common sense of the Spanish people, there won't be another civil war.' And with that he shook Walters' hand and ended the meeting.[1]

This was surprisingly perspicacious. Spain's society and social attitudes have changed radically in the past forty-five years, changes largely
driven by the expansion of the middle class to which the dictator
referred, as well as by liberty and democracy. In 1975 the country was
almost uniformly Catholic and its people almost wholly native-born
Spaniards. The Church exercised sway over public morality, as it had to
a large extent ever since Queen Isabella I asserted that to be Spanish
was necessarily to be Catholic by requiring the country's large Jewish
and Muslim populations to convert to Christianity on pain of expul-
sion. Women occupied a subordinate position, encouraged by both
Church and state to bear as many children as possible and required by
law to obey their husbands. A third of the population still lived in rural
areas and many city dwellers were relatively recent migrants from the
countryside.

All of this has changed in the past half century. Demographically
Spain has passed with extraordinary speed through the transition
that most countries experience when they get richer – in which
the birth rate declines, life expectancy increases and society ages.
Thanks to the arrival of large numbers of immigrants Spain is
now a multicultural country. Another change is geographic. The population is ever more concentrated in coastal areas and the Madrid
conurbation. A large swathe of the interior is now dubbed 'empty
Spain', made up of deserted villages, dying towns and disappearing
services – at least in the popular imagination. As Spaniards have become
city dwellers, and as climate change makes itself felt, attitudes to nature
are changing.

Since 1977 Spain has successively legalised contraception, divorce,
abortion, gay marriage and euthanasia. Although these changes were
opposed by the Church, they enjoyed widespread popular backing,
including among many PP voters. Although women still face some
discrimination, Spain has in many ways become a feminist country.
Superficially, at least, social attitudes today are more akin to Scandinavia

than to southern Europe. That may be a reaction to Franco's attempt to impose rules on private life. It may be too because Spaniards are generally open to new ideas, more so than Italians for example. One consequence of the isolation of the country under the dictatorship was a burning desire to join the rest of Europe, in customs and laws as well as politics and the economy. Dig beneath the surface and attitudes are more ambivalent. And the extended family remains the bedrock of society, which contributes to social cohesion.

Perhaps the single most dramatic change has been in the social position and roles of Spanish women. While Franco was alive only a quarter of adult women worked outside the home. Until a reform shortly before he died, women needed their husband's or father's permission to take a job, open a bank account, start a business, buy or sell property or even to travel far from their home region. Only fathers and not mothers had legal authority over their children. While adultery by women was in all circumstances a crime punishable by prison, for men it was so only if committed in the family home or openly flaunted.[2] A law in 1961 had allowed women to enter the professions but they were still barred from becoming judges or serving in the merchant marine or the armed forces.

In a conversation for this book, Elvira Lindo, a writer and feminist, described the changes women have experienced in her lifetime:

My mother didn't have any money of her own. My father gave her money each week to keep house. I remember her shrieking with joy when she was washing my father's clothes and found a banknote in a pocket. She wanted to be more independent and to have more personal sovereignty. She wanted her daughters to get an education to be able to have money. In her last years it made her very angry not to have her own money. For us, it was completely different.

With democracy, change was swift. Contraception was legalised in 1977 and homosexual relations ceased to be a criminal offence in 1979. Divorce followed in 1981, and with it legal equality between men and women within marriage. Felipe González's government legalised abortion with some restrictions in 1985. Social attitudes changed too, but at first less swiftly. Machismo remained, as Elvira Lindo said:

> The 'progressive culture' of the 1980s was very deceptive. It was apparently very left-wing but not with the concerns the left has now. Environmentalism took a long time to arrive, and feminism too. Women had to speak less, opine less and their words carried less weight than those of men. I went to work in radio, I became the director of a programme with men working for me. They would make sexual comments. You lived with this in a very lonely way, you had to take it home with you.

A second wave of change came with Zapatero's government. Half the ministers in his first cabinet were women, something that had hitherto happened only in Sweden. On his watch, Spain became only the third country in the world to legalise gay marriage. Further laws variously allowed abortion on demand, quickie divorce, stem-cell research, and promoted more gender equality in company boards and political party candidates' lists. A law against domestic violence increased penalties and included measures to protect victims. The PP and the Church opposed many of these changes but Rajoy did not undo them when he was in office. Both Aznar and Rajoy appointed women to important ministries.

From the outset, Pedro Sánchez described his government as feminist. In his first cabinet, in 2018, eleven of the seventeen ministers were women. It was an administration 'in the image of Spain', committed to social and gender equality as well as economic modernisation, the prime minister said. In 2021 Spain became only the fifth country in the world to legalise euthanasia. Again, the PP (and Vox) voted against but public opinion broadly approved.

Viewed cumulatively, the changes in Spanish society and social attitudes since the end of the dictatorship have been remarkable if still incomplete. 'Feminism has reached many layers of society,' according to Elvira Lindo. 'Change was from the bottom up.' More women than men now go to university. Women make up 40% of scientific researchers. In 1979 only 18 of the 350 members of the Chamber of Deputies were women; in April 2019 166 women were elected to the chamber, although that number fell to 154 in the repeat election in November 2019. The gap between the average salaries of women and men is closing, according to the INE. Some 43% of adult women work outside the home compared with 54% of men. Women make up only 31% of the boards of Spain's top thirty-five publicly quoted companies, but that is more than double the proportion in 2013. A majority of prosecutors and lower-court judges are women but this is not the case in the Supreme Court.[3] Only a decade ago, Spanish newspapers featured many photos of meetings and celebrations of the business, political and cultural elites in which all those portrayed were men. Such photos are much more likely to include several women now. However, domestic roles have not changed as much as those outside the home. Nine out of ten requests for time off from work to look after children or older relatives both before and during the pandemic were made by women.[4]

Spain is thus in the front rank of progress towards gender equality. It placed fourteenth in the World Economic Forum's Global Gender Equality index in 2021, ahead of France, the United Kingdom, the United States and Italy. In another study, by Georgetown University and the Oslo Peace Research Institute, it ranked fifth-best in the world for the welfare of women. A poll in 2019 found that 43% of all respondents (both women and men) considered themselves feminists, up ten points in five years. Among women aged under 25 the figure was 65%.[5]

Recent years have seen big demonstrations across the country on 8 March, for International Women's Day.

The advent of the coalition government saw tensions between different generations of feminists. Sánchez removed the equality portfolio from Carmen Calvo, his deputy, and gave it to Podemos as part of the coalition agreement. Pablo Iglesias gave the role to Irene Montero, his partner. Montero, aged 33, presented several bills that reflected fashionable concerns. One, which became law in 2022, aimed to define sexual consent and specified sexual harassment as a crime. Another would allow 'gender self-determination' from the age of 14 with parental consent, or from 16 without it. Older feminists, such as Calvo, thought that if a person's sex was defined as being a matter of choice then this would jeopardise laws against discrimination against women. These bills faced passive resistance within the government, even after Sánchez sacked Calvo to reduce tensions and rejuvenate the Socialist side of his government.

Vox represented a backlash against Spain's social transformation. Researchers found that its voters strongly opposed not just globalisation but also immigration and feminism. They also tended to be less well-educated and more religious than average.[6] Vox campaigned against sex education in schools and the domestic violence law, which it claimed discriminated against men. It wanted to overturn social liberalism in the name of traditional values. Despite this attempt to turn back the clock, the great majority of Spaniards seemed to be generally supportive of sexual equality and diversity. 'The changes were deep,' said Elvira Lindo. 'Perhaps there's a kind of feminism now that doesn't accept that, or thinks they weren't deep enough, but anyone of my age who compares their situation with their mother feels a big change.' Every time a woman is murdered, protests are held in town and city squares, normally led by the local authorities. These crimes, which now attract wide condemnation, are diminishing. In 2021 forty-three women were killed by their partners or former partners, the lowest figure since data began to be collected in 2003 and proportionately lower than in many other European countries.

There was some evidence homophobic crimes were increasing. That might reflect more reporting, after Sánchez's government created a unit in the interior ministry to fight these crimes. It may also have been part of a broader European trend, linked to social media, of groups of young people committing gang rapes or homophobic attacks. One such attack, the beating to death of Samuel Luiz, a 24-year-old nursing assistant, in A Coruña in July 2021 prompted national outrage. Nevertheless, such cases did not reflect the general mood. The Eurobarometer poll in 2019 found that 86% of respondents in Spain supported gay marriage. Another poll, by YouGov, found that 91% of Spanish respondents would be supportive if a son or daughter came out as gay, compared with 85% in Britain, 77% in Sweden, 75% in Germany and 57% in France. Spanish respondents were also the likeliest to say they were gay (10%) or know someone who is.[7] In an election in 2021 Isabel Díaz Ayuso, the PP regional president in Madrid, who is on the right of her party, spent a morning campaigning in Chueca, the capital's gay barrio. 'I don't care how people organise their lives in their home and in their bed,' she said, and added that it had been a mistake for the PP to have opposed gay marriage.[8] This more tolerant, diverse and equal society is also a more secular one.

Despite pandemic restrictions and damp weather, on Good Friday evening in 2021 several hundred people queued to enter the Basilica of Jesús de Medinaceli in the Barrio de las Letras in Madrid to pay their respects to a seventeenth-century image of Christ. Most of the faithful were over 40 but there was also a scattering of younger couples. The Christ of Medinaceli is 'very important for *madrileños*', said Magdalena, a regular worshipper. 'They say Spain is not a Catholic country anymore, but it's a lie.' Is it? Certainly there is a paradox. In the past forty-five years of democracy Spain has become a secular society with astonishing speed, faster than anywhere else in Europe, except perhaps Ireland. When Franco died, more than nineteen out of twenty Spaniards were baptised Catholics and 60% of them attended mass. In 2001 82% of respondents to the CIS poll still defined themselves as Catholic, but only half do now. Only about a fifth still go to mass regularly. Not only has the number of marriages declined each year over the past decade or so but in 2019 only a fifth of weddings were in a church. Nowadays almost half of children are born to women who are not married.

The 'national Catholicism' of the Franco regime swiftly dissolved into official secularism. Four concordats in 1979, linked to the constitution, separated Church and state. González's government implemented these; Aznar, contrary to the hopes of some in the Church, did not change them. Zapatero's government introduced a law which banned religious symbols in public places. And yet the Catholic Church retains considerable influence. That is perhaps unsurprising given how deeply woven into Spanish life it had been for centuries. Although there is no longer a Catholic party, Catholicism 'is what feeds Spanish political culture', according to Pablo Hispan, a PP deputy.[9] A recent academic study highlights the continuing 'entanglement of religious and national identities in public and political discourse'.[10] Almost every Spanish town still has its religious processions, such as in Holy Week, and an annual patronal festival with an official mass in which the mayor joins the priest. Despite Zapatero's law, it is not rare to find crucifixes in public buildings. The Church wields particular influence in social welfare, education and the management of heritage. Its charity, Caritas, helped to feed and/or provide practical help to 1.4 million poorer Spaniards in 2020. Church-run schools still educate around a quarter of Spanish children, including many from the elite. And the Church manages 3,300 historic buildings. All this may be why a third of taxpayers chose to donate 0.7% of their income tax to the Church, money that would otherwise go to the state. This amounted to €301 million in 2019.[11] The number of donors is rising.

It is an apparently stable compromise, but one that doesn't leave everyone happy. 'The Church invades the public space, laws, budgets and education,' argues Juanjo Picó of Europa Laica, a pressure group. Education is the most neuralgic subject. Religious instruction is an optional curriculum subject, but around half of children in state schools take it. Campaigners for a lay state say the place for religion is church, not school, and want it dropped from the curriculum. They complain that the Church has registered its ownership of some 35,000 properties, in some cases without legal title. In France and Portugal, they note, church buildings are owned by the state. In Spain, 'there's an entente cordiale' between Church and state, Picó argued. 'We have to move to a real separation.'

The Church itself has changed. After the Second Vatican Council of 1962–5, some Spanish priests and a new generation of bishops who had studied abroad began to oppose the dictatorship and support the opposition, especially but not just in Catalonia and the Basque Country. The Church as a whole was reconciled to change under González, who had belonged to Catholic Action, a lay movement, and studied at the Catholic University of Louvain in Belgium. Things were different during Zapatero's governments. He faced a generation of conservative bishops appointed under Pope John Paul II. The Church saw in Zapatero a return of anti-clericalism.

The confrontations of that era over gay marriage and abortion have ebbed. An uneasy peace prevails. Several things could upset it. Supporters of Vox are not necessarily all ultra-Catholic, but 'they do subscribe to the traditional Catholic identity of Spain against Islam', according to Julia Martiñez-Ariño, a sociologist of religion.[12] The Church hierarchy has been careful not to encourage Vox. Cardinal Juan José Omella, chosen as the president of the bishops' conference in 2020, met all the party leaders in his first eighteen months in the job, except Santiago Abascal, Vox's leader. The scandal of paedophile abuse by priests has had less impact in Spain than in many other countries, but that may soon change. The Church itself opened an investigation only after *El País*, the newspaper, presented to an aide to Pope Francis a dossier of cases dating back to the 1930s involving 602 perpetrators and 1,237 victims.[13] Some in the Church fear a resurgence of anti-clericalism. 'The attacks are from political elites which have an interest in attacking the Church because it still has prestige when it gives an opinion,' José Francisco Serrano, a Catholic journalist and historian, told me. 'They don't see the Church as a religious entity but as a political entity.' But under Sánchez the Socialists show little desire for confrontation with the Church and seem content to let social trends do their work.

These two sets of changes, in the position of women and of the Church, lie at the root of a swift demographic transition in which Spain has passed from high birth and death rates to low ones (excepting the deaths caused by the pandemic). The country's post-war baby boom peaked in 1975 when the fertility rate reached 2.9.[14] By 2000 it had fallen to 1.2, before recovering to 1.5 in 2010 and then falling again to 1.2 in 2019. This is the lowest fertility rate in the EU after Malta, and one of the lowest in the world. It is well below the 2.1 required to maintain the population constant. In the 1960s Spanish women married earlier and had more children than in any other country in Western Europe, except Portugal and Greece. The collapse in the fertility rate reflected the widespread use of contraception and the rejection by many women of their previously assigned primary role as child-rearers.

But it was also aggravated by the economic slump. The average age at which young people leave the parental home has risen to 30, which is three years above the EU average. Fully 64% of those aged 25 to 29 still live with their parents, many more than the EU average of 42% and fewer only than in Italy and Greece. The inability of this Peter Pan generation to emancipate means that on average Spanish women now do not have a first child until the age of 32, according to the INE. In the *El País* poll of young people cited in the previous chapter, almost two-thirds said they would like to have two children. Spain spends relatively little on childcare and on other incentives to have children. It could do much more. Instead, the demographic shortfall has been offset by immigration.

Even as the birth rate plunged, Spain's population grew explosively, from 40 million in 1999 to 47 million in 2010. The foreign-born population rose from just 165,000 when Franco died, to 800,000 in 1990, and peaked at 5.7 million (or 12.1% of the total) in 2012.[15] The slump prompted hundreds of thousands of immigrants to return home or move on to other countries. Economic recovery brought another increase in the immigrant population, to 5.3 million in 2021 (with a slight reduction during the pandemic), according to INE.

Along with the liberation of women and the decline of the Church, this amounted to a third historic change. Modern Spain had hitherto always been a country of emigration. Millions of Spaniards left in search of economic opportunity, mainly to Latin America from 1870 until the Civil War, and subsequently to Western Europe as well.[16] And those who went into exile, in Latin America or Europe in the aftermath of the Civil War, numbered at least 170,000.

Spain's experience of mass immigration came later and more suddenly than in other Western European countries. It has also been generally free of social tension. One reason for that was the recent memory of emigration and exile. Another was that the first wave of immigrants in the 2000s fitted in easily. The economy was growing, and two of the largest contingents were from Spanish-speaking Latin America (around 20%) and Romania, with linguistic and religious similarities. Some 200,000 Venezuelans have arrived since 2015, fleeing their country's dictatorship and economic collapse. In 2021, as for most of this century, the single biggest immigrant community was from Morocco (around 14% of the total). Surveys show that Spaniards are relaxed about immigrants, more so than most other Europeans. But there is no room for complacency.

The coming years will provide a double test of tolerance and integration. Most new arrivals still come through the airports, as visa overstayers. But a growing number come by sea from Africa, from very different cultures. Almost every week in 2020 and 2021 several hundred Africans made it to the Canary Islands, packed tightly into open fishing boats. Hundreds died in the attempt. After a previous surge in arrivals in the Canaries in 2006, Spain signed agreements with Morocco, Mauritania and Senegal under which those countries would accept their migrants back in return for aid and help patrolling the seas. But deportations halted during the pandemic, and anyway governments were reluctant.

Some of the new arrivals, especially from Mali, were fleeing violence. Most were economic migrants, driven to leave by overfishing and poverty. But in 2021, for the first time, three of the top five nationalities seeking asylum in Spain were African. At times reception facilities in the Canaries were overwhelmed. After weeks in temporary accommodation on the islands, most of the migrants eventually made it to the Spanish mainland. Many Africans moved on to the rest of Europe. But they are an increasingly visible presence in Spanish cities. They face a more uncertain welcome than the first wave of immigrants twenty years ago.

As the threat of Catalan separatism waned, Vox increasingly turned its attention to campaigning against unauthorised immigration, especially through social media. For the Madrid election in 2021 it put up posters contrasting the cost of looking after migrants who are unaccompanied minors with pensions for older Spaniards. It was a paradox that Vox did particularly well in areas along the Mediterranean coast where farmers depend on Moroccan and African labourers for the harvest.

Tumbling down the hillside to the south of the Calle Mayor, Lavapies was, in the early years of the twentieth century, 'the end of Madrid and the end of the world', in Arturo Barea's vivid description of the barrio in which his washerwoman mother lived and he went to school. One came to it from above or below in the social scale, he wrote:

Whoever came from above had stepped down the last step left to him before the final and absolute fall. Whoever came from below had scaled the first step upwards, which might lead to anywhere and anything.[17]

After a brief gesture at gentrification in the 1980s, and having acquired a role as a centre of alternative culture and leftist politics, in some ways Lavapies's sociology today would be recognised by Barea. It is a melting pot for recently arrived immigrants, Maghrebis, Latin Americans and now sub-Saharan Africans. The first African migrants came to Spain in 1984 and lived in a hostel in Lavapies because nobody would rent them rooms since they had no papers. They began to sell as *manteros* (street vendors), Malick Gueye told me. A Senegalese who arrived in Spain in 2005, he is the president of an association of *manteros*. In 2021 they opened a shop in Lavapies, selling T-shirts, bags and hoodies, decorated with anti-racist slogans.

Manteros have proliferated in Spain's cities, spreading their wares of fake designer bags and sunglasses on sheets roped at the corners for a quick getaway if the police appear. 'Nobody wants to be a *mantero*,' said Malick Gueye, complaining of police harassment. 'Everyone wants a dignified life where you get up and go to a job.' The problem was that it normally took three years to get a work permit. 'Racism isn't a monopoly of Vox,' but racists feel 'empowered' by its stance, he said. There has been an increase in racist attacks, though they remained rare. 'There's a breeding ground in favour of hatred in Europe from which Spain is not exempt,' Jesús Perea, the deputy minister for migration, told me.

One of Sánchez's first acts on becoming prime minister was to welcome to Valencia the *Aquarius*, a ship run by an NGO (non-governmental organisation) with 630 immigrants on board, which had been stranded off Italy for several weeks, denied a port. As migrant routes moved westwards towards Spain the government became more cautious. 'We have to strike a balance between security and solidarity,'

Perea said. But he remained optimistic. 'The general day-to-day attitude in Spain [towards immigrants] is better than in other countries.'
It helped that immigrants tended to be spread across the country,
rather than concentrated in ghettos. Though opinion poll evidence was
mixed, in general it tended to show a majority saying that immigration
was positive for the country. Many Spaniards remained welcoming.
One day in September 2021, I stumbled across a demonstration of
about 300 people outside the interior ministry calling for a change in
the rules to allow young migrants to be given work permits when they
turn 18 and leave reception centres. 'These youths shouldn't have to be
wandering the streets for three years until they get papers,' said Emilia
Lozano, a retired department store worker who had organised accommodation and training for some of them. A couple of months later the
demonstrators got their way as the government changed the rules.

The second generation of immigrants from the Maghreb was
starting to come of age. The terrorist atrocities in Catalonia in August
2017, in which fifteen people died, were committed by young men of
Moroccan extraction who had grown up in Ripoll, at the foot of the
Pyrenees. They were apparently well integrated. They spoke Catalan,
had jobs and played in a local football team. But they were recruited by
a jihadist preacher. That was a warning, even if they were exceptions. A
comprehensive study published in 2014 found 'no indicators of cultural
rejection or of reactive identities among immigrants or their children'.[18]
More recent research has detected that the children of immigrants face
a higher risk of dropping out of school. There are as yet few role models
of successful immigrants in senior jobs in business or politics. And
compare Spain's national football team with France's, for example.
With luck, this may be just a question of time.

The country's demographic problem means it will have to rely on
further inflows of immigrants. Without other changes, to meet its
pension bill it will need an extra 6 million to 7 million workers by
2040, according to Escrivá, whose ministry handled both pensions and

migration. Some are finding their way to the depopulating interior, where small towns and villages want immigrants to keep their schools, shops and bars open.

They came from the Spain of almost deserted medieval villages the colour of the harsh surrounding land, of lonely sierras, of forests of oak and elm, of the endless *meseta* and of declining towns. On a rainy Sunday in March 2019 some 50,000 of them marched down the Castellana boulevard in Madrid in what they called 'the rebellion of emptied Spain'. Their placards and banners displayed the poetry of Spanish place names and some prosaic demands. Villamayor del Rio wanted a pharmacy, Orihuela del Tremedal needed faster internet, Aranda del Duero demanded better infrastructure, 'Almanza resists' while 'Fuente de Béjar exists', as did Arévalo de la Sierra and El Royo. 'We feel a bit abandoned, we need doctors,' explained Paula Siles, a social care assistant from Las Parras de Castellote (population fifty-seven, down from eighty-six in 2004) in the Maestrazgo mountains of Teruel.

The history of the past century or more in many parts of the world has been one of migration from the countryside to the cities. In Spain this happened later, and more abruptly, than in many other countries in Europe. It began in the 1920s and then gathered force in the two decades from 1940 to 1960, when millions crowded into the centres of industry and economic growth in Barcelona, the Basque Country and Madrid. That human movement, the sum of countless individual decisions, has left a country whose population is geographically unbalanced. Large parts of rural Spain, in a vast arc to the north of Madrid stretching from the Portuguese border to the mountains of the Maestrazgo near the Mediterranean, are among the least populated parts of Europe, comparable only to Lapland and the Scottish Highlands. More than 90% of the country's population is crammed into 30% of the land. Some 4.6 million people are spread out across the remaining 70%, which has a population density of barely fourteen inhabitants per square kilometre. It is the Spain that flashes by from the motorway or the windows of high-speed trains.

This process has become self-reinforcing. As the population falls, schools, health centres, bank branches, shops and bars close and public transport withers, and so more people leave in search of services. In 1900, the province of Teruel had 246,000 people; today it has 134,000, or nine people per square kilometre. According to INE, out of a total of 8,131 municipalities, 5,002 had fewer than 1,000 people in 2019, while 1,360 had fewer than 100 people, up from 851 in 1996. Of these, more than half are situated in an upland swathe of the interior north-east of the country, including most or all of the provinces of Cuenca, Guadalajara, Soria and Teruel. Those who remain in such places are mainly old people, especially men. Julio Llamazares, a writer originally from León, once called the Castilla y León region 'the biggest geriatric home in the country'.[19] For a month or so in the summer, many of these villages fill up with the children and grandchildren of the residents or former residents. Many buy second homes in the *pueblo*, which holds a grip on the imagination but little connection to everyday life. Some provincial towns are losing people too. Over the past thirty years the population of León, a historic city, has fallen from 147,000 to 124,000.

The depopulation of much of interior Spain has become a political issue, as the march testified. In 2016 Sergio del Molino, a journalist from Zaragoza, published a book on the question called *La España Vacía* (Empty Spain). The term stuck. Activists quickly turned it into '*La España vaciada*', arguing that it was 'emptied out' or hollowed out by capitalism, Franco and government policies over decades.

This is too simplistic. Some parts of the countryside, and of interior Spain, are thriving, their population higher today than in the 1980s. And trying to halt the migratory flow would be as futile as Don Quixote's battle with windmills in now fairly empty La Mancha: the main cause of rural depopulation is the attraction of cities, which offer opportunity, services and cultural life that small towns and villages cannot. 'There was never a black hand which decided to empty out half of Spain,' according to Luis Antonio Saez of the University of Zaragoza.[20] Extensive cereal farming on arid land in Castile never offered much of a living. Franco's technocrats attempted to set up development poles for industries, such as car plants in Valladolid and Vigo, which might otherwise have gone to Catalonia or the Basque Country. They also flooded fertile valleys for hydro-electric dams, just as Iberdrola and Endesa are today planting massive windfarms on ridges across the country. But what else was an energy-poor country to do?

That said, policy decisions have sometimes had an effect in driving depopulation. The only historic kingdom not to gain its own regional government, León was a casualty of the territorial carve-up during the transition. It was lumped in with Old Castile while, absurdly, La Rioja and Santander (Cantabria) became regions in their own right. León, according to Llamazares, has since become a victim of centralisation in miniature, losing out to Valladolid, the capital of Castile and León. Second, railway investment has been concentrated in the high-speed train network leading to a kind of railway apartheid. Only two trains a day, taking three hours, connect Soria, a provincial capital, to Madrid 230 kilometres away. Teruel was even worse served: the sole daily train to the capital took four and a half hours. Some smaller towns have lost their train services altogether. Third, the government's decision to end coal-powered electricity generation, and thus coal mining, on sound environmental grounds led to the loss of several thousand jobs in Asturias, León and Teruel. And many in the rest of Spain believe that Madrid has benefited disproportionately from public policies over the past three decades.

The sense of grievance is widespread, catalysed in pressure groups set up over the past quarter of a century. One of the oldest established of these groups is Teruel Existe (Teruel Exists), which began protesting about the neglect of the province in the late 1990s. Two decades later it moved into electoral politics: 'We realised that the only things we got were nice words and pats on the back. If we wanted real political influence we had to be where decisions are taken,' said one of its leaders, Tomas Guitarte. In the election of November 2019 he won one of the province's three seats in the Congress of Deputies. The group also elected two senators. In the Congress Guitarte voted to invest Sánchez's coalition government. In return he extracted an agreement 'for re-population and territorial rebalancing' that involved promises of investment in infrastructure, transfers of government bodies to rural Spain and the creation of a junior ministerial post to supervise this. 'We achieved more in two years than in the previous twenty,' said Guitarte.[21]

The electoral success of Teruel Existe encouraged imitators. In a regional election in Castile and León in early 2022 Soria Ya won three of the province's five seats. A national umbrella group for the España Vaciada lobby is preparing to run candidates in half a dozen regions in the next general election. They want the government to spend an extra 1% of GDP or €11 billion a year to expand services in rural areas, and for depopulation to be included in the constitution as a factor in the complicated formula that governs regional financing. Because rural provinces are over-represented under the electoral law, one forecast was that España Vaciada could win up to twenty-five seats. Even if that proves an exaggeration, the political arithmetic of a fragmented parliament could give the rural lobby huge influence over future budgets. That is likely to distort public spending to the detriment of the broader national interest. España Vaciada emphasised infrastructure, although there is evidence that investment in education gives a higher return.[22] But the contrast with France's *gilets jaunes* movement was illuminating: instead of blocking roundabouts and trashing the Castellana, the equivalent of the Champs-Élysées, España Vaciada used the political system to express its complaints. And it had a point: the two main parties long treated interior Spain as a vote farm, parachuting in candidates from the centre who didn't necessarily have much connection to the areas they represented.

In interior Spain, 'the truth is that neither was the past so ideal nor is the future so dark', according to Ignacio Urquizu, a sociologist and former Socialist deputy who in 2019 was elected as mayor of his home town of Alcañiz in Teruel. He thought that the rate of depopulation could be halved with the right local policies.[23] Some small towns and villages have succeeded in attracting new residents, including immigrants. Rural Spain includes areas of economic dynamism, such as the wine-producing areas along the Duero, Ebro and Sil valleys. Rural tourism is growing: Castile and León has lost 2,000 bars since 2010 but gained rural hotels. More than transport infrastructure, two other things are sometimes missing: entrepreneurship and a high-speed internet connection, which are key to the vitality of the interior. The pandemic saw significant numbers of urban professionals move to rural Spain, with the aim of teleworking or setting up their own businesses. Rajoy's government began a €525 million project, continued by Sánchez, to bring high-speed internet connections to all municipalities or 95% of the population by 2021.[24] Almost half of rural homes were connected to the fibre-optic network by 2019, compared with only 17.5% in the EU as a whole. 'In Candelaria, Carboneras, Aguilar del Campóo or Villaconejos there's more of a fibre-optic network than in any [other] European capital,' boasted José María Álvarez Pallete, the boss of Telefónica.[25] A broader reform that gave more powers and resources to mayors would also be useful for interior Spain.

In Spanish literature and cinema, rural dwellers have often been depicted as *paletos* – country bumpkins, thicker than city slickers. In a hilarious satirical novel, *Un Hipster en la España Vacía* (A Hipster in Empty Spain), and its sequel, Daniel Gascón, a writer born in Zaragoza, dispelled that stereotype, contrasting the common sense and connections to the modern world of the people of a fictional small town in Teruel with the pretentious and patronising postmodernism of the urban cultural elite. Interior Spain deserves to be treated with realism rather than romanticism.

The largest saltwater lagoon in the western Mediterranean, the Mar Menor in the Murcia region was until the 1960s a natural paradise of crystalline water, submerged meadows, seahorses and abundant fish and molluscs. Then uncontrolled tourist development began with hotels and blocks of flats sprouting on its sand spit and shores. In the 1970s one of the dictatorship's biggest hydrological projects was completed, a 300 kilometre canal that takes up to 60% of the headwaters of the Tagus in central Spain to the River Segura in Murcia. This has irrigated some 60,000 hectares, turning the area around the Mar Menor into a giant fruit and vegetable garden, growing lettuces, melons, broccoli and peppers. The area supplies around 20% of Spain's horticultural exports and, by one estimate, 100,000 farm jobs.[26]

Now the Mar Menor is dying. In 2016 the lagoon turned into a green soup, clogged with algae. In 2019, and then again in 2021, several tonnes of dead fish washed up on its shores. 'It's the symptom of an environmental catastrophe,' declared Noelia Arroyo, the PP mayor of the nearby city of Cartagena, calling it 'a national emergency'.[27] Some 50,000 marched in protest in Cartagena and a local campaign to try and save the lagoon gathered strength. The problem, scientists said, is that nutrient-rich fertiliser run-off from the farms leaches into the Mar Menor, stimulating the growth of algae that block sunlight and deprive the water of oxygen and thus of marine life. The PP regional government has tended to side with the farmers, while the national government looked the other way. In 2021 at last that changed. Teresa Ribera, the environment minister, met Murcia's president, Fernando López Miras, and they agreed on measures to help save the lagoon. The regional government agreed to restrict fertiliser use close to the Mar Menor. Ribera complained that it had failed to act against farmers who have irrigated some 8,000 hectares without licence.

Whether or not enforcement follows, it may to be too late: the underground aquifer is now contaminated with nitrates which find their way into the lagoon. But the politicians felt under public pressure to be seen to be acting. And that is fairly new in a country which in some ways was a pioneer in environmental protection, but has hitherto lacked much modern environmental consciousness.

Spain has great environmental diversity but also suffers environmental stress. Large parts of the country lack sufficient water. 'Spain is a vast stretch of sterile terrain surrounded by a narrow strip of fertile land,' according to Ramón y Cajal.[28] The solution, many thought, was water diversion schemes such as the Tagus-Segura, and the planting of trees to stabilise the headwaters of rivers. Both the Restoration regime and the Second Republic approved hydraulic plans for large-scale irrigation, and the Republic approved a reforestation scheme. Franco continued these, with the building of large reservoirs for irrigation and power, and the reforestation of 3 million hectares. Under the influence of the Romantic movement's attachment to wild, mountainous landscape, and following the example of the United States, the Restoration regime created two national parks in 1918, in Covadonga in the Picos de Europa mountains in Asturias and Ordesa in the Pyrenees in Aragon. Spain was only the third European country to do so, after Sweden and Switzerland. Further parks followed in the 1950s and 1960s, protecting the volcanoes of the Canary Islands and Doñana, the large wetland at the mouth of the Guadalquivir river in Andalucía. Today over a quarter of Spain's land area is protected, either as national or regional parks or sites of special interest. The original concern with landscape has yielded to one of biodiversity and ecology.[29] But it took a long time before efforts were made to protect the coastline. By one count 28% of Spain's coasts have been built upon. Nowadays developers face opposition. In an emblematic case, the courts ruled that a giant hotel built in Cabo de Gata national park in Almería should be demolished, although that had yet to happen at the time of writing.

221

Modelling suggests that the western Mediterranean is likely to face a bigger change in its climate than the rest of Europe. Spain already suffers aridity, with around a fifth of its land classified by researchers as desertified.[30] Forest fires and floods are frequent problems. The summer of 2022 was the hottest since records began in 1961, with temperatures above 40°C for weeks on end in much of the country in what seemed like a foretaste of an uncomfortable future. Sánchez's government approved a climate change law which promoted green energy. But policy remains patchy. The government lifted tolls on more than 1,000 kilometres of motorway as contracts ran out. But it postponed a decision to implement a national motorway toll because of the opposition of truckers, Podemos and Basque and Catalan nationalists. Although concern about climate change is growing, it lags behind that in other European countries. A Eurobarometer poll in 2021 found that only 3% of Spanish respondents thought climate change to be a top problem, compared with a European average of 13%. It was striking that Spain lacked a Green Party, though Más País, a splinter from Podemos aspired to be one (see next chapter). It did, however, have an animal-rights party, which came close to reaching the national Congress and could claim to have had an impact on public attitudes.

Only about a fifth of the seats in the great bull ring of Las Ventas in Madrid had been sold on a warm Saturday evening of lowering cloud in June 2017. A water seller outside said the crowd was normal for an ordinary *corrida* outside the fashionable San Isidro festival in the spring and with 'run of the mill' bullfighters. 'It's sad for those of us who love it and live from it that it doesn't attract more people.' The crowd was mainly working-class Spaniards, with a scattering of Asian tourists. The *corrida* began with a trumpet blast and the entry of two middle-aged men on white horses and dressed in black sixteenth-century tunics with a long red feather in their black hats. The three *toreros* and their retinue followed them, in tight uniforms of green and pink with lashings of gold braid and flashing sequins, and their magenta and gold capes. The band played a *paso doble* and then another trumpet blast announced the first bull. Frisky and aggressive, it crashed its horns against the wooden fence that protects the *banderilleros*. After the preliminary skirmishes, the matador stood, puffed up, in front of the bull, which was weakened, bemused and panting. He jabbed his sword into the animal's broad neck. It staggered around and then slowly subsided. The second torero was artless, his bull losing ruby blood from the hole in its back made by the picador. Several times he inserted his sword, only for the infuriated bull contemptuously to toss it off. The crowd whistled and slow-handclapped. The torero looked nervous. The whole exercise had become an embarrassing exercise in seemingly pointless cruelty. At last he killed the beast, at the seventh attempt, and slunk away before a silent crowd. His successor in the ring immediately imposed himself. He swaggered on tiptoe towards his bull, engaging it with veronicas as if asking it to dance. The bull repeatedly rushed past him, its horns almost brushing his arched body, man and bull moving as if magnetically attracted to each other in a dance of death, the man knowing any slip or lapse of concentration could be fatal, the bull complicit in its own impending demise. The bullfighter went in for the kill and at the second attempt the bull crumpled against the fence. He turned away. But then the bull staggered up, its life force resisting to the end, a murmur going through the crowd. And then the bull subsided again and the rain fell harder. It was an average and representative bullfight, without the glamour of famous names and top-notch bulls, a mixture of macho valour, dramatic art, fumbling and cruel butchery.

Until recently bullfighting almost defined Spain in foreign eyes. Some foreigners, like Hemingway, were entranced by it; others appalled. What is less well known abroad is that Spaniards, too, have long been divided about bullfighting. The anti-taurine tradition is as strong as the taurine one. Emilia Pardo Bazán, the nineteenth-century writer, called it 'the national dementia' rather than 'the national fiesta'. That has become the majority view. In one poll, in 2014, 90% said they didn't attend *corridas*. In another, in 2019, 56% said they were against bullfighting and only 25% were in favour. But for its devotees, bullfighting is an art, not a sport, and it is covered in the cultural pages of the newspapers.

In this century professional bullfighting has steadily declined. In 2007 there were bullfighting festivals in 902 Spanish towns. By 2019 that number had fallen to 377. The pandemic dealt a heavy economic blow to the industry and some breeders of fighting bulls seemed likely to go out of business. At local level, however, bull-baiting events of various kinds are still common at village and small-town festivals in the summer. That is true, too, of Catalonia, despite a vote in the Catalan parliament to ban bullfighting in 2010, a decision taken more for nationalist than animal-rights reasons. Bullfighters have faced aggressive abuse on social media and one or two have been physically attacked by animal rightists. Other Spaniards still revere them: I was once having lunch in a bar in Seville when Julián López, El Juli, the most famous of contemporary Spanish bullfighters walked in. He was greeted with adoration.

Rajoy's government declared bullfighting to be part of Spain's cultural patrimony. But the *corrida*'s committed defenders are not confined to the PP and Vox. Bullfighting 'is culture, it's tradition, it's participation, it's conservation, it's ecosystem, it's [the] economy and of course it's passion', wrote Emiliano García-Page, the Socialist regional president of Castile-La Mancha.[31] The unofficial leader of Tendido 7, the section of Las Ventas where the most knowledgeable and critical fans gather, is Faustino Herranza, known as El Rosco. He claimed to have gone to every *corrida* at the San Isidro festival for more than forty years. He had been a deputy mayor for Izquierda Unida in a town in the Sierra de Guadarrama and voted for Podemos.[32]

While bullfighting is unlikely to disappear altogether, its time as a mass activity seems sure to draw to a close. Rosa Montero, a novelist who is the daughter of a *torero*, has written that her father taught her to love animals; that *toreros* and aficionados are not murderers and psychopaths but, she argued, they belong 'to a world that is now obsolete' with a level of violence that was disturbing.[33]

As Spain became an urban country and many young people grew up with little knowledge of the countryside, attitudes to animals were changing in other ways too. In 2021 the national government banned the hunting of wolves north of the River Duero, the only part of the country where it was still allowed. The decision faced objections from the regional governments in Castile and León, Galicia, Asturias and Cantabria, and from farmers. There were between 2,000 and 2,500 wolves in more than 300 packs in Spain, mostly in these northern areas, and farmers regularly lose livestock to them. 'The wolf has been a cursed species for centuries. . . . It has gone from being a symbol of cruelty in rural societies to one of conservation,' Juan Carlos Blanco, a biologist, told *El País*.[34]

Spaniards now see animals as pets, not as threats or to provide sport. Hunting, too, is in decline. The agriculture ministry issued 769,000 licences in 2018, almost 300,000 less than in 2005. But the number of pets grew by a staggering 40% in the five years to 2018, most of them dogs. There were more pets than children under 15, a sign perhaps of the growing loneliness of Spanish city life.[35]

Spain has become a country of smaller families and more individualism. In 2020 almost 5 million Spaniards lived on their own, forming a quarter of all households, according to INE. Yet the family remains the bedrock of Spanish society, and one of the secrets of its success. Grandparents share parenting duties, especially picking up children from school. At weekend lunch times, restaurants are full of large family parties, often comprising three generations. The relative lack of state childcare facilities means that women continued to play a principal role as carers. This is 'an ambivalent society', according to Ángeles

González-Fernández, a historian at the University of Seville. 'Postmodern, yes, but at the same time traditionally Spanish.'[36]

It is a society that lives much of its life outdoors, in the street. That is facilitated by the weather. It is also because many people live in fairly small flats. The bar has traditionally been at the centre of Spanish life, as if it functioned as the living room. In many ways it still is, though their numbers are slowly falling: in 2017 there were 184,430, down almost 10% since 2010. On the other hand, the number of restaurants is rising each year.

In all, 65% of Spaniards live in flats, the highest figure in the eurozone after Latvia, and 45% in large blocks of more than ten flats. Spain has very high rates of owner-occupation, but housing has become an issue of growing importance since the 2008–13 slump. One of the strands in the formation of Podemos was groups of activists who mobilised against evictions for non-payment of mortgages. The rise of short-term holiday lets in cities like Barcelona and Madrid was a factor in a steep rise in rents. In the big cities, many of the poor live in overcrowded rented housing, with six or seven crammed into flats of 60 or 70 square metres, with cubicle-like bedrooms. All this highlighted the lack of public housing.

Despite their reputation for proud, rebellious individualism, Spaniards are good at following norms. To many people's surprise, a ban on smoking in bars and other public places introduced in 2011 was widely respected. The country has managed to reduce the numbers killed each year in road accidents from 5,940 in 1989 to 1,004 in 2021. The introduction of penalty points which could lead to the loss of driving licences by Rubalcaba was a crucial step in this. During the pandemic, Spaniards were early and conscientious adopters of face masks.

Spaniards are good at demonstrating, and do so often. Except during the slump, and sometimes in Catalonia and in the past in the Basque Country, the demos are nearly always peaceful and orderly. But organised civil society is relatively weak. The political parties carry out many tasks that in other countries would fall to think-tanks, NGOs or civic groups. That is partly because there are few tax incentives for charitable donations, as opposed to that for the Church. 'For a strong civil society, you need money,' Eduardo Serra, a former chairman of the Prado, told me.

Like France, but unlike Italy, some Spaniards are attracted to a version of the American dream. The democratic period has seen the spread of American-style car-dependent suburbs around Madrid, for example. But many younger Spaniards are bike- or scooter-riding urbanites. The two visions of the city clashed when the PP regained the Madrid city council in 2019 after a period of left-wing rule. It tried to scrap a scheme barring most cars from the city centre, but was thwarted by protests, and the courts and later reinstated it under a different name.

The quality of life is generally high. Spaniards are healthier, better fed and taller than in the past: their average height has increased from 1.69 metres in 1977 to 1.73 metres in 2017.[37] Men born in 1996 averaged 1.76 metres, 14 centimetres more than those born a century before, while women measured 1.63 metres on average, 12 centimetres more. A Spaniard born today can expect to live for eighty-three years, the second-longest lifespan in the OECD after Japan, which it is set to overtake it by 2040, according to a study by the University of Washington in the United States.[38] The Mediterranean diet is now more myth than reality. But Spaniards do eat a lot of fresh food, and they care a lot about the provenance and quality of the ingredients of their diet. A generally good health service helps. But so does the strength of family networks, which is surely a factor in the fact that most Spaniards tell pollsters that they are happy, even younger people. The poll of 18–34-year-olds for El País newspaper published in July 2021 found that 85% declared themselves 'satisfied' with their life: they know that, unlike their parents or grandparents, they are growing up in a free, democratic society, and the extended family offers a support network. In many ways Spanish society has become more tolerant and relaxed about differences. But this does not apply to politics.

CHAPTER 9

THE 'CASTE' AND ITS FLAWED CHALLENGERS

Their cries were '*No nos representan*' ('They don't represent us') and 'Real democracy now!' After a demonstration on 15 May 2011, thousands of mainly young, middle-class Spaniards set up an improvised camp in the Puerta del Sol, in the heart of Madrid. They called it a 'citizens' assembly'. It was in protest at austerity, the sense of entitlement among politicians and bankers, and what they saw as the unfairness of a country that bailed out the savings banks while cutting spending on schools and hospitals. They stayed there for weeks. Amplified through social media, the protests spread across the country. The protesters would soon be dubbed *los indignados* (the indignant ones), and 15 May 2011 – or 15M in the Spanish shorthand habit for referring to important dates – would come to be seen as a turning point in contemporary Spanish history. The *indignados* initially enjoyed broad public support, with polls showing 70% to 80% agreeing with them.[1] It 'was a great outburst of dismissal', said Carolina Bescansa, a sociologist who took part. 'The consensus was on what we didn't want. We didn't want more cuts, we didn't want corruption, and we didn't want that way of doing politics behind the backs of citizens.'[2]

Just six months after 15M and with the Zapatero government deeply unpopular, the PP won an absolute majority at a general election.

Superficially it was as if nothing much had changed politically. In fact, the *indignados* crystallised smouldering discontent, and in due course their legacy would include a redrawing of the political map. Out of that discontent would emerge two new national political parties, Podemos on the left and Ciudadanos on the centre-right. In a general election in 2015 these two grabbed 34% of the vote between them. A stable political system based on the Socialists and the PP fragmented. The result was three further general elections in the next four years, none of which produced a majority government.

A small group of youngish professors or postgraduates of the Faculty of Political Science and Sociology of Madrid's Complutense University, one of whom was Bescansa, saw in the *indignados* the potential for radical change in Spain. Pablo Iglesias, aged 32 in 2011, had studied the Italian far left and taken part in anti-globalisation protests across Europe. Juan Carlos Monedero had worked for the government of Hugo Chávez, Venezuela's leftist populist strongman. Iñigo Errejón, aged 27, had studied Bolivia under Evo Morales, its leftist leader, and also worked in Venezuela. All three were influenced by the work of Antonio Gramsci, the Italian Marxist philosopher who developed the concept of cultural hegemony, that to be successful the left had to implant its ideas and values in society as a whole and not just rely on the economic struggles of the working class. While Iglesias was in many ways a Leninist, Errejón was a fan of Ernesto Laclau, an Argentine Gramscian who argued for a leftist populism which he saw in Peronism in his own country. From the contemporary Latin American left, and from the example of Chávez in particular, the group took the importance of charismatic leadership and of inserting (or disguising) socialist ideas in a broader national-populist framework. Iglesias stressed, too, the importance of communication and of television in particular. The three of them founded two weekly television programmes, one that went out on a small local channel in Vallecas, a working-class district of Madrid, and the other on

HispanTV, a channel which was reported to have been set up by the Iranian government.[3] Iglesias quickly became a media pundit, debating in the *tertulias* (chat shows) that proliferate on mainstream Spanish television and radio. With his trademark ponytail, he became nationally known.

The Complutense group saw the emergence of the *indignados* as a point of rupture, as evidence that Spain was not just suffering political, economic and social crises but an overarching 'crisis of the regime' and was 'on the verge of a second transition', as Iglesias put it.[4] Bescansa conducted polls which seemed to suggest that the political consensus underlying Spanish democracy had greatly weakened because this was no longer identified with wellbeing. The group thought this weakness opened up the possibility of the overthrow of the transition settlement from the left by those who could connect with the new public mood, as had happened in several Latin American countries. At first Iglesias and Errejón worked as advisers to Izquierda Unida, an electoral alliance dating from 1986 and based on the Communist Party. Then, at an event in January 2014 in a theatre in Lavapies in Madrid, they launched Podemos, meaning '(Yes) we can'. Within four months, and with Iglesias's face on the ballot slip, the new party won 1.3 million votes (8% of the total) in a European election. By late 2014, less than a year after its birth, it had 28% support in the opinion polls and was in first place.

Podemos claimed to embody a new kind of politics that rejected the divide between left and right in favour of one that pitted, in Laclau's formulation, *los de abajo* (those at the bottom) against *los de arriba* (those at the top). It flirted with direct democracy, setting up 'circles' of supporters rather than a conventional party organisation. In its most effective slogan, it denounced the 'caste' – a small self-serving elite of politicians, bankers and businesspeople which was held to exploit and oppress 'the people' at the bottom. The term 'the caste' was borrowed from Italy's populist Five Star Movement.[5] While many voters at first welcomed Podemos as a cry of anger and for renewal, its political project represented a wholesale rejection of the liberal democracy forged in the transition. It was the hard left in soft, populist focus. Iglesias stressed that what interested him was capturing the power of the state, implicitly in a permanent way as Chávez had done, not just winning an election. 'You don't conquer heaven by consensus,' he said at Podemos's first Congress in 2014. 'You storm it.'

Iglesias set out his critique of Spanish democracy in a book published in 2015.[6] He stated that he was 'eager to settle scores with the reverence for the transition evinced by most of the political forces in Spain'. What characterised the transition, he went on, 'was its unrelenting tutelary oversight by economic and political elites symbolically subject to the crown'. He saw the monarchy as 'a crucial element for Francoist institutional continuity'. The system was operated by and for 'the caste' – 'the thieves who erect political frameworks for stealing democracy from the people'. The constitutional reform of 2010 that gave priority to debt payments was 'a coup'. Podemos was Eurosceptic. Iglesias warned against 'Spain's wholesale conversion into a colony of German Europe; a country stripped of sovereignty' – a statement that might have come from Nigel Farage and British Brexiteers or Victor Orban in Hungary. Corruption was 'a form of government' and 'an intrinsic feature of our political regime and ruling political caste'. The corrupt and the powerful enjoyed impunity. 'It has always been exceptional in this country for politicians or bankers to end up with firm prison sentences.'

So here was a third rejection of the transition settlement, along with those of ETA and the more extreme strand in Basque nationalism, and of Catalan separatism. Though Iglesias claimed to identify uniquely Spanish failings, derived from the original sin of the transition, much of his argument was part of the European *Zeitgeist* in 2015, as Brexit gathered force and populists of left or right gained strength from Greece to Italy to Poland. Iglesias's critique contained some falsehood and much exaggeration. But there was enough truth in it to resonate with a significant minority of Spaniards. Podemos quickly became 'the political force of the losers from the crisis', as Ignacio Urquizu, a sociologist and a Socialist MP, wrote.[7]

Another critique came from Ciudadanos, but a moderate one aimed at reforming, not casting aside, the transition settlement. Founded by fifteen intellectuals and journalists in Barcelona in 2005 as a regional party, Ciutadans as it was called in Catalan was originally broadly liberal or social democratic in outlook. The founders were dismayed by the swerve of the Catalan Socialist party, with which several of them identified, towards Catalan nationalism, and by Pasqual Maragall's coalition with Esquerra. None of the founders wanted the job of leader of the new group, for which Albert Rivera, a fast-talking young Barcelona lawyer, volunteered and was accepted. Ciutadans won three seats in the Catalan parliament in 2006. A decade after its founding Rivera saw an opportunity to recreate Ciutadans as Ciudadanos, a national party, exploiting the discredit of the PP and the credit his group had gained in the rest of Spain for opposing the separatists in Catalonia. It burst into national politics in the 2015 election, winning 14% of the vote and forty seats. Opposition to peripheral nationalisms and the defence of the unity of Spain was a central plank in the Ciudadanos platform, which meant that some of its opponents branded it as a Spanish nationalist party. It also believed in free markets, in modernising reforms of the state, the labour market and education and in a crackdown against corruption and wasteful duplication of spending by the central government and the regions. In contrast to the PP, it espoused individual freedoms and rights such as gay marriage and abortion. Rivera, who became increasingly histrionic, talked of emulating Emmanuel Macron's success in overcoming traditional parties of right and left in France. 'We have to move away from the old left–right axis,' he told me in 2018. 'The big battle of the twenty-first century is between liberalism and the open society, and populism-nationalism and the closed society.' Yet he would fail to put this into practice.

Spanish democracy, like many others, does have structural flaws which have become more apparent over the past decade, although they are not necessarily those stated by Iglesias, as the rest of this chapter will explain. It is not that Spain is not democratic, as the wilder Catalan separatists and Iglesias (at first) claimed. Think-tank rankings and academic studies show that it enjoys a full democracy, on a par with others in Western Europe.[8] But like all democracies, Spain's has imperfections. They have less to do with the transition settlement than with the way the political system has evolved over the past forty years. Three problems stand out: the role and character of the political parties; the public administration; and the judiciary.

Mindful of the lessons of the Second Republic, the architects of the transition placed political stability above all other considerations, including the accountability of government. As the system evolved, it concentrated power in the hands of the parties and especially of the party leaders in what has increasingly come to be seen as a *partidocracia* (partydocracy) that serves the interests of the politicians rather than them serving those of the citizens. For a start, Spain has far more politicians than it needs as Miriam González, a Spanish lawyer who has worked mainly in Brussels and London, has pointed out. There are no official figures but she estimates there are between 300,000 and 400,000 of them. That means Spain has more politicians than federal Germany and, in proportion to population, twice as many as in France or Italy.[9] This surfeit is partly because when the regional governments were set up, it was decided that each would have a legislative assembly. It was also because regionalisation was not accompanied by rationalisation of the previous structure of local government. Uniquely in Europe, Spain has four levels of government. At the bottom, there are over 8,000 municipalities. Even Brazil, with more than four times as many people as Spain, and where creating new municipalities has been a growth industry, gets by with 5,570. The provincial *diputaciones* or assemblies should have been abolished when the *Comunidades Autónomas* or regions were created by the constitution. But they survive in those regions that comprise more than one province. These assemblies have up to fifty-one members and provide services to municipalities. At all levels, Spanish politicians tend to have a larger court of advisers and hangers-on on the public payroll than in many other European democracies.

Second, the political parties have spread their tentacles laterally, into other supposedly independent institutions, ranging from the civil service to the judiciary and to universities. The leverage of politicians over the public administrations has been a prime facilitator of corruption. Up to 20,000 public service jobs, including many senior ones, are *cargos de libre designación*, a term which interestingly has no vernacular equivalent in English but means that they are discretionary political appointments, whose occupants can be hired and fired at will by their political masters. That is far more than in any other Western European country. They are the modern equivalents of the *pretendientes*, the swarms of would-be office holders whose hopes were raised by every change of government in the nineteenth century.

When Rajoy and the PP were ejected from office in 2018, some 6,000 people lost their jobs, including 437 presidential advisers, according to Miriam González.[10] When the Socialists were turfed out of the regional government in Andalucía in the same year, 660 people were immediately fired. When Sánchez became prime minister in 2018, he placed Socialist loyalists at the head of RTVE, the state broadcaster; the CIS, the state social research company which carries out opinion polls; and even the Paradores, the chain of mainly historic hotels. These bodies are all supposed to represent the broad public interest. The case of the CIS was particularly scandalous. Having been previously respected by academics, its opinion polls proceeded to show a bias towards the left.

Franco bequeathed an archaic and under-resourced public administration. But it included a small nationally appointed corps of professional senior civil servants, which dated from before the Civil War and whose function was to check the arbitrary power of *caciques* over local government. As Antonio Muñoz Molina, a novelist whose first job was in the small cultural office of Granada city council, has recalled, in each municipality members of this national corps held three crucial posts: they were responsible for certifying the legality of the mayor's actions, for approving spending and for controlling the purse strings. They had job security and couldn't be hired or fired by the mayor.[11] Once democracy became established, and just as Spain began to get richer, they were gradually pushed aside and replaced with *cargos de libre designación*. These political appointees have little incentive to act as a check on the politicians who control their livelihood. And since they are not appointed transparently, or on grounds of merit, their quality is variable, at best.

Or take universities. Carlos III University and King Juan Carlos University, both in Madrid and both founded in the 1990s, were identified with the Socialists and the PP respectively. King Juan Carlos University was embroiled in scandal when several PP politicians, including Pablo Casado, were alleged to have obtained Master's degrees from the university's Institute of Public Law despite doing very little of the required academic work. Casado admitted he had been credited with eighteen of twenty-two assignments but insisted he had done nothing wrong. The case of Cristina Cifuentes, the PP president of the Madrid regional government from 2015 to 2018, was particularly telling. She had vowed 'zero tolerance' of corruption and had facilitated a judicial investigation of her predecessor for alleged kickbacks. Once in office she was charged with forging documents to obtain a similar degree from the Institute of Public Law. She was eventually absolved but an aide and a university teacher were convicted of the forgery.[12] Subsequently someone – it was thought to be someone from within the government or the PP – leaked old footage from a security camera in a supermarket that showed her being interrogated for allegedly having stolen two jars of cold cream years earlier.[13] Cifuentes said this had been an 'involuntary mistake' but resigned from her post. This revelation looked political and seemed to send a message about her attempt to wage a campaign of zero tolerance of corruption.[14]

This appeared to be an example of the way that some politicians crossed boundaries and abused the powers of the state, such as the security services, for their partisan interest. Jorge Fernández, the interior minister in Rajoy's first government, faced trial for having allegedly set police to spy on Luis Bárcenas, the PP's rogue treasurer. Bárcenas had €22 million in a Swiss bank account, the apparent fruit of illicit contributions from construction and other companies, and claimed to have made secret top-up payments to party leaders, including Rajoy (who denied this). He was sentenced by the Supreme Court to thirty-three years in prison in 2018 for the receipt of bribes, illicit enrichment and money laundering.[15]

In Spain, as elsewhere, many politicians are honest and motivated by a vocation for public service. But not all of them. In all, more than 900 PP politicians faced corruption charges, Sánchez claimed when he proposed the censure motion against Rajoy (although he provided no details).[16] Most cases involved regional or local government. A former regional president of Madrid faced charges relating to alleged irregularities in the award of contracts, several of them relating to a wild spree of business deals involving the capital's staid water utility.[17] Three of the past four presidents of the PP in Valencia faced charges relating to public contracts. All denied wrongdoing. But the PP did not have a monopoly of corruption cases. A former Socialist president of Andalucía and four of his councillors received prison sentences for maladministration and misuse of public funds over a scandal involving the abuse of a €680 million fund for redundant workers to make payments to political clients.[18] In some cases corruption was linked to the rising cost of political campaigns. Spaniards are relatively reluctant to join or donate to political parties, which are more reliant on public financing than in many other countries. But the system facilitated corruption, and not just because of the *cargos de libre designación*. Until the law on public contracting was tightened in 2017, it allowed low-ball bids and large cost overruns. There was no law to protect whistleblowers. Some suffered the loss of their job and persecution.[19]

Public concern over, and awareness of, corruption soared in the aftermath of the financial crisis. A Eurobarometer poll in 2018 found that 94% of respondents in Spain thought corruption was widespread in their country, compared with an EU average of 71%. But only 5% said they had had experienced or witnessed an act of corruption in the previous twelve months, in line with the EU average. Spain is not Italy: corruption is not systemic, and it tends eventually to be punished by the courts.

There was another dimension to the slogan *No nos representan*. In this century the Spanish political class has become increasingly disconnected from the public, operating in a self-referential cocoon that has little bearing on the concerns of citizens. That is how the public perceives them. The electoral system contributes to the disconnection. Elections are conducted on the basis of a 'closed list', in which voters choose a party rather than a particular candidate. It is the party leaders who decide where on the list a given candidate is placed, and therefore their prospects of election. This means that there is no particular link between representative and the represented.

Though their salaries were relatively low, politicians enjoyed protection and perks. More of them enjoy official cars and security details than in many European countries. Muñoz Molina, who headed the New York office of the Cervantes Institute in the 1990s, recounted the promotional trips that regional presidents and mayors began to make to the city as Spain got richer. They hired expensive PR people and expensive venues and arrived with large entourages from home. Most of the others who attended would be from the small group of resident Spaniards in the city, rather than the American public or investors. 'The noise they made in New York was mainly heard in their places of origin,' inside their bubble.[20]

Indefensibly, thousands of politicians enjoy *aforamiento* – the right to be tried only by the Supreme Court or regional Superior Courts. When he negotiated a stillborn agreement with Ciudadanos, Sánchez promised to reform the constitution to abolish *aforamiento*. It hasn't happened. Miriam González argues that it is the politicians who boss around the businesspeople, through obsessive economic regulation, rather than the other way round. In other words, rather than a small caste, it is a cast of hundreds of thousands of politicians who run Spain.

There are few mechanisms of accountability, apart from elections and, to an extent, the media. Newspapers, both printed and digital, in Spain are highly partisan, as they are, for example, in Britain. After the financial crisis they became even more dependent on advertising by governments, at all levels. Although some newspapers have conducted important investigations, they also practise a degree of self-censorship. Nobody ever touches Spain's largest private companies, a former minister once told me, partly because of their advertising budgets and power of patronage. In the broadcast media, with a few honourable exceptions, endless *tertulias* of opinionated punditry outweigh analysis of facts. Parliamentary committees are toothless and formulaic. Ministers rarely feel the need to resign when they make mistakes. Spain only approved a Freedom of Information Law in 2013 and its operation has been flawed. In 2021 AccessInfo Europe, an NGO, criticised what it saw as the lack of independence from the government of the Transparency Council, the body charged with handling requests for information. In one of the few holdovers from Franco, the official secrets law dates from 1969, though it was amended in 1978. It doesn't set a time limit for documents automatically to become public.

Historians have repeatedly called for a new law. While governments have paid lip service to this, it hasn't happened.[21]

What has made all this worse is that the parties themselves have become less internally democratic. When Felipe González was prime minister he often had to battle to get his way in the executive of the Socialist party. His deputy, Alfonso Guerra, was his chief rival in the party. Now leaders tend to dominate their parties. Both Sánchez and Rajoy brought in rule changes that make it harder for party committees to eject leaders. The adoption of primaries to choose party leaders has introduced presidential-style leadership into a parliamentary system. Leaders now owe their jobs to rank-and-file members rather than to mid-level party officials who are more likely to understand the broader interests of voters.

After Sánchez regained the leadership of the Socialist party through a primary in 2018 he ruthlessly purged those who had sided with his rivals. Casado was similarly harsh in culling congressional lists for the 2019 general election. Rivera and Iglesias, too, were intolerant of dissent. There were very few free-thinkers left in national politics. One was Cayetana Álvarez de Toledo, an outspoken aristocratic historian who combined libertarianism with an *afrancesado* hostility to regional differences. Surprisingly Casado appointed her as PP parliamentary spokesperson, a job which required tact. She lasted thirteen months before being sacked. Unusually she chose to remain in politics, on the back benches. 'In Spain we are not used to the exercise of freedom inside the parties,' she said. 'We confuse disagreement with dissent and freedom with indiscipline.'[22] Almost the only other critical voices within parties tended to be regional presidents (dubbed 'barons') who had their own local political followings. Otherwise, the parties were top-down entities.

Sánchez's leadership was particularly presidential in style. He brought his election guru, Iván Redondo, into the Moncloa, making him chief of staff with power over the official machine. Redondo had previously worked for PP politicians and was disliked and mistrusted by many Socialists but he had stuck with Sánchez during the bitter battles over the party leadership in 2017 and 2018 and the prime minister valued loyalty above all other qualities. But Redondo made mistakes. He was influential in Sánchez's decision to repeat the 2019 election. And his fingerprints were all over a hapless Socialist campaign that saw the party placed third in a Madrid regional election in 2021. In a reshuffle a couple of months later, Sánchez sacked Redondo and brought into government Socialist politicians who had opposed him in the 2018 primary. It was a visible attempt to unite the party.

'Synthetic diagnosis of Spain: we have a 21st-century society, but a 20th-century economy and a 19th-century public administration,' was a pithy summary by Victor Lapuente, a Spanish political scientist at the University of Gothenburg.[23] Apart from the political capture of its upper reaches, the civil service suffered from rigidity and an archaic focus on procedure rather than outcome. The civil service was not especially large, although the regional governments had too many appendages (such as public companies or foundations) whose chief purpose was to provide employment. There were around 3.3 million employees in all three levels of the public administration, of whom almost half worked for the regional governments. The problem was the poor quality of administration. Because of the freeze on recruitment following the financial crisis, the average age of civil servants was 58, with many due to retire over the next decade.[24] Many of these workers were on temporary contracts, which have been abused by the regions, and have not enjoyed much in-service training to keep them up to date. Permanent staff were recruited through public examinations (known as *oposiciones*), which gave priority to memorisation rather than problem-solving. They cannot be moved to other jobs without their consent. For users of public services it often appeared as if the bureaucrats were the helpless slaves of dysfunctional computer systems. As one computer scientist put it, if Larra lived today rather than 'Vuelva usted mañana' he would call his skit 'Error 404'.[25]

The limitations of the system were exposed by the pandemic. At the start, the health ministry struggled to procure protective equipment. It turned out that after decades of decentralisation the ministry had been reduced to a handful of elderly penpushers with no experience of purchasing. Both the ministry and the regional governments struggled with contact-tracing; an app for that purpose was trialled and abandoned. Their difficulty in logging basic information was illustrated by the high level of 'excess deaths' during the early months of the pandemic (i.e. the difference between reported pandemic deaths and the abnormal increase in the mortality rate as reported by public registries). Many other European governments faced similar difficulties, and Spanish hospital staff offered dedicated care in extraordinarily testing circumstances. And after a slow start because of the mistakes of the European Commission, Spain's vaccination campaign was impressive. It was the first large country to jab 70% of its population. But Spaniards' faith in their health system, previously often described as one of the best in the world, was shaken, temporarily at least.

Similarly, the difficulty the social security administration experienced in implanting the minimum-income scheme revealed the limitations of another ageing and rigid branch of the state. The lethargy of the bureaucracy showed, too, in its notorious slowness in approving applications for Spanish nationality. In 2015 the Congress approved a law which gave descendants of Sephardic Jews expelled in 1492 the right to acquire nationality. Pierre Assouline Zerbib, a French writer born in Casablanca, applied. It took five years for his application to be processed. He discovered that a fax (yes!) approving the issue of his passport had taken a year to get from the Ministry of Justice in Madrid to the Spanish consulate in Paris.[26]

The underlying problem, as Lapuente highlighted, was that democratic governments failed to reform the public administration to bring it into the twenty-first century. Apart from the archaic recruitment policy, there was a lack of professional senior managers in the public sector. And there were few procedures for information-sharing and cooperation between the staff of different public entities.[27] The government promised billions of EU money for a digital upgrade of the public administration, and also promised its reform. But providing new computers may prove to be easier than changing entrenched working practices.

Another problem with the working of the Spanish state was the lack of evaluation of the effectiveness of public policies, a regular criticism in the European Commission's reports. After much prodding from Brussels, in 2013 Rajoy's government agreed to set up AIREF, an independent fiscal watchdog modelled on the Congressional Budget Office in the United States and Britain's Office for Budget Responsibility. It proceeded to embark on Spain's first-ever spending reviews, which turned up much waste. In repeated letters to *The Lancet*, dozens of Spanish and other public health experts called for a lesson-learning public inquiry into the management of the pandemic, a call to which the government turned a deaf ear. Sánchez set up an annual exercise involving outside academics to assess to what extent the government was implementing its programme but this was formulaic and superficial.

The judiciary's image, too, has been damaged by the suspicion of political capture. The constitution insists on a strict separation of powers. Initially twelve of the twenty members of the General Council of the Judiciary, which makes judicial appointments and oversees the system, were chosen by the judges themselves and eight by the Congress of Deputies. But a Socialist government in the 1980s pushed through a change under which all twenty members are chosen by a qualified majority of the Congress (meaning by agreement between the two main parties). It justified this by arguing that in those days the majority of the judges were still those appointed by Franco, and had a conservative bias. But over time this change politicised the process. Each region has a high court; each of their chambers has three judges, one chosen by the regional parliament and the others by the national judicial council.[28]

The PP claimed to favour a reform under which judges should choose the General Council, whose members serve for a five-year term. But when Rajoy enjoyed an absolute majority he did nothing to implement this. Instead, he negotiated an agreement with Alfredo Pérez Rubalcaba, the Socialist leader from 2011 to 2014, over appointments to the council. In 2018 the government and the PP came close to an agreement on renewing the council, which collapsed when a PP senator boasted on WhatsApp that in the carve-up his party had managed to achieve 'behind-the-scenes control' of the second, penal, chamber of the Supreme Court.[29] Thereafter, the PP refused for more than three years to agree to renew the membership of the council. This rendered hypocritical the PP's constant claim to be the pre-eminent defender of the constitution. In frustration the government talked of introducing a law that would require only a simple majority of parliament to approve membership of the council. This brought a sharp rebuke from the European Commission, which was grappling with the political capture of the courts by governments in Hungary and Poland, and Sánchez dropped the idea. The commission has urged Spain to ensure that at least half the members of the council are judges elected by their peers in line with a recommendation by the Council of Europe.

In a manner that is typical of Spain, judges have organised themselves in four separate associations, of which one leans left, another leans right and two are non-political. But they tend to agree on many things. In practice, most judges and prosecutors are fiercely independent – as the corruption convictions showed. In 2020 the judiciary carried out a poll of 1,000 judges which found that 99% of them said they felt complete independence in doing their job. But that is not how many Spaniards see them. A Eurobarometer poll found that 58% of respondents in Spain thought the judiciary was not very independent, and only 20% were satisfied with the way it works. In national polls, it is consistently the worst evaluated public service. Critics noted that the president of the Constitutional Tribunal between 2013 and 2017 was previously a member of the PP, for example. The public prosecutor is appointed by the government, and can be sacked by it. There was criticism when Sánchez appointed Dolores Delgado to the job after she had been his justice minister. Spanish law allows third parties to attach themselves to criminal prosecutions under a procedure known as *acusación popular* (popular prosecution). That has sometimes increased the pressure on prosecutors in corruption cases, but it also contributed to the image of politicisation, as when Vox acted as the 'popular prosecutor' in the Catalan separatist trial (although its intervention was juridically irrelevant).[30]

Rather than a lack of independence, the judiciary's biggest problem was gross understaffing. In a jointly authored article in *El País* in 2016, the presidents of all four judges' associations pointed out that there were only 12.5 judges per 100,000 people. That was well below the EU average of 21.6, although similar to the ratio in France and Italy. But Spaniards are more litigious: there were 182 legal cases per 100,000 people in 2015 compared with 100 in Italy. There were too many judicial districts, which meant that there were eight separate digital networks within the judiciary.[31] The result was that justice moved slowly, and that was often a matter of public frustration. Corruption cases involving PP politicians were still working their way through the courts a decade or more after the events concerned, for example.

The judiciary does tend to have a conservative stance. This is no longer a legacy of Franco: no currently serving judge was appointed by the dictatorship. A new penal code was approved in 1995. The civil code dates from 1889 but has undergone several reforms since 1978. Rather, judiciaries in most countries tend to be conservative by nature;

after all, their prime task is to apply the legal status quo and defend public order. Apart from the case of the Catalan separatist leaders, sometimes clumsy verdicts by the courts have led to controversies in two areas in particular: freedom of expression and sexual violence. A partial reform of the penal code in 2015 increased the penalties for 'hate speech' or glorification of terrorism and removed the requirement to show that there was a specific threat against an individual. These are sensitive issues for Spaniards, who are still scarred by ETA's terrorism and by jihadist attacks. Nevertheless, the reform was illiberal. In its first three years more than 50 people were convicted. Those convictions were the work of a minority of ultra-conservative judges rather than a concerted attack on freedom of expression. And some similar cases ended in acquittals.

In one case a rapper known as Valtònyc was sentenced to forty-two months for glorifying terrorism in YouTube posts. He fled to Brussels where a Belgian court refused to extradite him. Willy Toledo, an actor and provocateur, was acquitted of blasphemy after writing a Facebook post 'shitting on God and the Virgin' in support of three women charged over parading a giant plastic vagina in place of the Virgin Mary during the Holy Week procession in Seville (they were eventually acquitted as well). Perhaps the most notorious case involved the jailing for nine months of a rapper known as Pablo Hasél for repeated incitements to violence in YouTube posts and tweets. They included messages saying 'it would be deserved if the car of Patxi López [a Basque Socialist leader] exploded' and 'someone should put an icepick in José Bono's head' (Bono was a former Socialist minister). In parallel Hasél was fined, but not jailed, for insulting the monarchy. The sentence was careful and selective, if debatable. It prompted six nights of violent rioting in Barcelona by a mixture of anarchists and separatists.

Another notorious case concerned a gang rape during the San Fermín bull-running festival in Pamplona. A court in Navarre convicted the six accused men, dubbed *la manada* (meaning herd or pack), only of sexual abuse, imposing a nine-year sentence and freeing them pending appeal. That prompted a public outcry. The Supreme Court later corrected the verdict, stiffening the charge and imposing an immediate fifteen-year sentence. Partly as a result of this case, the government eventually changed the law on rape and sexual consent, at the instigation of Irene Montero, the Podemos minister for equality.

In other contexts Spanish courts often show great respect for individual rights and liberties. During the pandemic some regional courts struck down restrictive measures such as curfews or bans on movement. In a divided and hotly disputed verdict the Constitutional Tribunal ruled that the government erred in invoking a 'state of alarm' to impose a nine-week total lockdown at the start of the pandemic, rather than a tougher 'state of exception'. The ruling had no immediate practical effect but it did mean that public health law would have to be reviewed in preparation for any future epidemic.

A decade after the *indignados*, Spain is in many ways a different country. Their legacy is palpable but far from straightforward. Some of the sources of their anger were addressed, at least partially. The law was reformed so that banks no longer treated their mortgage-holders so abusively. 'Corruption still exists but there's no longer impunity,' as Bescansa noted in 2021.[32] Six years on from publication of Iglesias's book, nearly all the individuals he cited as corrupt and unpunished are, or have been, in jail. According to the *Financial Times*, of the forty-seven bankers sentenced to prison terms worldwide by 2018 as a result of the financial crisis eleven were in Spain, the second-biggest number after Iceland (twenty-five).[33] They included Miguel Blesa, Bankia's former chairman, who committed suicide shortly before he was due to begin his sentence, and Rodrigo Rato, the economy minister in Aznar's governments and a former managing director of the IMF, who succeeded Blesa at Bankia. According to one count, ninety politicians or former officials were in jail in 2017.[34] Perhaps this was because of a change of attitude by the courts and prosecutors, as Bescansa implied. Or perhaps because, while Spanish justice grinds slowly, it grinds inexorably.

But *No nos representan* remained in some ways an unanswered criticism. Many Spaniards continued to see the political system as distant from their concerns. A Eurobarometer poll in late 2020 found that 53% of respondents in Spain were dissatisfied with their democracy. That compared with an EU average of 41%, though it showed a similar level of discontent as in France or Greece. Though satisfaction with democracy had increased since 2014 it remained well below its level of 2008, before the financial crisis. Eurobarometer also found that Spaniards had significantly less trust in their government (both national and regional), their parliament and their political parties than the average European.

Political renewal proved elusive. The best chances were squandered. Both Podemos and Ciudadanos would come to display many of the vices of the 'old politics' they claimed to despise. Ten years after 15 May, both Rivera and Iglesias had resigned as party leaders. After the 2015 election Pedro Sánchez, who had become the Socialist leader the previous year, at first tried to reach an agreement with Podemos to form a government. With 159 of the 350 seats in the Congress of Deputies between them, and the prospect of Catalan and Basque nationalist support, on paper this was plausible. But since Podemos had come so close to overtaking the Socialists, for Sánchez it was a dangerous rival more than an ally. And Iglesias, with sixty-nine seats, overplayed his hand: he wanted control of the defence, interior and justice ministries, the sources of hard power, which only served to alarm everyone else about his intentions.[35] When these talks failed, the Socialists (with ninety seats) turned to Ciudadanos (forty). They agreed on a coherent and broad programme of reforms (including the abolition of the *diputaciones*). But neither Podemos nor the PP would back their potential coalition. After a repeat election in June 2016, at which Podemos failed to gain seats and the Socialists (down five) and Ciudadanos (down eight) lost ground, Rajoy would eventually limp on for another two years.

A better chance came in the election of April 2019. Its result offered Spain a matchless opportunity to get the strong, reforming coalition government it needed. Between them the Socialists (123 seats) and Ciudadanos (57) had an absolute majority. But by then Rivera had become set on trying to replace the PP as the leading force on the centre-right, just as the PP had done to Suárez's UCD in the 1980s. He never forgave Sánchez for outwitting him in the censure motion against Rajoy. At the start of the campaign for the election he flatly ruled out ever allying with Sánchez. Sánchez himself wasn't keen and by then he and Rivera detested each other.[36] But for a would-be centre party, Rivera's refusal to look to both sides for allies was incomprehensible and would be near fatal. With reason, voters blamed him more than anyone else for the lack of a government and for being obliged to trudge to the polls again in November 2019 for the fourth general election in as many years. Ciudadanos was all but wiped out, reduced to ten seats. It lost 60% of the 4.2 million votes it had gained in April. Rivera resigned from all his political roles. His replacement, Inés Arrimadas, the young victor of the Catalan election of 2017, was less petulant and more centrist, but had been dealt a very weak hand.

Rivera's mistake gifted Pablo Iglesias the chance for Podemos to enter government in coalition with Sánchez. But Podemos was no longer the broad, collegial, idealistic project of its early days. Iglesias had forced out those who challenged his leadership or his political line. They included Errejón, whom Monedero accused in the best Stalinist fashion of 'building a party within a party'. Errejón wanted a collective leadership, for Podemos to take more account of parliamentary politics, and to continue to appeal to Spaniards who didn't traditionally back the left. Iglesias wanted an all-powerful leader (himself), and for Podemos to keep one foot in the political battles of the streets. Errejón lost the power battle at a second party Congress held at Vista Alegre, a former bullring in Madrid, in early 2017. The delegates chanted 'Unity, unity', but what happened was a split. 'We risk committing some of the mistakes of the traditional left in Spain,' Errejón had warned on the eve of the Congress. 'The culture of the internal enemy and of the steam-roller is damaging Podemos.'[37] Having been demoted at the Congress, Errejón eventually resigned to form his own regional party in Madrid. Bescansa left, too. Iglesias installed Irene Montero, his romantic partner, as his deputy, a move that smacked of a patrimonial approach to power.

Instead of building a national party organisation, Podemos had chosen to form loose affiliations with local hard-left movements in, for example, Andalucía, Catalonia, Galicia and Valencia. This had allowed it to grow rapidly though it became a liability when these groups peeled away or withered. Only a small number of the Podemos mayors elected across the country in 2015 were re-elected four years later. Those who were included Ada Colau, a housing activist who became mayor of Barcelona. She claimed to be creating a new model of urban manage-ment, reducing car usage, increasing public housing, banning new hotels in the city centre and controlling illegal holiday apartments. She set up a mediation team which she said had stopped 10,000 evictions. She was a good talker, and shrewdly kept her political base happy. But her critics accused her of neglecting basic tasks, such as security and street cleaning. By 2021 much of the centre of Barcelona had a scruffy, neglected air.

Iglesias turned Podemos into a copy of Izquierda Unida with which he allied from 2016 on, a merger which Errejón had opposed. Its support declined, though it seemed to have a solid floor of 10–12% or so. Iglesias's credibility was damaged when in 2018 he and Montero bought a €600,000 chalet with a swimming pool in Galapagar, an affluent suburb of Madrid. To many it seemed that he had joined the caste. Entering government did not seem to boost Podemos's support. It claimed credit for the increase in the minimum wage and for the socially progressive outlook of the government, though the Socialists disputed that. With the exception of Yolanda Díaz at the Labour Ministry, its ministers were unimpressive and had small jobs, carved out of bigger ministries.

Iglesias was palpably happier as an agitator than as an administrator. The Podemos ministers often pushed their own political line, rather than the government's, publicly criticising the monarchy and NATO. To Socialist outrage, Iglesias compared Puigdemont to the Republican exiles after the Civil War. This constant rhetorical activism partly stemmed from an understandable concern that Podemos should not lose its identity and public profile, as tends to happen to the smaller partner in coalitions. But it created a permanent sense of instability at the heart of Sánchez's government. More than a cohesive coalition in the mould of northern Europe, it often seemed like a loose alliance. It transpired that Sánchez lacked the authority to sack Podemos ministers. Iglesias seemed increasingly ill at ease personally, his smile often turning into a snarl. He and Montero faced daily, noisy protests by a small group of far-right demonstrators near their chalet, a form of aggression which might have attracted more sympathy for them had Iglesias not in the past praised similar protests against bankers and the shouting down of political opponents at the Complutense.

In March 2021 Inés Arrimadas, in a bungled attempt to show that Ciudadanos was a hinge party in the centre, concocted with the Moncloa a plan to bring down the PP regional government in Murcia with which it was in coalition. What followed was an example of chaos theory, in which this seemingly minor movement rippled across Spanish politics. Isabel Díaz Ayuso, the young president of the Madrid region, from the PP's conservative wing, instantly ended her coalition with Ciudadanos and called a snap election. Iglesias announced that he was stepping down as deputy prime minister to stand in the Madrid election. With no sense of irony, he called on Más Madrid, Errejón's party, to back him. But Más Madrid had its own candidate, Mónica García, a hospital anaesthetist. She elegantly slapped down Iglesias, saying 'Women are tired of doing the dirty work only to be told to step aside at historic moments.'[38] Iglesias had posed as a feminist, changing the formal name of his party from Unidos Podemos to Unidas Podemos (feminine). But few were taken in by this move by one of the most macho of Spanish politicians. 'We shouldn't add . . . more testosterone,' García said pointedly. Errejón had his revenge for the Vista Alegre congress. Iglesias proclaimed portentously that the Madrid election was a contest between 'democracy and fascism'. But the voters preferred Díaz Ayuso's call for 'freedom' to keep the bars open during the pandemic and to keep taxes low, and García's commitment to more spending on health care. The PP won by a landslide (with 45% of the vote), while Más Madrid (17%) beat not just Podemos (in fifth place with 7%) but the Socialists. To nobody's surprise Iglesias announced his retirement from politics, though he was soon back as a television pundit. His departure didn't solve Podemos's problems. Yolanda Díaz, a Communist who sometimes seemed to belong in the Socialist party, wanted to create a broad left-wing movement. She clashed with what remained of the Podemos party apparatus. As for Ciudadanos, it was annihilated in Madrid and looked to be on the way to extinction and/or absorption by the PP at national level.

The two traditional parties were battered and diminished. Their combined vote had plunged from 84% in 2008 to 49% in November 2019. But they had survived and still, in essence, ran the political system. That pointed to the partydocracy's structural strength, helped by an electoral system that is the most majoritarian among those European countries that use proportional representation. The provinces are its constituencies, with a minimum of three seats per province. That means that less populated provinces, mainly in Castile, are over-represented, which favours the PP. In provinces with six to nine seats, the two main parties benefit, while the rest are approximately proportional. This system penalised national parties that won less than 15% of the vote and whose support was evenly spread, such as Ciudadanos (especially) and to an extent Podemos.

But their survival was also testament to the traditional parties' ability to adapt. One legacy of 15M to Spanish politics was a cult of youth, though with that came inexperience. Turning 50 in February 2022, Sánchez was the oldest of the party leaders who fought the 2019 elections. He led a weakened party but he had seen off any such threat of a *sorpasso* by Podemos as might have existed and could claim to have prevented the near obliteration suffered by the Socialists' counterparts in Greece and France. This was not inevitable. Rubalcaba, his predecessor, was in many ways a more substantial politician. A traditional social democrat, he was doomed by the opprobrium the Socialists received over Zapatero's U-turn and embrace of austerity, forced on the government by the European authorities and the financial markets. 'We've lost credibility with part of our electorate, as happened to all parties in power in Europe,' Rubalcaba told me in 2012. 'It's a double reproach: for taking un-socialist, disliked measures and because they didn't work.' He counselled patience, saying it would be 'very dangerous' to go further to the left.

Yet that was the course that Sánchez adopted, at least superficially. He only achieved his domination of the party after a bitter internal battle that almost tore it apart. He was a little-known *diputado* from Madrid when he was chosen as secretary general by a narrow margin at a congress in 2014, after Rubalcaba resigned following defeat in a European election. Sánchez won mainly because Susana Díaz, the powerful president of Andalucía, traditionally an important repository of Socialist votes, swung her weight behind him because she wanted a placeholder until she could take over. But Sánchez had other ideas. In some ways a wooden and limited politician, he is also bold, imperturbable and extraordinarily resilient. In the general elections of 2015 and 2016 he suffered even worse defeats than Rubalcaba; he claimed them as victories because Podemos had not overhauled the Socialists. But Susana Díaz and many of the Socialist barons concluded that he should be replaced.

When asked to abstain to allow Rajoy to govern, Sánchez had tweeted 'No is No. What part of No don't you understand?' As Spain drifted, without a government for ten months, Sánchez told Rubalcaba and other Socialist leaders that in the end the party would abstain. But then he changed his mind. He discovered that 'No is No' was popular among the party rank and file, who saw it as the recovery of the party's dignity. 'Society had *podemizado* and the Socialist party had *podemizado*,' Óscar López, who is close to Sánchez, told Antonio Caño, Rubalcaba's biographer.[39] Díaz and the Socialist barons thought the party had a responsibility to abstain for the sake of Spanish democracy. They spied in Sánchez's intransigence an opportunity to oust him, which they did at a fratricidal party meeting in October 2016. They miscalculated: Sánchez rallied the rank and file against the party establishment and won his job back in a primary in May 2017. The experience clearly scarred him.

Sánchez was not ideological. His political beliefs were those of a conventional European social democrat. As leader, his politics were determined by his circumstances, more than is usually the case. That led him to draw close to Podemos and accept the support of nationalists, an option that Rubalcaba had dubbed a 'Frankenstein government'. It was an option that, for example, Germany's social democrats, who had had plenty of time to learn that communism is a prison, ruled out. His critics, inside as well as outside the Socialist party, claimed that Sánchez lacked principles, that his word could not be trusted, that he was a mere tactician determined to cling to power at any price. There was evidence for such charges. Yet he could claim to have read the post-15M political mood in Spain more accurately than they. When I interviewed him in November 2018, before he had entered a formal coalition with Podemos, he defended agreements with it saying: 'This shows that our political system is able to include forces that might have placed themselves at the margins of the system . . . but which are evolving.' The point was, he said, that 'Spain is experiencing a change in its political system.' Three years later he could claim to have tamed Podemos, and helped to turn it into a party of the institutions, or at least some of them. But there were costs to the alliance with Podemos. The government spent so much time and political energy consulting internally on decisions that it sometimes seemed to forget to consult externally.

Perhaps the only significant democratic red line Sánchez crossed was to have allowed negotiations for the support on the budget and other votes of EH Bildu, ETA's successor party (see chapter 6). And he placed short-term political expediency above the defence of the democratic state in his mishandling of the claim, published in the *New Yorker* in April 2022 and made by Citizen Lab, a watchdog, that the Spanish government had between 2017 and 2020 spied on the mobile phones of sixty-five people linked to Catalan separatism.[40] The Lab said that in sixty-three cases it had detected the use of Pegasus, surveillance software made by an Israeli company which sells it only to governments. The Catalan and Basque nationalist parties and Podemos expressed outrage. Esquerra threatened to break off all cooperation with the government, which meant that it might find it hard to win parliamentary votes. Sánchez responded defensively, seeming to give credibility to the Citizen Lab report. He sent Félix Bolaños, the minister of the presidency, to meet the Generalitat in Barcelona and to promise several investigations.[41] In a bizarre turn, Bolaños then announced that the phones of Sánchez and the defence and interior ministers had suffered an 'illicit and external' interception in May and June 2021.

The head of the intelligence service, Paz Esteban, appeared before a closed congressional committee to say that it had monitored the phones of eighteen (not sixty-five) Catalan leaders and activists, including Pere Aragonès, the Generalitat's president, at the time of the violent protests in Catalonia against the sentencing of the separatist leaders in 2019. It had done so with judicial orders and had done nothing illegal, she was reported to say. It was left to Margarita Robles, the defence minister, to point out that the intelligence service was only doing its job: 'What should a state, a government, do when someone violates the constitution, when someone declares independence, cuts the public highway, when they carry out public disorders?'[42] Nevertheless, the government made Esteban the sacrificial victim of whole affair, sacking her without any stated cause. That undermined Robles, who had been one of the government's most popular ministers. A group of Spanish academics questioned the accuracy and impartiality of the Citizen Lab report, in which a tech entrepreneur who sympathised with Catalan separatism was closely involved.[43] Citizen Lab insisted its investigation was independent.[44]

The flip side of Sánchez's imperturbability was a public perception of lack of empathy. For the first two months of the pandemic and lockdown he appeared on television every weekend, giving statements and answering questions. But when the first wave of the pandemic ebbed, and the PP refused to support a continuation of the state of emergency, he seemed to throw in the towel, handing over responsibility to the regions. He became the good-news prime minister: he popped up to talk of European aid and vaccination, but was nowhere to be seen when successive waves of Covid-19 hit the country.

As for the PP, it suffered, with a lag, the same kind of loss of direction that had dogged Rubalcaba. The corruption scandals damaged its credibility. After Rajoy resigned, the party elected as its leader Pablo Casado, aged just 37 at the time, in a primary. He was an accomplished orator but inexperienced as a strategist. His party had been a broad church under Aznar and Rajoy, uniting economic libertarians, Christian democrats and Catholic Spanish nationalists. Yet that coalition had splintered with the rise of Ciudadanos and then Vox. Like Sánchez, Casado was faced with trying to ensure his party remained pre-eminent in its half of the political spectrum while needing sometimes to cooperate with a more radical rival (Vox, in his case) in regional governments. His answer was to engage in frenetic opposition to everything the government did, sensible or not, while swerving between trying to copy Vox and trying to appeal to the centre. That reflected different currents within the PP. It governed in Andalucía (after 2018), Castile and León, and Galicia under moderate leaders (in the first two in coalitions with Ciudadanos). In Madrid, Díaz Ayuso represented the party's right wing. She had broad appeal in Castile, but not necessarily in coastal Spain.

Casado insisted that his party's corruption was in the past. To try to draw a symbolic line, he announced that it would leave its headquarters in Calle Génova in Madrid, following accusations that it had been refurbished with illicit donations. The PP was well placed to absorb the rump of Ciudadanos. But Vox was a bigger problem for it. When Santiago Abascal, Vox's leader, filed a censure motion against Sánchez in October 2020, Casado used the debate to launch a scorching attack on the hard-right party. By splitting the right, 'you offer the left a guarantee of perpetual victory', he said. He accused Abascal of dividing Spaniards. 'We don't want to be like you,' he went on. 'It's come to this. Either Vox, or Spain.'[45] The PP did not apply that policy at regional level.

A senior PP official argued that to recapture its lost voters the party had to show itself to be a plausible alternative government to Sánchez and the Socialists. Yet Casado offered sound and fury rather than statesmanship. He never grew into his job. In early 2022 his leadership imploded. First he ill-advisedly pushed the PP regional president in Castile and León into calling an early election in which the big winner was Vox. And then his simmering feud with Díaz Ayuso, his protégé turned rival, exploded into open civil war which could have only one winner. The party's regional leaders turned against Casado, forcing him to resign, proving that hard though it is to unseat Spanish party leaders, it is not impossible. Of the four young national leaders who had fought the 2019 general elections, only Sánchez remained.

At an extraordinary party Congress Alberto Núñez Feijóo took over as the PP president by acclamation, resigning from his job in Galicia and moving to the Senate. 'Nobody should count on me to take part in this infantile entertainment into which Spanish politics has degenerated,' he said.[46] He quickly sketched out a more mature, moderate stance, focusing his critique of the government on the economy and defending 'the political, cultural and linguistic identity of the regions'.[47] He offered the best hope of the PP staving off a *sorpasso* by Vox. Vox's support edged up in the opinion polls to 18% by the end of 2021. It offered PP-led governments in Andalucía, Madrid and Murcia, and initially of the Madrid city council, confidence and supply agreements to sustain them in office. In return it didn't extract more than the odd gesture, such as the cutting of €600,000 earmarked for helping immigrants in Andalucía and the blocking of a declaration against gender violence in Madrid, for example.[48] But in Castile and León it insisted on entering the regional government. However, Vox's leaders were generally unimpressive and it faced problems in building a national organisation, with splinters and splits in some provinces. Feijóo's arrival as the PP's national leader quickly gave his party a boost in the opinion polls and support for Vox began to fall. In June 2022 the PP won a sweeping victory and an absolute majority in an election in Andalucía under its moderate leader there, Juanma Moreno. It seemed likely that the next general election, due by November 2023 at the latest, would see a recovery in the combined vote share of the two traditional parties, the Socialists and the PP.

The most visible legacies of 15M were political polarisation and *crispación*, or permanent confrontation. *Crispación* began in the 1990s with José María Aznar and gathered force under Zapatero (see chapter 1). But even then, behind the scenes there was cross-party communication and, on big issues such as fighting terrorism, agreement. This approach was personified by Rubalcaba, the last holdover from Felipe González's cabinet still in frontline politics. As leader, he met Rajoy almost once a month to discuss the Catalan crisis, and co-managed with the prime minister the abdication of King Juan Carlos in 2014.[49] Despite their political disagreements, they had a cordial personal relationship.

Those days have gone. Sánchez's slogan in 2016 of 'No is No' set a new tone. Sánchez did collaborate with Rajoy over Catalonia in 2017. But he and Casado went for months on end without talking to each other. They were unable to forge agreements on issues over which national accord should have been easy, if not automatic. Each of them sought political advantage from the pandemic, for example. A nadir in this unbridled confrontation came when Sánchez's government included a tirade against the PP, suitable for a party election pamphlet, in the preamble to the text of a law published in the official gazette.[50] Another was the PP's irresponsible blocking of the renewal of the membership of the General Council of the Judiciary. European diplomats expressed surprise at the PP's disloyal opposition in Brussels. This went beyond normal politicking in the European Parliament and extended to lobbying the European Commission against government policies. But *crispación* was not a tool restricted to the two main parties: polarisation of debate and the denigrating of opponents were the stock in trade of both Podemos and Vox.

The left–right divide is more pronounced in Spain than in many other countries. Although the data is limited, there is some polling evidence that what political scientists call 'affective polarisation' – the tendency of voters of one party to distrust and reject the attitudes of those of another – has been growing. This applies particularly to questions of identity and national unity, and to a lesser extent the level of taxes and immigration.[51] The average Spanish voter is slightly to the left of centre, further left than in other European countries. That is a reaction to the Franco dictatorship, but it also shows a preference for the welfare state. This helps to explain why the Socialists have governed for twice as long as the PP. It also explains why, until 2015, when the PP was in opposition it resorted more to *crispación* than the Socialists did when they were.[52] When power changed it was not generally because voters switched sides but because disillusioned voters of the party in office stayed at home.

The emergence of a multi-party system might have been expected to blunt *crispación* and promote cooperation. But it has done the opposite. There are now two multi-party blocks where there were two parties. That has led to a centrifugal political dynamic, in which the Socialists compete as well as collaborate with Podemos and the PP with Vox, so both worry that conciliatory stances will have an electoral cost. There is a generational factor, too. Many of today's leaders entered politics in their parties' youth movements, which tend to be ideologically uncompromising. Casado's PP never forgave Sánchez for winning power in the censure motion with the votes of Catalan and Basque separatists and of Podemos, which it saw as an anti-system party. Certainly, those were steps that some of Sánchez's Socialist predecessors would not have taken. But political circumstances have changed: Sánchez has been in a parliamentary minority throughout his premiership. For their part, the Socialists see the PP's reliance on the votes of Vox in regional governments and, foreseeably, in a future national government, as similarly illegitimate. *Crispación* meant that the politicians often seemed to be talking at each other in an echo chamber, rather than to the country. The leaders jousted in parliamentary debates in which their MPs loudly and obediently clapped them. While there were occasional flights of parliamentary oratory, the spectacle was often unseemly. The polls show that most Spaniards thought confrontation had gone too far and the quality of their political leadership was declining.

At times in the decade since 15M, Spain's politics seemed to resemble Gramsci's observation regarding the collapse of the liberal order in inter-war Italy: 'The crisis consists precisely in the fact that the old is dying and the new cannot be born; in this interregnum a great variety of morbid symptoms appear.' The question was whether Spain's crisis, to use Gramsci's term, can be resolved through a partial renewal of the old. Sánchez at least was able to offer a certain short-term stability while steering Spain through the pandemic and implementing some social improvements for the poorer half of the country. But putting the country back on a clear path of sustainable economic growth and progress required more far-reaching reforms and agreements. And trapped as they were in their bubble, the politicians seemed oblivious to changes in the outside world that threatened Spain.

CHAPTER 10

THE NARCISSISM OF SMALL DIFFERENCES

They came in their hundreds, swimming around the border fence or walking across the beach at low tide under the permissive eyes of Moroccan border guards who would normally have stopped them. In thirty-six hours in May 2021 some 8,000 would-be migrants descended on the Spanish city of Ceuta, an enclave of 85,000 people on the African shore of the Strait of Gibraltar. About 1,500 of them were unaccompanied minors who were not easy to deport legally. Clearly rattled by Morocco's sudden weaponisation of migration, the government deployed 3,000 troops with armoured cars from the garrison in Ceuta and sent 200 police reinforcements. Sánchez flew to the city, vowing to defend its 'territorial integrity' as the authorities grappled with a humanitarian headache.

Morocco's King Muhammed VI had opened the border because he was furious that Spain had secretly admitted Brahim Gali, the leader of Polisario, a group which has fought for the independence of Western Sahara, for medical treatment for Covid-19. Western Sahara was a Spanish colony until Franco's death. When Spain relinquished the territory, King Hassan II, Muhammed's father, annexed it by mobilising 350,000 civilians in a 'Green March' of occupation.

Polisario, which is sponsored by Algeria, holds sway over some squalid refugee camps and around 20% of the territory in the desert interior. Spain, in common with the EU, does not recognise Moroccan sovereignty over Western Sahara and supports the UN's call for a referendum on its future. It is a conflict that has festered, seemingly unresolvable, for decades. But shortly before the end of his term, Donald Trump reversed US policy on the issue and, without consultation, recognised Moroccan sovereignty over the Sahara in return for Morocco's recognition of Israel. This empowered Muhammed, who began to push for Europe to follow suit.

The Ceuta incident highlighted three things about Spanish foreign policy. First, that EU membership continues to be its cornerstone. Sánchez quickly garnered high-level support in Brussels. 'Spanish borders are European borders,' declared the EU's Home Affairs Commissioner. Ursula Von der Leyen, the commission president, said pointedly that the issue of migration would be 'crucial' in the EU's future relationship with Morocco. The EU is its biggest aid donor and an important trade partner. The kingdom grumbled that Spain was 'Europeanising a bilateral issue', but backed down, closing the border again. Second, Morocco's intelligence services had clearly done a better job than Spain's, having quickly found out about Gali's presence in a hospital in Logroño. Spanish officials admitted to having been taken by surprise when the migrant surge happened. A blame game ensued about who decided to let Gali in. It ended with Arancha González Laya, the foreign minister, losing her job.

The third and most important lesson concerned the existential importance of the Maghreb for Spain, though it was less talked about as a foreign policy priority than Europe and Latin America. Spain faced a difficult balancing act in the Maghreb. Morocco is a vital but awkward neighbour. It is a rising power in North Africa. It was Spain's ninth largest export market. More importantly Spain was home to over 750,000 people of Moroccan origin and, despite everything, officials

261

considered it to be a crucial partner in controlling unauthorised migration. And Morocco claimed Ceuta and Melilla, the other Spanish enclave, as its own. But on the other hand Algeria, Morocco's foe, had traditionally supplied up to half of Spain's imports of natural gas. This came into sharp focus when, months after the Ceuta incident, Algeria broke off diplomatic relations with Morocco. It then opted not to renew an expiring agreement under which it pumped gas to Spain and Morocco through a pipeline that runs across Moroccan territory. This pipeline took almost half of Algeria's gas exports to Spain. Algeria promised to expand the capacity of the undersea pipeline to Almería that took the remainder, and to make up the shortfall with shipments of liquid natural gas. But this increased the cost at a time when energy prices were soaring. And then Sánchez abruptly changed Spain's position on the Sahara, praising Morocco's plan for the territory to become autonomous but under its sovereignty. In an attempt to placate Algeria, which withdrew its ambassador, the government deported there several political exiles. But Algeria reduced its gas shipments to Spain and blocked Spanish exports. All this was a harsh lesson in *Realpolitik* and Spain's relative lack of weight in the world.

Democracy transformed Spain's international profile. It developed three foreign policy priorities: enthusiastic membership of the European Community; less enthusiastic membership of NATO; and attempting to act as a bridge between Europe, the United States and Latin America. At first this worked well. Felipe González was a big player in the European Community, taken seriously by Helmut Kohl, François Mitterrand and Margaret Thatcher. And González was also influential in Latin America, as a counsellor in the region's democratisation and a cheerleader for corporate Spain as it began to invest there. Aznar's Atlanticism may have failed but it was an attempt to project Spain on the world stage. Loss of influence began under Zapatero. His decision to withdraw Spanish forces from Iraq, abruptly and without consultation, was popular at home but damaged Spain's image as a reliable ally for the United States. Influence continued to decline under Rajoy, who showed little interest in foreign policy. When Sánchez came into office some commentators enthused that Spain would at last become a player in Europe again. He was the first Spanish prime minister of the current democratic period to speak fluent English and he was a convinced pro-European. He was more active than Rajoy but in the event Spain continued to be a rule-taker more than a rule maker in the EU. In 2020 the European Council approved a Franco-German initiative for pandemic aid grants financed by mutualised perpetual debt rather than Spain's proposal for common Eurobonds.

There were some structural factors at play. The economic slump forced big cuts in foreign aid. Spain's need for European aid twice in a decade, minority governments and the Catalan conflict all weakened Spain's hand. It didn't help that the diplomatic service was old-fashioned, corporatist and politicised. José Manuel García-Margallo, Rajoy's first foreign minister, said he regretted not having modernised the service, which he said corresponded to the world of fifty years before. Arancha González, who had been a senior international trade official at the UN and the World Trade Organisation, did try to shake up the service, introducing boards for appointments. She was neither a diplomat nor a member of the Socialist party and faced resistance. 'The system expelled her as a foreign body,' an academic told me.

Spain's position in Latin America has also weakened. Felipe González launched annual summits with Latin American leaders, formalised in the Iberoamerican community. Attendance dropped off and the summits became biennial. Officials pointed out that in a fractured Latin America it was the one venue which all countries attended, but that smacked of a lowest common denominator. Few Latin Americans considered themselves to be 'Iberoamericans'. Spain tended to take Latin America for granted, and assumed it understood it and could speak for it. Neither was true. To make matters worse, foreign policy towards the region has become politicised, in two ways. Under Sánchez, Spain has had twin policies towards Latin America: an official one follows the EU and US position of support for democracy and freedoms, while a parallel one undertaken by Podemos and, less comprehensibly, Zapatero, espoused sympathy for the populist and authoritarian left in the region. Zapatero's actions as a self-appointed mediator in Venezuela were highly controversial: he secured the release of dozens of prisoners but the regime promptly arrested others. The opposition saw him as a stooge for Nicolás Maduro's dictatorship. Spain's failure to stand fairly and squarely for liberal democracy damaged its reputation in the region. On the other hand, Venezuela has become a domestic political issue in Spain, as Cuba long has been. Many of the leaders of the more intransigent wing of the Venezuelan opposition now live in Madrid where they have influence over the PP and Vox.

Spain did have international assets. Madrid became a more and more important crossroads for Latin Americans, in cultural and people-to-people terms. The Spanish language remained a powerful cultural tool. Spain had soft power, which it could make more of: a poll taken each year by the Elcano Royal Institute, a think-tank, regularly showed that foreigners had a higher opinion of the country than Spaniards themselves. And Spain could point to some modest diplomatic successes. Notwithstanding the Ceuta incident, its migration-linked cooperation programmes with African countries were well-conceived. The Sánchez government's approach to post-Brexit Gibraltar was mature. García-Margallo had peremptorily demanded co-sovereignty leading to full sovereignty. This was not just unacceptable to Gibraltarians but also short-sighted. It would set a precedent that would have haunted Spain in relation to Ceuta and Melilla. Gibraltar's economy depends on some 10,000 workers who cross the border each day. In turn, those jobs are important for what is one of the poorest parts of Spain in the Campo de Gibraltar opposite the Rock. Sánchez's team negotiated a pragmatic agreement with the UK under which Gibraltar would form part of the Schengen zone of passport-free travel.

Its external border – the port and airport – would be policed by Frontex, the EU's border force, in deference to Gibraltarian sensitivity over the deployment of Spanish police. Both sides hoped the agreement would become a treaty between the EU and the UK.

Spain's loss of international influence came as its international integration was ever greater, as an open economy dependent on energy imports and whose large companies derived much of their revenues abroad. 'We depend on the outside world a lot more than the outside world depends on us,' wrote Emilio Lamo de Espinoza, the founding director of the Elcano Royal Institute, an international affairs think-tank in Madrid. 'This is perhaps the fundamental contradiction of Spain's current situation: being a country enormously dependent on the outside world, it has neither the resources nor the capacity to manage this condition adequately.'[1] The contradiction was sharpened by Spain's internal problems. In an unprecedented joint article published in 2012, all the living foreign ministers of Spanish democracy stated that they were 'convinced that to be influential beyond our borders we need to be strong internally . . . projecting an image of a vigorous, politically stable, legally secure and open country'.[2] And not only was that not the case, but the Spanish public did not seem to see it as a problem.

The Atocha station in Madrid is a daily marvel. With meticulous punctuality a fleet of sleek AVEs, as the high-speed trains are called, streak off at up to 300 kilometres per hour to a dozen different destinations in southern and eastern Spain. This spectacle has recently begun to be matched at Chamartín station, on the other side of Madrid, where AVEs leave for Galicia and the north. There are plenty of criticisms that can be made of Spain's bet on high-speed rail. It has led to a two-speed railway system, many of the lines may not repay the investment for decades and there is some evidence that Madrid has benefited more than the provincial capitals. Yet there can be no doubt that the AVEs, along with an extensive motorway network, have shrunk the country in terms of journey times and joined up the nation for the first time. They symbolise much that is good about modern Spain.

Yet, paradoxically, as Spain has become both more integrated internally and more connected to the world, in some ways Spaniards are more strongly attached than ever to their *terruño* (local patch). Foreign observers have long remarked on this characteristic. In his *Handbook for Travellers in Spain*, first published in 1845, Richard Ford declared: 'Spain is today, as it always has been, a collection of small bodies tied to a string of sand which lacking union lacks strength.' He noted that 'from the earliest period down to the present, all observers have been struck with this *localism*, as a salient feature in the Iberian character'.[3] This localism continues, and if anything has become stronger today than forty years ago. It is expressed in a fierce attachment to cultural traditions, to the town fiesta and to local food and wine. It is one of the appealing features of Spain, it gives it social cohesion and perhaps these strong local identities have made the changes brought by globalisation easier to bear. They go beyond Catalonia and the Basque Country. In the past forty years, under the aegis of the *estado autonómico* and the devolution of powers, places such as Andalucía, and even Madrid, which never had strong regional political identities in the past, have acquired them. But localism can also weaken the nation state.

The preceding chapters have argued that contemporary Spain is not burdened by an atavistic exceptionalism nor by Franco's ghost. But like all countries it has its specificities, mainly derived from history and geography. As we have seen, a legacy of the relative weakness of the state in the nineteenth century in a country of many geographical obstacles was the survival of regional identities which evolved into rival nationalisms. They were strong enough to resist but not to impose themselves. They cannot simply be ignored or repressed, as Franco tried to do. But nor do they justify breaking up what is on the whole a successful country.

Seen in the context of the past two centuries, the transition settlement was a historic success. If there was a ghost guiding it, surely it was that of Manuel Azaña and his vision of a liberal Spain that embraced its diversity, a *patria* of citizenship and the rule of law. Under its auspices, the centuries-long hold of national Catholicism over political life and public morality was at last broken, Spain joined the Western European mainstream and society modernised at the speed of a flood from a breached dam. After more than forty years it needs reform, but not replacement as Podemos, Catalan and Basque separatism and Vox all argue.

The *estado autonómico*, the heart of the transition settlement and Spain's contemporary democracy, was a bold attempt to reconcile diversity and unity, to respect regional languages, cultures and differences while asserting a common national culture that unites all Spaniards. It can claim to have been broadly successful. By bringing public services closer to the people, it improved them. It encouraged a healthy competitive rivalry and experimentation: Castile and León, for example, a largely rural region with an income per person slightly below the national average, has some of the best educational results in Spain. Regional inequalities fell, at least at first. Andalucía remains one of Spain's poorer regions but it is nothing like as poor as it was. Income per head has overhauled that of Italy's *mezzogiorno*. Fernán-Núñez now has a health clinic, and access to a district hospital in Montilla, 15 kilometres away, both run by the regional government. Some of these positive outcomes were due in part to Spain's entry into the EU and its structural and cohesion funds for poorer regions. But polls tend to show that Spaniards rate their regional government more highly than the national one.

The system has defects, too. Some are obvious. They include the unnecessary proliferation of regulation and the wasteful reproduction of the paraphernalia of quasi-independence, from public television stations to contemporary art museums. There are too many regions. In many of them there is insufficient political competition, which has engendered a rebirth of the *cacique*. And the system gives mayors of big cities too few powers. Other drawbacks are more insidious. The biggest is the open-ended constitutional framework of the *estado autonómico*, which lacks a clearly defined division of powers between centre and region. That has led to a permanent tug of war over powers, and meant that the Constitutional Tribunal has become an overworked and, to some, discredited referee. Because of the way the political system has evolved, open-endedness has become centrifugal. In twenty of the forty years since the 1982 election, the governing party has lacked a majority in Congress. It has relied on Basque and Catalan nationalist parties in a trade of parliamentary votes for the transfer of powers. Some of those parties now want to destroy the Spanish nation state. In throwing in its lot with peripheral nationalisms the left – the Socialists and especially Podemos – has turned its back on its long history of commitment to universal rights, and the pre-eminence of social class over national feeling. For many of their nationalist allies, home rule – the constitution's *autonomía* – is an intermediate stop, not a destination.

The *estado autonómico*'s boost to localism has also generated a narrowness of mind, a blinkered parochialism. Regional governments often seem to be creating self-contained worlds. When in summer 2019 the Madrid regional government began hiring music teachers for the first time since before the slump, it in effect made it impossible for musicians from other parts of Spain to apply. Or take languages. Regional governments in Valencia and the Balearics are promoting the local variant of Catalan. In Asturias some want to give official status to *bable*, a local tongue derived from Latin. In each case there is an argument for protecting a linguistic culture. But divisive policies, such as attaching linguistic requirements for public sector jobs, tend to follow.

The impulse is often to stress what divides rather than what unites, what Sigmund Freud called 'the narcissism of small differences'. This is most obviously so with Basque and Catalan nationalists, but it applies more widely in Spain today. The country risks becoming 'a kingdom of *taifas*', Felipe González often warned, referring to the mosaic of small warlord states that emerged in Muslim Spain following the collapse of the Ummayad caliphate in 1009.[4] This fissiparous tendency ignores the many things that all Spaniards have in common, as women or men, parents and children, workers, professionals, consumers, ecologists, cyclists, football fans and basketball players, eaters of tortillas, tomatoes, squid, fish or steaks. And the focus on the local and regional has come at the cost of Spain's national and international interests.

Some on the right believe the answer is re-centralisation, as Vox would like. It is surely not coincidental that today, as in the time of José Ortega y Gasset's *España Invertebrada*, many of the most vocal centralisers are Basque and Catalan journalists and intellectuals. But their unitarianism flies in the face of both history and social realities. The right should understand that federalism, which it instinctively rejects, is the answer to many of its anxieties. Formal federalism would involve a clear demarcation of powers and clear rules for dispute-resolution. It would involve reforming the Senate, a toothless and rather functionless body which serves chiefly as a parking place for second-tier politicians, to turn it into a chamber that represented the regions, along the lines of Germany's Bundesrat. Federalism might also bring about a change in the underlying philosophy of how to govern Spain, from being a radial country centred on the hub of Madrid to a networked one with competing power centres, in which for example Barcelona might feel more like Munich than Marseilles and state agencies were spread around the country rather than clustering in Madrid. That would not placate hardcore separatists but it would satisfy many Catalans who became disillusioned with regional autonomy. In twenty-first-century Europe it really shouldn't be impossible to reconcile regional diversity, sub-national identities and national unity. But once national identity and nationalism become dominant strands of the political system, it is hard to reverse that. If the current fissiparous trend continues, Spain risks gradually coming apart, for lack of glue. It is time to value the whole as well as, and not instead of, the parts. The country needs to find ways of making itself more attractive to the 3 million or so Catalans and Basques who say they want to leave it, without hurting the interests of the other 43 million Spaniards.

For several generations, the answer was held to lie in Ortega y Gasset's observation that 'Spain is the problem, Europe is the solution.' That has become a cliché, its shelf life long over, along with much of Ortega's thinking, marked as it was by the pessimism of the 1898 Generation of intellectuals. Spain has become a far better place since then. Entry to Europe provided Spain with a shared national project during the transition. The EU has helped Spain a lot, in many ways. It has, of course, been a source of development aid, the EU structural funds helping to pay for infrastructure and improvements in the poorer parts of the country. Not surprisingly, Spaniards are among the most enthusiastic Europhiles in the EU, though that may owe something to their mistrust of their own governments and institutions. Perhaps more importantly the European Commission has acted as a kind of superego, in Freudian terms, preventing unbridled populism and restraining separatism. Pressure from Brussels was important in pushing Spanish governments to undertake economic reforms both during the financial crisis and the pandemic.

The difficulty with Ortega's dictum is what happens when you have joined Europe and there are still problems at home. In other words, Europe is not the solution to all of Spain's problems. And Europe's future in a rapidly changing world is far from assured. Some Spaniards argue that having achieved democracy, considerable prosperity and integration into Europe, Spain needs a new grand national project. That, too, reflects Ortega's influence. 'Only great enterprises awake the deepest vital instincts of great human masses,' he wrote.[5] Like Ortega, many Spanish intellectuals tend to be obsessed with what Spaniards *are,* with problems of essence, rather than what they *do* and with their need for a better quality of government at all levels.

Spain cannot rely on either Europe, or on some nebulous national project, to paper over national discord. The political crisis of paralysis, polarisation and fragmentation which manifested itself in 2016 may have been temporarily stilled by Sánchez, but in many ways it continues. 'Ultimately, the spirit of 15M [the *indignados*] continues to float in the atmosphere,' as Ignacio Urquizu puts it.[6] The country's main problem today is the inability of the politicians to reach even minimal agreements across what has become a bitter partisan divide. That makes even the smallest constitutional reform almost unthinkable, let alone a leap forward requiring multiple trade-offs such as formal federalism. It even makes it hard to imagine serious moves towards the better government the country needs. Lasting improvements in education and training, and necessary rationalisations of public spending, with less directed to pensioners and more to young people, are unlikely without broad cross-party pacts. Some pundits called for a grand coalition to carry out reforms, but that carried the risk of strengthening the extremes. More useful, and more possible, would be a few cross-party agreements on the main reforms. These were the dilemmas Spain seemed likely to face in the coming years in a political system featuring a partial restoration of the two-party system, the continuing presence of Basque and Catalan nationalists, and the existence of two disruptive parties at the extremes in Podemos and Vox.

The narcissism of small differences expressed by nationalisms and localisms within Spain is mirrored in *crispación*, the need to fetishise political disagreements even where they scarcely exist. The divide between left and right has proved harder to bridge in Spain than in France, with the triumph of Macron, in Germany, with its grand coalitions, or in Italy, with its protean governments. Spanish politicians may have started to learn the art of coalition building at national level but so far this has simply deepened the trenches that separate left and right. Some argue that this ideological trench, and not the issues of historical memory, may be the most pernicious legacy of the Civil War. But rather than a hangover from the last century, this looks more like a consequence of 15M, of the financial crisis and the *indignados*.

More than a decade after discontent surfaced with the irruption of the *indignados*, the populist challenges to Spain's constitutional settlement – Podemos, Catalan separatism and Vox – seemed no longer to be advancing, for the time being at least. ETA's abandoning of violence appeared to be definitive. All this pointed to the resilience of Spanish democracy. But to survive is not necessarily to thrive. Alliances of short-term expediency provide no long-term foundation for the country's progress. 'No is No' continues to haunt Spanish politics.

The pandemic, the slowness of economic recovery and the return of inflation all took their toll on the government's support. Opinion polls pointed to the possibility that at the next general election Spain would move back to the right. But which right? Throughout 2020 and 2021 Vox steadily crept up in the polls, thanks largely to Casado's ineffectual leadership of the PP. That was a problem for the country not just the PP. Many on the left argued that Vox was a far more potent threat to democracy than Podemos. That was debatable. Certainly, Vox was hostile to some elements of liberal democracy, such as minority rights, and said it wanted to ban peaceful peripheral nationalist parties. But in the view of one study it is of the radical rather than extreme right: 'discursively, it doesn't attack democracy'.[7] Podemos's initial disdain for an independent judiciary and its alliances with Latin American dictatorships similarly questioned its commitment to liberal democracy. To seek power, Pablo Iglesias reconciled himself to the constitution, and the same might well become true of Vox. But Podemos was tamed by being the minority partner in a minority government, with less than a third as many parliamentary seats as the Socialists. A majority government in which Vox had almost as many seats as the PP would be deeply disturbing for democrats. In those circumstances many would call for a *cordon sanitaire* around Vox, an agreement not to ally with it. Unlike some other mainstream conservative parties in Europe the PP has not adopted that position, at least in regional government. But neither did Sánchez place a *cordon sanitaire* around Podemos as Olaf Scholz did with Die Linke, Germany's hard-left party. For a *cordon sanitaire* against Vox to be credible and effective the implication would be that if the PP were the most-voted party and the left lacked a parliamentary majority, then the Socialists would have to back a PP government.[8] In this context Núñez Feijóo's arrival at the head of the PP looked providential. It gave the PP a poll boost and held out the possibility that support for Vox would start to decline, or at least stop growing.

Another uncertainty concerned the future of the monarchy. For many on the right and in the centre it was a crucial bulwark of the constitution and against extremism. Juan Carlos's misdeeds inflicted lasting damage to the institution, especially to its reputation among young people. Will this prove to be terminal? Much will depend on how effective Leonor, King Felipe's elder daughter, proves to be as a representative of the monarchy. Its second weapon is inertia, and that may be decisive in its survival.

Spanish society is resilient and overwhelmingly moderate. Fortunately, the polarisation among the politicians was on the whole not reflected in everyday life. For many Spaniards life is good. But the country may be becoming over-reliant on these qualities. In a scathing opinion article in 2021 Antonio Caño, the former editor of *El País*, wrote that 'for lack of other motives, partying and sun are becoming the only symbols of identity and the only escape valves from an appalling reality'.[9] Many would say this was hyperbolic, and others might argue that partying and sun have much going for them. But Caño had a point.

Exactly a century ago the inability of the Restoration politicians to reach agreements on reforms opened the way to the dictatorship of Primo de Rivera. There is no reason for history to repeat itself, but that ought to serve as a warning to Spain's political class. National character is a suspect notion, given human diversity the world over. But history, geography and customs do shape attitudes and behaviours. Rightly or wrongly, Spaniards are known for pride, stubbornness and unwillingness to compromise (a word that doesn't have an equivalent in Spanish). But they have many qualities. In normal everyday interactions, they are unfailingly patient, humane and kind. Those qualities have long been noted by outsiders. César Vallejo, a great Peruvian modernist poet, wrote of a visit to Madrid in the 1920s that 'the permanent values of humanity take preference over the smoke of the locomotive, the banking hall, the klaxon of the motor car and the fixed wing of the aircraft'. In many ways that remains the case today. Spaniards have been remarkably patient over the past decade. But unless their demands for change are addressed, at some point their patience may snap.

NOTES

Prologue

1. On *Las Meninas*, see Michael Jacobs, *Everything is Happening: Journey into a painting*, Granta, London, 2015.
2. José Varela Ortega, *España: Un relato de grandeza y de odio*, Espasa, Barcelona, 2019, p. 25.
3. Jason Webster, *Violencia: A new history of Spain – past, present and the future of the West*, Constable, London, 2019, Introduction.
4. 'Orientalism', according to Said, an intellectual of Palestinian origin, is a system of representation which deploys imaginative projection and patronising tropes to deny the value and logic of other societies, seen as inferior.
5. Tom Burns Marañón, *Hispanomanía, con un Prólogo para Franceses*, Galaxia Gutenburg, Barcelona, 2014, p. 59. All translations from Spanish sources are mine.
6. Franz Borkenau, *The Spanish Cockpit: An eyewitness account of the Spanish Civil War*, Phoenix Press, London, 2000, pp. 299–300.
7. Burns (2014), pp. 106 and 109.
8. Wade Davis, *Magdalena: River of dreams*, Bodley Head, London, 2020, p. xiii.

1 The unravelling

1. https://elpais.com/elpais/2018/12/05/opinion/1544031394_526596.html
2. The death toll is a matter of some dispute and much exaggeration. Enrique Moradiellos, in a recent Spanish account, provides the following casualty figures for the Civil War: 150,000 to 200,000 killed in military action (including bombardments), of whom 60% were on the Republican side; 155,000 dead in repression during the war, of whom around 100,000 were killed in the nationalist zone. In addition Spain suffered up to 380,000 'excess deaths' between 1936 and 1939, compared with the preceding years, because of hunger and disease. Enrique Moradiellos, *Historia Mínima de la Guerra Civil Espanola*, Turner/El Colegio de México, Mexico, 2016, p. 275. The estimate of 20,000 for those executed in post-war repression is from Paul Preston, *The Spanish Holocaust*, W.W. Norton, New York, 2012, p. xi.
3. Juan Carlos was the grandson of Alfonso XIII, the Bourbon monarch ousted by the declaration of the Republic in 1930.

4. Charles Powell, *España en Democracia, 1975–2000*, Plaza y Janés, Barcelona, 2001, pp. 209–16.

5. OECD, *Economic Surveys: Spain*, May 2021, p. 37. www.oecd.org/economy/surveys/Spain-2021-OECD-economic-survey-overview.pdf

6. On the transition see Javier Tussell, *Spain: From dictatorship to democracy*, Blackwell, Oxford, 2007; Powell (2001) and Charles Powell, 'Revisiting Spain's transition to democracy', in Senén Florensa (ed.), *The Arab Transitions in a Changing World: Building democracies in light of international experiences*, IEMed, Barcelona, 2016.

7. William Chislett, *Spain: What everyone should know*, Oxford University Press, Oxford, 2013.

8. Ibid., p. 156.

9. William Chislett, *Spain and the United States: The quest for mutual rediscovery*, Real Instituto Elcano, Madrid, 2005.

10. See Oscar Calvo-Gonzalez, *Unexpected Prosperity: How Spain escaped the middle-income trap*, Oxford University Press, Oxford, 2021.

11. See, for example: www.eldiario.es/politica/frob-cajas-crisis-bancos-bankia-cclm-can-pp-psoe-upn-iu-banco-de-valencia-banca-civica_1_5690328.html

12. www.reuters.com/article/us-spain-corruption-idUSL243227820061214

13. Interview with the author, November 2020.

14. www.bbc.com/news/world-europe-39068843

15. www.economist.com/leaders/2015/12/16/feliz-navidad-espana

16. See: Spain, Annex to the EU Anti-Corruption Report, Brussels, 2 March 2014.

17. https://elpais.com/politica/2016/01/27/actualidad/1453925502_689607.html

18. www.poderjudicial.es/cgpj/es/Poder-Judicial/Audiencia-Nacional/Noticias-Judiciales/La-Audiencia-Nacional-condena-a-penas-de-hasta-51-anos-de-prision-a-29-de-los-37-acusados-en-el--caso-Gurtel-

19. In October 2020 the Supreme Court reviewed the case. It upheld the individual sentences, varying them only slightly. It found that the PP had benefited from €245,000 in illegal financing for campaigns in two Madrid suburbs. But it said that the PP could not be held to be institutionally corrupt since it was not a party to the case. Rajoy took this as vindication. See: www.elmundo.es/espana/2020/10/15/5f87f14321efa0ed538b467a.html

20. www.lavanguardia.com/comer/al-dia/20180601/443979431132/comida-rajoy-restaurante-madrid-mocion-de-censura.html

21. Bárcenas, the PP's former treasurer, claimed that Rajoy figured on a list of under-the-counter payments he said he made to party leaders, but Rajoy denied this and there was no independent corroboration.

22. https://elpais.com/ideas/2020-08-08/recuerda-que-eres-mortal.html

23. www.elmundo.es/espana/2020/07/11/5f0a07fbfdddffe9b38b46e0.html

24. www.elmundo.es/espana/2020/03/18/5e7261affc6c83774d8b4628.html

25. See para 9 of the sentence: www.poderjudicial.es/cgpj/es/Poder-Judicial/Tribunal-Supremo/Noticias-Judiciales/El-Tribunal-Supremo-condena-a-Inaki-Urdangarin-a-5-anos-y-10-meses-de-prision-por-malversacion--prevaricacion--fraude--dos-delitos-fiscales-y-trafico-de-influencias-en-el--caso-Noos-#:~:text=El%20Tribunal%20Supremo%20condena%20a,influencias%20en%20el%20%E2%80%9Ccaso%20N%C3%B3os%E2%80%9D

26. www.bbc.com/news/world-europe-53415781

27. www.nytimes.com/2021/12/13/world/europe/switzerland-money-laundering-case-juan-carlos.html

28. www.reuters.com/world/europe/spanish-prosecutor-drops-fraud-case-against-former-king-juan-carlos-2022-03-02/

29. www.economist.com/europe/2020/07/23/spains-king-felipe-is-distancing-himself-from-his-father

30. www.elmundo.es/espana/2021/02/26/6038d5c8fdddffb7608b4647.html

31. https://letraslibres.com/revista/a-nice-young-fellow/

2 A Catalan autumn

1. Enric Ucelay-Da Cal, *Breve historia del separatismo catalan*, Ediciones B, Barcelona, 2018, p. 16.
2. https://elpais.com/ccaa/2016/12/24/catalunya/1482594032_989718.html
3. In March 2022 the European Parliament ordered an investigation into Russian involvement in the Catalan *procés*. It had emerged that Puigdemont met Russian emissaries in October 2017, though he insisted he turned down offers of help from them.
4. Lola García, *El Naufragio: La deconstrucción del sueño independentista*, Ediciones Península, Barcelona, 2018, p. 174.
5. www.elmundo.es/internacional/2017/03/30/58dcff9b46163f6c328b4627.html
6. www.reuters.com/article/us-spain-politics-catalonia-eu-idUSKBN1CO31E
7. García (2018), pp. 215–16.
8. https://elpais.com/espana/2020-07-30/los-129-dias-de-mediacion-baldia-entre-rajoy-y-puigdemont.html
9. www.casareal.es/sitios/listasaux/Documents/Mensaje20171003/20171003_Mensaje_de_Su_Majestad_el_Rey.pdf
10. www.elconfidencial.com/espana/cataluna/2019-10-18/rosa-foc-tactica-violentos-incendiar-barcelona-717_2288576/
11. Daniel Gascón, *El Golpe posmoderno*, Debate, Barcelona, 2018.
12. Centre d'Estudis d'Opinió, Baròmetre d'Opinió Política. 2a Onada 2022, Gencat. https://ceo.gencat.cat/ca/barometre/detall/index.html?id=8428

3 The invention of Catalonia

1. Centre d'Estudis d'Opinió, Generalitat de Catalunya, Baròmetre d'Opinió Política, 3a Onada 2020.
2. This phrase was coined by Aureli Maria Escarré, the abbot of the Benedictine monastery of Montserrat, who played an important role in reconstructing Catalan nationalism during the Franco dictatorship
3. García (2018), p. 147.
4. Francesc-Marc Álvaro, *Ensayo General de una Revuelta: Las claves del proceso catalán*, Galaxia Gutenberg, Barcelona, 2019, p. 43.
5. www.theguardian.com/commentisfree/2017/nov/06/carles-puigdemont-catalonia-democracy-spain-catalans.
6. https://cronicaglobal.elespanol.com/politica/todos-alcaldes-franquistas-absorbio-ciu_143348_102.html
7. Álvaro (2019), p. 52.
8. Eric Hobsbawm, 'Inventing traditions', in Eric Hobsbawm and Terence Ranger (eds), *The Invention of Tradition*, Cambridge University Press, Cambridge, 1983, p. 6.
9. Norman Davis, *Vanished Kingdoms: The history of half-forgotten Europe*, Allen Lane, London, 2011, chapter 4.
10. Jordi Canal, *Historia Minima de Cataluña*, Turner/El Colegio de México, Mexico, 2015, p. 36.
11. The term 'composite monarchy' was popularised by J.H. Elliott.
12. J.H. Elliott, *Scots and Catalans*, Yale University Press, New Haven and London, 2018, p. 64.
13. Raymond Carr, *Spain 1808–1939*, Oxford University Press, Oxford, 1966, p. 30.
14. Robert Hughes, *Barcelona*, Harvill Press, London, 2001, chapter 7.
15. Quoted in Gascón (2018), p. 97.
16. Hughes (2001), p. 298.
17. Carr (1966), p. 538.
18. Ibid., pp. 546–7.

19. Manuel Chaves Nogales, *Qué Pasa en Cataluña?*, Editorial Almuzara, Madrid, 2013, p. 99.
20. www.economist.com/europe/2017/11/02/the-man-who-wasnt-there
21. Gerald Brenan, *The Spanish Labyrinth: The social and political background to the Spanish Civil War*, Cambridge University Press, Cambridge, 2008, p. 282.
22. Quoted in Jordi Amat, 'Fascistas, sí; fascismo, no', *La Vanguardia* 11 August 2017.
23. Ucelay-Da Cal (2018), pp. 146–51.
24. All quotes from Chaves Nogales (2013).
25. Canal (2015), pp. 203–4.
26. Jordi Amat, *Largo Proceso, Amargo Sueño: Cultura y política en la Cataluña contemporanea*, Tusquets Editores, Barcelona, 2018, p. 105.
27. On the rebuilding of Catalanism and the role of Pujol, see Amat (2018).
28. It collapsed in 1982, amid allegations of mismanagement and fraud. A criminal investigation ended with charges against Pujol and the bank's other directors being dropped.
29. Amat (2018), pp. 345–6.
30. Quoted in Hughes (2001), p. 25.
31. Jean-Benoît Nadeau and Julie Barlow, *The Story of Spanish*, St Martin's Press, New York, 2013, chapter 5.
32. Generalitat de Catalunya, Statistical Institute of Catalonia, *Language Uses of the Population*, 2019. www.idescat.cat/indicadors/?id=aec&n=15781&lang=en
33. www.europapress.es/sociedad/educacion-00468/noticia-tc-recuerda-castellano-no-puede-dejar-ser-tambien-lengua-aprendizaje-ensenanza-cataluna-20191007194309.html
34. www.elmundo.es/espana/2020/10/29/5f9af79ffc6c83bb758b45d9.html
35. https://elpais.com/opinion/2021-12-16/inmersion-linguistica-todo-por-el-pueblo-pero-sin-el-pueblo.html
36. www.lavanguardia.com/local/barcelona/20180907/451686440606/el-48-de-los-libros-vendidos-en-catalunya-son-en-catalan.html
37. https://cvc.cervantes.es/lengua/anuario/anuario_20/
38. www.lavanguardia.com/edicion-impresa/20181003/452162897167/barcelona-capital.html
39. Author interview, Barcelona, 2012.
40. www.elmundo.es/cataluna/2021/04/25/60844ae0fdddffc6ae8b45ba.html
41. Raphael Minder, *The Struggle for Catalonia: Rebel politics in Spain*, Hurst, London, 2017, p. 33.
42. Jordi Amat, La Conjura de los Irresponsables, Editorial Anagrama, Barcelona, 2017, p17.
43. This paragraph and the next draw on Amat (2017).
44. Jordi Canal, *Con permiso de Kafka: El proceso independentista en Catalonia*, Ediciones Península, Barcelona, 2018, p. 142.
45. Gascón (2018), pp. 57–8.
46. Quoted in Álvaro (2019), p. 127 and p. 142.
47. Amat (2017), p. 54.
48. https://confilegal.com/20210616-la-audiencia-nacional-abre-juicio-oral-a-jordi-pujol-y-sus-siete-hijos-e-impone-una-fianza-de-75-millones-al-primogenito/
49. https://elpais.com/politica/2019/08/15/actualidad/1565879983_942585.html And: https://elpais.com/espana/2020-07-16/de-la-mata-propone-juzgar-a-jordi-pujol-su-mujer-y-sus-hijos-por-enriquecerse-mediante-la-corrupcion.html
50. 'La Audiencia de Barcelona ordena el ingreso en prisión de Oriol Pujol', Poder Judicial de España, Archivo de Notas de Prensa, 9 January 2019.
51. García (2018), pp. 136–7.
52. See: www.economist.com/europe/2017/01/07/in-their-search-for-independence-catalans-can-resemble-brexiteers
53. Álvaro (2019), chapter 8.
54. www.elmundo.es/cataluna/2018/04/17/5ad4e148e5fdea22598b4603.html

55. Quoted in José Alvárez Junco, *Dioses Útiles: Naciones y nacionalismos*, Galaxia Gutenberg, Barcelona, 2016, p. 227.
56. Gascón (2018), chapter 8.
57. www.elperiodico.com/es/politica/20180514/quim-torra-articulos-contra-espanoles-6817795
58. https://elpais.com/espana/elecciones-catalanas/2021-02-07/breviario-indepe.html
59. Amartya Sen, *Identity and Violence: The illusion of destiny*, Penguin Books, Harmondsworth, 2006, pp. xii–xiii.
60. Álvarez Junco (2016), pp. 51–2.

4 Why Spain is not France

1. 'A Orillas del Duero', in *Campos de Castilla*, first published in 1912. Antonio Machado, *Poesia*, Alianza Editorial, Madrid, 2017, p. 55.
2. Richard Ford, *A Hand-book for Travellers in Spain*, Centaur Press, London, 1966, vol. 1, p. 6. Ford's book was first published in 1845.
3. Juan Pablo Fusi, *Historia Mínima de España*, Turner, Madrid, 2012, chapter 4; Richard Herr, 'Flow and ebb, 1700–1833', in Raymond Carr (ed.), *Spain: A History*, Oxford University Press, Oxford, 2000.
4. On Goya, see Robert Hughes, *Goya*, Knopf, New York, 2006.
5. José Álvarez Junco, *Mater Dolorosa: La idea de España en el siglo XIX*, Taurus, Barcelona, 2001, p. 73.
6. Ibid., p. 137.
7. Carr (1966), p. 35.
8. See Nigel Townson (ed.), *Is Spain Different? A comparative look at the 19th and 20th centuries*, Sussex Academic Press, Eastbourne, 2015.
9. Quoted in Álvarez Junco (2001), p. 533.
10. Adrian Shubert, *Espartero el Pacificador*, Galaxia Gutenberg, Barcelona, 2018, p. 25.
11. Quoted in frontispiece of Shubert (2018).
12. Gregorio Alonso, 'The crisis of the old regime: 1808–1833', in Adrian Shubert and José Álvarez Junco (eds), *The History of Modern Spain: Chronologies, themes, individuals*, Bloomsbury Academic, London, 2018.
13. There were almost a hundred *pronunciamientos* between 1820 and 1936 according to Álvarez Junco (2016), p. 163.
14. Javier Barón, *Una Pintura para una Nación*, Museo del Prado, Madrid, 2019, Foreword.
15. On the parallels between the two wars see Mark Lawrence, *The Spanish Civil Wars: A comparative history of the First Carlist War and the conflict of the 1930s*, Bloomsbury Academic, London, 2017.
16. Fusi (2012), p. 191.
17. Julio Aróstegui, 'El carlismo y las guerras civiles', in Aróstegui, Jordi Canal and Eduardo G. Calleja, *El Carlismo y las Guerras Carlistas*, La Esfera de los Libros, Madrid, 2011.
18. See Shubert (2018).
19. Lawrence (2017), p. 32 and p. 66.
20. Quoted in Shubert (2018), p. 154
21. Roger Price, *A Concise History of France*, 3rd edn, Cambridge University Press, Cambridge, 2014, p. 225.
22. See Aróstegui et al. (2011); and Maria Cruz Romeo Mateo, 'The civil wars of the 19th century: An exceptional path to modernisation?', in Townson (ed.) (2015).
23. Although Franco ruled as if he were an absolute monarch.
24. Mark Lawrence, 'Juan Álvarez Mendizábal', in Shubert and Álvarez Junco (eds) (2018).
25. On the development of the state, see Diego Palacios Cerezales, 'The state', in Shubert and Álvarez Junco (eds) (2018).

26. Bravo Murillo's motto may be the origin of the celebrated slogan attributed to Porfirio Díaz, Mexico's dictator from 1884 to 1911, 'little politics, much administration'.

27. Isabel Burdiel, *Isabel II: Una biografía*, Taurus, Barcelona, 2019, Introduction.

28. María Sierra, 'The time of liberalism 1833–74', in Shubert and Álvarez Junco (eds) (2018), p. 42.

29. Carr (1966), pp. 492–5.

30. Townson, 'Introduction', in Townson (ed.) (2015).

31. Leandro Prados de la Escosura, *Spanish Economic Growth, 1850–2015*, Palgrave Macmillan, Basingstoke, 2017, p. 41.

32. Palacios Cerezales (2018), p. 314.

33. This paragraph and the next draw heavily on Eugen Weber, *Peasants into Frenchmen: The modernisation of rural France 1870–1914*, Stanford University Press, Stanford, 1976.

34. Ibid., p. x.

35. Quoted in ibid., p. 95

36. Ibid., p. 336.

37. www.ft.com/content/102f4bb2-d351-11e7-8c9a-d9c0a5c8d5c9

38. https://elpais.com/cultura/2020-10-09/fallece-el-historiador-joseph-perez-premio-principe-de-asturias-de-ciencias-sociales-de-2014.html

39. https://elpais.com/internacional/2021-04-08/francia-aprueba-una-ley-para-proteger-las-lenguas-regionales-y-facilitar-su-ensenanza.html

40. https://elpais.com/internacional/2021-05-21/el-constitucional-frances-veta-parcialmente-la-ley-que-permitia-la-inmersion-linguistica-en-francia.html?rel=lom

41. The rest of this paragraph draws on Palacios Cerezales (2018).

42. Álvarez Junco (2001), p. 541.

43. Ibid., p. 547.

44. Arturo Barea, *The Forging of a Rebel: The forge*, Pushkin Press, London, 2018, p. 119.

45. Spain retained northern Morocco, Western Sahara and a few small African colonies.

46. Quoted in Carr (1966), p. 473.

47. Mary Vincent, *Spain 1833–2002: People and state*, Oxford University Press, Oxford, 2007, pp. 87–91.

48. For a particularly trenchant demolition of Ortega, see José María Ridao, *República Encantada: Tradición, tolerancia y liberalismo en España*, Tusquets Editores, Barcelona, 2021, pp. 193–219.

49. José Ortega y Gasset, *España Invertebrada y Otros Ensayos*, Alianza Editorial, Madrid, 2014, p. 62.

50. Ibid., p. 76.

51. Álvarez Junco (2001), p. 603.

52. Diario de Sesiones del Congreso de los Diputados, 27 May 1932, pp. 5855–77.

53. Xosé M. Núñez Seixas, 'Nation and nationalism', in Shubert and Álvarez Junco (eds) (2018).

54. Quoted in Weber (1976), p. 96.

55. Núñez Seixas (2018).

5 Let's talk about Franco

1. https://politica.elpais.com/politimca/2018/06/19/actualidad/1529397533_593099.html

2. Silva and Sánchez-Albornoz's comments in conference with foreign correspondents, October 2018.

3. See Xosé M. Núñez Seixas, *Guaridas del Lobo: Memorias de la Europa autoritaria, 1945–2020*, Crítica, Barcelona, 2021.

4. Enrique Moradiellos, *Franco: Anatomy of a dictator*, I.B. Tauris, London, 2018, Introduction.

5. For a succinct account of the law, see Chislett (2013), pp. 160–3.

6. https://elpais.com/espana/2022-01-09/las-huellas-del-horror-franquista-10000-esqueletos-recuperados-en-20-anos.html
7. https://elpais.com/espana/2020-09-02/la-juez-declara-al-estado-propietario-legitimo-del-pazo-de-meiras.html
8. See Omar Encarnacion, *Democracy without Justice in Spain: The politics of forgetting*, University of Pennsylvania Press, Philadelphia, 2014.
9. https://elpais.com/opinion/2021-10-31/datos-necesarios-para-la-memoria-historica.html
10. Moradiellos (2016), chapter 2; quote on p. 42.
11. Paul Preston, *Comrades: Portraits from the Spanish Civil War*, HarperCollins, London, 1999, p. 195.
12. Santos Juliá, *Vida y Tiempo de Manuel Azaña 1880–1940*, Taurus, Barcelona, 2008.
13. Quoted in Carr (1966), p. 607.
14. Lawrence (2017), p. 28.
15. Moradiellos (2016), pp. 63–4.
16. Ibid., p. 63.
17. Anthony Beevor, *The Battle for Spain*, Penguin, Harmondsworth, 2006, chapters 6 and 7.
18. Moradiellos (2016), p. 21.
19. Paul Preston, *A People Betrayed: A history of corruption, political incompetence and social division in modern Spain, 1876–2018*, William Collins, London, 2020, chapter 10.
20. Manuel Chaves Nogales, *A Sangre y Fuego: Héroes, bestias y mártires de España*, Libros del Asteroide, Barcelona, 2011, Prólogo.
21. Quoted in Juliá (2008), p. 400.
22. See, for example, Fernando del Rey, *Retaguardia Roja: Violencia y revolución en la guerra civil española*, Galaxia Gutenburg, Barcelona, 2019.
23. Moradiellos (2016), pp. 275–6.
24. Juliá (2008), p392.
25. https://elpais.com/elpais/2017/12/22/opinion/1513954465_461537.html
26. Preston (2012), p. 499.
27. See Paul Preston, *Franco: A biography*, HarperCollins, London, 1993, and Enrique Moradiellos (2018).
28. As portrayed in *Mientras Dure la Guerra* ('While the war lasts'), a 2019 film by Alejandro Amenábar.
29. Preston (2020), p. 371.
30. Several thousand Republicans who had escaped to France ended up, after the German invasion, being sent to Mauthausen concentration camp in Austria. Others joined the French Resistance and were among the first troops to enter Paris in the liberation in 1944.
31. Moradiellos (2018), p. 42.
32. Preston (2020), p. 349.
33. Centro de Investigaciones Sociológicas (CIS), *Memorias de la Guerra Civil y el Franquismo*, April 2008, question 12.
34. Javier Cercas, 'Un pacto sobre el pasado', *El País Semanal*, 9 April 2017.
35. To cite a trivial example, I cannot be certain that the snapshots from my own memory I referred to in the prologue are factually accurate.
36. Quoted in David Rieff, *In Praise of Forgetting: Historical memory and its ironies*, Yale University Press, New Haven and London, 2016, p. 22.
37. CIS (2008), question 21.
38. https://elpais.com/cultura/2017/02/09/babelia/1486671469_920588.html
39. https://elpais.com/opinion/2020-10-12/ni-heroes-ni-villanos.html
40. 'Truth commissions: the agony of silence', *The Economist*, 15 May 2021.
41. Interview with the author, November 2018.
42. https://elpais.com/diario/2002/11/21/espana/1037833222_850215.html
43. Rieff (2016), p. 39

44. Ibid., p. 36
45. www.ft.com/content/b0be351e-d256-4833-aace-8c03386c9ad4
46. www.lavanguardia.com/politica/20201204/49864525002/jemad-miguel-angel-villar-roya-expresiones-militares-confunden-opinion-publica.html
47. https://elpais.com/internacional/2021-04-29/francia-promete-sanciones-para-los-mili-tares-que-alertaron-del-desmoronamiento-del-pais.html
48. https://elpais.com/internacional/2021-06-27/la-doble-vida-de-franco-a-y-el-extremismo-en-el-ejercito-aleman.html
49. https://blogs.lse.ac.uk/europpblog/2021/11/17/who-votes-for-the-populist-radical-right-in-portugal-and-spain/
50. https://elpais.com/espana/2020-11-18/los-presupuestos-protagonizan-la-sesion-de-control-al-gobierno-en-el-congreso.html

6 The Basque paradox and *galeguismo*

1. Eduardo Madina and Borja Sémper, *Todos los Futuros Perdidos: Conversaciones sobre el final de ETA*, Plaza y Janés, Barcelona, 2021, p. 26.
2. http://politica.elpais.com/politica/2017/04/10/actualidad/1491779940_303824.html
3. This paragraph draws on Álvarez Junco (2016), pp. 234–52; quote on p. 251.
4. Quoted in Paddy Woodworth, *The Basque Country: A cultural history*, Signal Books, Oxford, 2007, p. 13.
5. André Flores-Bello and others, 'Genetic origins, singularity and heterogeneity of Basques', *Current Biology*, 31(10), 2021, pp. 2167–77.
6. Álvarez Junco (2016), pp. 239–40.
7. Woodworth (2007), p. 27.
8. See John Hooper, *The New Spaniards*, 2nd edn, Penguin, Harmondsworth, 2006, chapter 17.
9. Mark Kurlansky, *The Basque History of the World*, Vintage, 2000, chapter 9.
10. Interview with the author, Bilbao, May 2018.
11. Hooper (2006), p. 245.
12. Interview with the author, Bilbao, May 2018.
13. Woodworth (2007), pp. 175–6.
14. https://elpais.com/opinion/2021-06-04/el-legado-de-la-herida-del-terrorismo-en-espana.html
15. www.elmundo.es/opinion/2021/06/12/60c390a121efa0656d8b465d.html
16. https://politica.elpais.com/politica/2018/04/28/actualidad/1524940722_226849.html
17. https://politica.elpais.com/politica/2018/02/21/actualidad/1519238990_863473.html
18. Juan Pablo Fusi and José Antonio Pérez (eds), *Euskadi 1960–2011: Dictadura, transición y democracia*, Biblioteca Nueva, Madrid 2017, pp. 30 and 284.
19. Kurlansky (2000).
20. Madina and Sémper (2021).
21. Fernando Aramburu, *Patria*, Tusquets, Barcelona, 2016.
22. Tobias Buck, *After the Fall: Crisis, recovery and the making of a new Spain*, Weidenfeld & Nicolson, London, 2019, chapter 7.
23. Antonio Caño, *Rubalcaba: Un político de verdad*, Plaza y Janés, Barcelona, 2020, p. 214.
24. See figure in Woodworth (2007), p. 115.
25. Author interview with Iván Jiménez, Bizkaia Talent, May 2018.
26. Briefing for foreign correspondents, June 2020.
27. Euskobarometro poll, 2019, www.ehu.eus/es/web/euskobarometro/
28. https://elpais.com/espana/2021-10-18/arnaldo-otegi-realiza-una-declaracion-solemne-con-motivo-de-la-decimo-aniversario-del-fin-de-eta.html

29. https://elpais.com/espana/2021-10-25/eh-bildu-ensancha-el-tablero-politico-vasco.html
30. Álvarez Junco (2016), pp. 252–70.
31. https://elpais.com/elpais/2020/07/01/eps/1593617739_343431.html

7 The fading of the Spanish dream

1. See, for example: https://elpais.com/economia/2021-02-14/santana-10-anos-de-un-motor-gripado-en-linares.html
2. Interview with the author, May 2018.
3. William Chislett, 'Challenges and opportunities for Spain in times of COVID-19', Real Instituto Elcano Working Paper, April 2021.
4. www.huffingtonpost.es/entry/quien-es-ana-iris-simon-pedro-sanchez-discurso_es_60ab516be4b0d56a83eba511
5. Manuel García-Santana et al., 'Growing like Spain: 1995–2007', *International Economic Review* 61(1), 2020, pp. 383–416.
6. Michael Reid, 'The strain in Spain: A special report', *The Economist*, 28 July 2018.
7. Politikon, *El Muro Invisible*, Editorial Debate, Barcelona, 2017, chapter 4.
8. https://elpais.com/economia/2021-07-12/pedro-sanchez-presenta-el-plan-estrategico-para-impulsar-el-coche-electrico-con-los-fondos-europeos.html
9. www.expansion.com/empresas/distribucion/2020/01/29/5e309dec468aebd76f8b462f.html
10. Miguel Almunia et al., 'Venting out: Exports during a domestic slump', National Bureau of Economic Research Working Paper 25372, December 2018.
11. Peter Eppinger et al., 'The great trade collapse and the Spanish export miracle', *The World Economy* 41(2), February 2018.
12. www.astimobilerobotics.com/blog/abb-to-acquire-asti-to-drive-next-generation-of-flexible-automation
13. www.economist.com/europe/2018/08/18/can-other-cities-imitate-bilbaos-cultural-tourism-success
14. https://elpais.com/economia/2020-11-08/la-banca-cierra-en-12-anos-el-50-de-oficinas-y-echa-al-40-de-empleados.html
15. www.elmundo.es/opinion/2020/02/10/5e40084efc6c83be6b8b458b.html
16. Klaus Schwab et al., *Global Competitiveness Report 2019*, World Economic Forum, Geneva, 2019.
17. www.elmundo.es/economia/actualidad-economica/2021/05/09/6093b16cfc6c83f8668b4602.html
18. https://elpais.com/economia/2020-08-01/el-verano-mas-negro-del-turismo.html
19. Interview with the author, July 2021.
20. OECD (2021).
21. www.psoe.es/media-content/2019/12/30122019-Coalici%C3%B3n-progresista.pdf
22. OECD, *Economic Surveys: Spain*, 2017, Paris, OECD, p. 63.
23. https://elpais.com/espana/2021-07-04/yolanda-diaz-el-gobierno-no-puede-parecer-mas-cerca-de-la-elite-que-de-la-gente.html
24. According to José Luis Escrivá, the social security minister, www.elmundo.es/opinion/2020/05/30/5ed11211fc6c83e3588b4584.html
25. Interview with the author, July 2021.
26. OECD (2017), p. 78.
27. https://elpais.com/economia/2019/04/17/actualidad/1555529390_753721.html
28. Ángel de la Fuente and Rafael Doménech, 'Cross-country data on skills and the quality of schooling: A selective survey', BBVA Research Working Paper, November 2021.
29. Buck (2019), pp. 91–2.
30. Interview with the author, May 2018.

31. https://elpais.com/educacion/2021-02-07/el-curso-de-la-pandemia-elevo-los-aprobados-a-maximos-historicos.html
32. www.shanghairanking.com/rankings/arwu/2021
33. www.lamoncloa.gob.es/serviciosdeprensa/notasprensa/inclusion/paginas/2022/101022-escriva-pensiones.aspx
34. OECD (2021) and OECD, *Pensions at a Glance: How does Spain compare?* November 2021.
35. Kiko Lorenzo and Raúl Flores, Caritas Madrid, conference with foreign correspondents, May 2020.
36. Interview with the author, June 2020.
37. Chislett (2021), p. 16.
38. European Commission, *Country Report Spain 2019*.
39. https://ec.europa.eu/eurostat/databrowser/view/sdg_08_10/default/table?lang=en

8 Scandinavia in the sun?

1. Walters gave this account of the meeting in an interview with *ABC*, a Spanish newspaper, published on 15 August 2000.
2. Hooper (2006), p. 126.
3. Data from Instituto de Mujeres, Minsterio de Igualdad.
4. https://elpais.com/sociedad/2021-08-25/conciliacion-la-asignatura-pendiente-lastrada-por-la-pandemia.html
5. https://elpais.com/sociedad/2019/03/03/actualidad/1551638433_568255.html
6. Heyne and Manucci, Europpblog, LSE, November 2021.
7. https://yougov.co.uk/topics/international/articles-reports/2021/08/31/international-survey-how-supportive-would-britons-
8. www.elmundo.es/elecciones/elecciones-madrid/2021/04/13/6075d78121efa0e2778b4628.html
9. Interview with the author, Madrid, April 2021.
10. Mar Griera, Julia Martínez-Ariño and Anna Clot-Garrell, 'Banal Catholicism, morality policies and the politics of belonging in Spain', *Religions* 12, 2021.
11. Figures in 'La iglesia católica en España', Conferencia Episcopal Española, May 2021.
12. Interview with the author, April 2021.
13. https://elpais.com/sociedad/2021-12-19/la-iglesia-espanola-afronta-una-gran-investigacion-de-la-pederastia-con-251-nuevos-casos-aportados-por-el-pais.html
14. The fertility rate is the average number of children that a woman will give birth to.
15. William Chislett, *Forty Years of Democratic Spain*, Real Instituto Elcano, Madrid, 2018.
16. Aitana Guia, 'Migrations', in Álvarez Junco and Shubert (eds) (2018), chapter 19.
17. Barea (2018), p. 103.
18. Rosa Aparicio and Alejandro Portes, *Growing Up in Spain: The integration of the children of immigrants*, La Caixa Foundation, Barcelona, 2014.
19. https://elpais.com/elpais/2020/01/03/opinion/1578068213_476762.html
20. www.elmundo.es/opinion/2021/04/10/606b4dc0fdddffc7998b4645.html
21. https://elpais.com/espana/2021-11-21/el-15-m-rural-desafia-al-psoe-y-al-pp.html
22. Angel de la Fuente and Xavier Vives, 'Infrastructure and education as instruments of regional policy: Evidence from Spain', *Economic Policy* 10(20), April 1995.
23. Ignacio Urquizu, *Otra Política es Posible*, Debate, Barcelona, 2021, chapter 5, and interview with the author, March 2019.
24. www.lavanguardia.com/magazine/experiencias/salvar-meseta-laponia-sur.html
25. www.elmundo.es/economia/2020/06/23/5eef92f3fdddff02588b4579.html
26. https://elpais.com/elpais/2020/02/14/eps/1581678745_698258.html
27. https://elpais.com/clima-y-medio-ambiente/2021-08-21/seis-dias-de-desastre-ecologico-en-el-mar-menor-con-miles-de-peces-muertos.html

28. Quoted in Josefina Gómez de Mendoza, 'The environment', in Álvarez Junco and Shubert (eds) (2018), chapter 14.
29. Ibid.
30. www.ft.com/content/0d38e8d3-3f20-4818-8751-740d05f8ac13?shareType=nongift
31. www.elmundo.es/opinion/columnistas/2022/01/07/61d6c971fdddff3e3d8b4575.html
32. https://elpais.com/ccaa/2019/05/20/madrid/1558363176_904628.html
33. *El País Semanal*, 30 October 2016.
34. https://elpais.com/clima-y-medio-ambiente/2021-05-28/el-lobo-de-bestia-feroz-a-simbolo-de-la-naturaleza-salvaje.html
35. https://elpais.com/politica/2019/05/16/actualidad/1558033959_289970.html
36. Ángeles González-Fernández, 'Población y sociedad 1960–2010', in Jordi Canal (ed.), *Historia Contemporánea de España*, vol. 2: *1931–2017*, Taurus, Barcelona, 2017. Quote on p. 425.
37. https://elpais.com/politica/2017/06/12/actualidad/1497288605_348268.html
38. https://elpais.com/sociedad/2018/10/16/actualidad/1539678495_813483.html

9 'The caste' and its flawed challengers

1. José Ignacio Torreblanca, *Asaltar los Cielos: Podemos o la política después de la crisis*, Editorial Debate, Barcelona, 2015, p. 121.
2. Interview with the author, May 2021.
3. This paragraph and the next draw on Torreblanca (2015). See also 'Pablo Iglesias habla sobre su relación con Irán', YouTube, 2 November 2014, www.youtube.com/watch?v=jjeVbE3dL4Q
4. Pablo Iglesias, *Politics in a Time of Crisis: Podemos and the future of a democratic Europe*, Verso, London, 2015, p. 136.
5. The Five Star Movement copied the term from a book published in 2007 by two Italian journalists, Sergio Rizzo and Gian Antonio Stella. Miguel de Unamuno, a Spanish writer of the Generation of 1898, had criticised 'the ancient historic caste'.
6. Iglesias (2015).
7. Ignacio Urquizu, *La Crisis de Representación en España*, Catarata, Madrid, 2016, p. 100.
8. See, for example, reports on the state of democracy in the world by the V-Dem Institute of Gothenburg University or the Economist Intelligence Unit.
9. Miriam González Durántez, *Devuélveme el Poder: Por qué urge una reforma liberal en España*, Ediciones Península, Barcelona, 2019, chapter 1.
10. Ibid., p. 29.
11. Antonio Muñoz Molina, *Todo lo que era sólido*, Seix Barral, Barcelona, 2013, pp. 46–9.
12. www.elconfidencial.com/espana/2021-02-15/cifuentes-caso-master-audiencia-madrid_2951416/
13. https://elpais.com/politica/2018/04/25/actualidad/1524643078_623889.html
14. 'Spain: A question of degrees', *The Economist*, 22 September 2018. The Institute of Public Law was shut down after these scandals; its director, Enrique Álvarez Conde, was charged with fraud but died before coming to trial.
15. https://www.poderjudicial.es/cgpj/es/Poder-Judicial/Tribunal-Supremo/Noticias-Judiciales/El-Tribunal-Supremo-confirma-penas-de-hasta-51-anos-de-prision-para-los-procesados-en-el--caso-Gurtel
16. 'Discurso de Pedro Sánchez en el debate de la Moción de Censura contra el Gobierno de Mariano Rajoy', Congreso de los Diputados, 31 May 2018, p. 6.
17. www.rtve.es/noticias/20210806/juicio-ignacio-gonzalez-adjudicaciones-campo-golf-canal-isabel-ii/2153481.shtml
18. www.poderjudicial.es/cgpj/es/Poder-Judicial/Sala-de-Prensa/Archivo-de-notas-de-prensa/La-Audiencia-Provincial-de-Sevilla-notifica-la-sentencia-del-caso-de-los-ERE

19. Raphael Minder, *Esto es España? Una década de corresponsalía*, Ediciones Península, Barcelona, 2020, pp. 317–34.
20. Muñoz Molina (2013), pp. 109–19.
21. https://elpais.com/espana/2021-04-05/el-gobierno-inicia-la-reforma-de-la-ley-franquista-de-secretos-oficiales.html
22. https://elpais.com/espana/2020-08-15/urge-un-gobierno-de-concentracion-moral-y-constitucional-en-espana.html?rel=mas
23. https://elpais.com/opinion/2021-08-17/las-reformas-son-para-el-verano.html
24. www.lavanguardia.com/politica/20201101/4977267538/funcionarios-empleo-publico-burocracia-pandemia.html
25. https://elpais.com/opinion/2021-06-04/larra-en-el-ciberespacio.html
26. https://elpais.com/opinion/2021-04-11/mi-espana.html
27. https://elpais.com/opinion/2020-11-23/administracion-digital-secuestrada.html
28. Hooper (2006), p. 336.
29. https://elpais.com/politica/2018/11/20/actualidad/1542742122_009936.html
30. See, for example: www.publico.es/politica/juicio-independencia-rigor-vox-proces-acusar-organizacion-criminal-no-cuadre-relato-juez-instructor.html
31. https://elpais.com/politica/2016/12/02/actualidad/1480701452_072845.html
32. Interview with the author, May 2021.
33. https://ig.ft.com/jailed-bankers/
34. www.publico.es/politica/90-politicos-funcionarios-prision-espana-delitos-corrupcion.html
35. https://elpais.com/politica/2016/01/22/actualidad/1453461680_098827.html
36. Ramon González Férriz, *La Ruptura: El fracaso de una (re)generación*, Flash e-book, Penguin Libros, 2021.
37. www.eldiario.es/politica/ideologico-podemos-preocupado-mostrarse-partidos_128_3591344.html
38. https://elpais.com/espana/2021-03-16/mas-madrid-desbarata-el-intento-de-iglesias-de-liderar-el-asalto-de-madrid.html
39. Caño (2020), p. 283 and chapter 9.
40. www.newyorker.com/magazine/2022/04/25/how-democracies-spy-on-their-citizens
41. www.mpr.gob.es/prencom/notas/Paginas/2022/240422-reunion-generalitat-catalunya.aspx
42. www.elperiodico.com/es/politica/20220427/catalangate-robles-espionaje-cni-independentismo-13574015
43. https://paginadelforodeprofesores.wordpress.com/carta-a-citizenlab-sobre-catalangate/
44. https://elpais.com/espana/2022-05-15/ronald-deibert-fundador-de-citizen-lab-los-gobiernos-usan-pegasus-porque-tienen-apetito-de-espiar.html
45. www.pp.es/actualidad-noticia/casado-abascal-no-su-mocion-es-no-sanchez-sus-socios-visibles-que-esta-sombra-que
46. https://elpais.com/espana/2022-04-03/el-nombramiento-de-feijoo-lleva-aires-de-cambio-de-ciclo-en-la-tensa-relacion-entre-pp-y-psoe.html
47. https://elpais.com/espana/2022-05-06/feijoo-reivindica-en-barcelona-la-identidad-territorial-frente-a-mentalidades-centralistas.html#?rel=mas
48. José Rama, Lisa Zanotti, Stuart J. Turnbull-Dugarte and Andrés Santana, *Vox: The rise of the Spanish populist radical right*, Routledge, Abingdon, 2021, p. 144.
49. Caño (2020), chapters 7 and 8.
50. The law repealed a restriction on coercive picketing during strikes. www.elmundo.es/espana/2021/04/23/60828fd7fdddff88778b458e.html
51. https://dobetter.esade.edu/es/polarizacion-espana
52. Urquizu (2021), chapter 1.

10 The narcissism of small differences

1. Emilio Lamo de Espinoza, *Entre Águilas y Dragones: El declive de Occidente*, Espasa, Barcelona 2021, p. 330.
2. Ibid., p. 330.
3. Ford (1966), p. 7. Italics in the original.
4. Simon Barton, *A History of Spain*, Palgrave Macmillan, Basingstoke, 2004, p. 45. *Taifa* means 'party' or 'faction' in Arabic.
5. Ortega y Gasset (2014), p. 154.
6. Urquizu (2021), p. 178.
7. Rama et al. (2021), p. 143.
8. Urquizu (2021), chapter 4.
9. https://elpais.com/opinion/2021-03-15/un-proyecto-fallido.html – not long after this op-ed was published *El País* ceased publishing Caño's articles.

BIBLIOGRAPHY

Álvarez Junco, José. *Mater Dolorosa: La idea de España en el siglo XIX*, Taurus, Barcelona, 2001
—— *Dioses Útiles: Naciones y nacionalismos*, Galaxia Gutenberg, Barcelona, 2016
Álvaro, Francesc-Marc. *Ensayo General de una Revuelta: Las claves del proceso catalán*, Galaxia Gutenberg, Barcelona, 2019
Amat, Jordi. *La Conjura de los Irresponsables*, Editorial Anagrama, Barcelona, 2017
—— *Largo Proceso, Amargo Sueño: Cultura y política en la Cataluña contemporánea*, Tusquets Editores, Barcelona, 2018
Aparicio, Rosa and Alejandro Portes. *Growing Up in Spain: The integration of the children of immigrants*, La Caixa Foundation, Barcelona, 2014
Aramburu, Fernando. *Patria*, Tusquets Editores, Barcelona, 2016
Aróstegui, Julio, Jordi Canal and Eduardo G. Calleja. *El Carlismo y las Guerras Carlistas*, La Esfera de los Libros, Madrid, 2011
Barea, Arturo. *The Forging of a Rebel*, Pushkin Press, London, 2018
Barón, Javier. *Una Pintura para una Nación*, Museo del Prado, Madrid, 2019
Barton, Simon. *A History of Spain*, Palgrave Macmillan, Basingstoke, 2004
Beevor, Anthony. *The Battle for Spain*, Penguin, Harmondsworth, 2006
Borkenau, Franz. *The Spanish Cockpit: An eyewitness account of the Spanish Civil War*, Phoenix Press, London, 2000
Brenan, Gerald. *The Spanish Labyrinth: The social and political background to the Spanish Civil War*, Cambridge University Press, Cambridge, 2008
Buck, Tobias. *After the Fall: Crisis, recovery and the making of a new Spain*, Weidenfeld & Nicolson, London, 2019
Burdiel, Isabel. *Isabel II: Una biografía*, Taurus, Barcelona, 2019
Burns Marañon, Tom. *Hispanomanía, con un Prólogo para Franceses*, Galaxia Gutenberg, Barcelona, 2014
Calvo-Gonzalez, Oscar. *Unexpected Prosperity: How Spain escaped the middle-income trap*, Oxford University Press, Oxford, 2021
Canal, Jordi. *Historia Minima de Cataluña*, Turner/El Colegio de México, Mexico, 2015
—— (ed.). *Historia Contemporánea de España*, vol. 2: *1931–2017*, Taurus, Barcelona, 2017
—— *Con Permiso de Kafka: El proceso independentista en Cataluña*, Ediciones Península, Barcelona, 2018

BIBLIOGRAPHY

Caño, Antonio. *Rubalcaba: Un político de verdad*, Plaza y Janés, Barcelona, 2020

Carr, Raymond (ed.). *Spain 1808–1939*, Oxford University Press, Oxford, 1966

—— *Spain: A History*, Oxford University Press, Oxford, 2000

Chaves Nogales, Manuel. *A Sangre y Fuego: Héroes, bestias y mártires de España*, Libros del Asteroide, Barcelona, 2011

—— *Qué pasa en Cataluña?*, Editorial Almuzara, Madrid, 2013

Chislett, William. *Spain and the United States: The quest for mutual rediscovery*, Real Instituto Elcano, Madrid, 2005

—— *Spain: What everyone should know*, Oxford University Press, Oxford, 2013

—— *Forty Years of Democratic Spain*, Real Instituto Elcano, Madrid, 2018

—— 'Challenges and opportunities for Spain in times of COVID-19', Real Instituto Elcano Working Paper, April 2021

Davis, Norman. *Vanished Kingdoms: The history of half-forgotten Europe*, Allen Lane, London, 2011

Davis, Wade. *Magdalena: River of dreams*, Bodley Head, London, 2020

Elliott, J.H. *Scots and Catalans*, Yale University Press, New Haven and London, 2018

Encarnacion, Omar. *Democracy without Justice in Spain: The politics of forgetting*, University of Pennsylvania Press, Philadelphia, 2014

Ford, Richard. *A Handbook for Travellers in Spain*, Centaur Press, New York, 1966

Fusi, Juan Pablo. *Historia Minima de España*, Turner, Madrid, 2012

Fusi, Juan Pablo and José Antonio Pérez (eds). *Euskadi 1960–2011: Dictadura, transición y democracia*, Biblioteca Nueva, Madrid, 2017

García, Lola. *El Naufragio: La deconstrucción del sueño independentista*, Ediciones Península, Barcelona, 2018

Gascón, Daniel. *El Golpe posmoderno*, Editorial Debate, Barcelona, 2018

González Durántez, Miriam. *Devuélveme el Poder: Por qué urge una reforma liberal en España*, Ediciones Península, Barcelona, 2019

González Férriz, Ramón. *La Ruptura: El fracaso de una (re)generación*, Flash e-book, Penguin Libros, 2021

Hobsbawm, Eric. 'Inventing traditions', in Eric Hobsbawm and Terence Ranger (eds), *The Invention of Tradition*, Cambridge University Press, Cambridge, 1983

Hooper, John. *The New Spaniards*, 2nd edn, Penguin, Harmondsworth, 2006

Hughes, Robert. *Barcelona*, Harvill Press, London, 2001

—— *Goya*, Knopf, New York, 2006

Iglesias, Pablo. *Politics in a Time of Crisis: Podemos and the future of a democratic Europe*, Verso, London, 2015

Jacobs, Michael. *Everything is Happening: Journey into a painting*, Granta, London, 2015

Juliá, Santos. *Vida y Tiempo de Manuel Azaña 1880–1940*, Taurus, Barcelona, 2008

Kurlansky, Mark. *The Basque History of the World*, Vintage, London, 2000

Lamo de Espinoza, Emilio. *Entre Águilas y Dragones: El declive de Occidente*, Espasa, Barcelona 2021

Lawrence, Mark. *The Spanish Civil Wars: A comparative history of the First Carlist War and the conflict of the 1930s*, Bloomsbury Academic, London, 2017

Machado, Antonio. *Poesía*, Alianza Editorial, Madrid, 2017

Madina, Eduardo and Borja Sémper. *Todos los Futuros Perdidos: Conversaciones sobre el final de ETA*, Plaza y Janés, Barcelona, 2021

Minder, Raphael. *The Struggle for Catalonia: Rebel politics in Spain*, Hurst, London, 2017

—— *Esto es España? Una década de corresponsalía*, Ediciones Península, Barcelona, 2020

Moradiellos, Enrique. *Historia Minima de la Guerra Civil Espanola*, Turner/El Colegio de México, Mexico, 2016

—— *Franco: Anatomy of a dictator*, I.B. Tauris, London, 2018

Muñoz Molina, Antonio. *Todo lo que era Sólido*, Seix Barral, Barcelona, 2013

Nadeau, Jean-Benoît and Julie Barlow. *The Story of Spanish*, St Martin's Press, New York, 2013

Núñez Seixas, Xosé M. *Guaridas del Lobo: Memorias de la Europa autoritaria, 1945–2020*, Crítica, Barcelona, 2021

OECD. *Economic Surveys: Spain*, OECD, Paris, May 2021

Ortega y Gasset, José. *España Invertebrada y Otros Ensayos*, Alianza Editorial, Madrid, 2014

Politikon. *El Muro Invisible: Las dificultades de ser joven en España*, Editorial Debate, Barcelona, 2017

Powell, Charles. *España en Democracia, 1975–2000*, Plaza y Janés, Barcelona, 2001

—— 'Revisiting Spain's transition to democracy', in Senén Florensa (ed.), *The Arab Transitions in a Changing World: Building democracies in light of international experiences*, IEMed, Barcelona, 2016

Prados de la Escosura, Leandro. *Spanish Economic Growth, 1850–2015*, Palgrave Macmillan, Basingstoke, 2017

Preston, Paul. *Franco: A biography*, HarperCollins, London, 1993

—— *Comrades: Portraits from the Spanish Civil War*, HarperCollins, London, 1999

—— *The Spanish Holocaust: Inquisition and extermination in twentieth century Spain*, W.W. Norton, New York, 2012

—— *A People Betrayed: A history of corruption, political incomp etence and social division in modern Spain, 1876–2018*, William Collins, London, 2020

Price, Roger. *A Concise History of France*, 3rd edn, Cambridge University Press, Cambridge, 2014

Rama, José, Lisa Zanotti, Stuart J. Turnbull-Dugarte and Andrés Santana. *Vox: The rise of the Spanish populist radical right*, Routledge, Abingdon, 2021

Rieff, David. *In Praise of Forgetting: Historical memory and its ironies*, Yale University Press, New Haven and London, 2016

Rey, Fernando del. *Retaguardia Roja: Violencia y revolución en la guerra civil española*, Galaxia Gutenberg, Barcelona, 2019

Ridao, José María. *República Encantada: Tradición, tolerancia y liberalismo en España*, Tusquets Editores, Barcelona, 2021

Sen, Amartya. *Identity and Violence: The illusion of destiny*, Penguin, Harmondsworth, 2006

Shubert, Adrian. *Espartero el Pacificador*, Galaxia Gutenberg, Barcelona 2018

Shubert, Adrian and José Álvarez Junco (eds). *The History of Modern Spain: Chronologies, themes, individuals*, Bloomsbury Academic, London, 2018

Torreblanca, José Ignacio. *Asaltar los Cielos: Podemos o la política después de la crisis*, Editorial Debate, Barcelona, 2015

Townson, Nigel (ed.). *Is Spain Different? A comparative look at the 19th and 20th centuries*, Sussex Academic Press, Eastbourne, 2015

Tussell, Javier. *Spain: From dictatorship to democracy*, Blackwell, Oxford, 2007

Ucelay-Da Cal, Enric. *Breve historia del separatismo catalán*, Ediciones B, Barcelona, 2018

Urquizu, Ignacio. *La Crisis de Representación en España*, Catarata, Madrid, 2016

—— *Otra Pólitica es Posible*, Editorial Debate, Barcelona, 2021

Varela Ortega, José. *España: Un relato de grandeza y de odio*, Espasa, Barcelona, 2019

Vincent, Mary. *Spain 1833–2002: People and state*, Oxford University Press, Oxford, 2007

Weber, Eugen. *Peasants into Frenchmen: The modernisation of rural France 1870–1914*, Stanford University Press, Stanford, 1976

Webster, Jason. *Violencia: A new history of Spain – past, present and the future of the West*, Constable, London, 2019

Woodworth, Paddy. *The Basque Country: A cultural history*, Signal Books, Oxford, 2007

INDEX

INDEX

INDEX